100 YEARS OF STRUGGLE

MANDELA'S ANC

100 YEARS OF STRUGGLE

MANDELA'S ANC

Heidi Holland

PENGUIN BOOKS

PENGUIN BOOKS

Published by the Penguin Group
Penguin Books (South Africa) (Pty) Ltd, 24 Sturdee Avenue, Rosebank, Johannesburg 2196, South Africa
Penguin Group (USA) Inc, 375 Hudson Street, New York, New York 10014, USA
Penguin Group (Canada), 90 Eglinton Avenue East, Suite 700, Toronto, Ontario, Canada M4P 2Y3 (a division of Pearson Penguin Canada Inc)
Penguin Books Ltd, 80 Strand, London WC2R 0RL, England
Penguin Ireland, 25 St Stephen's Green, Dublin 2, Ireland (a division of Penguin Books Ltd)
Penguin Group (Australia), 250 Camberwell Road, Camberwell, Victoria 3124, Australia (a division of Pearson Australia Group Pty Ltd)
Penguin Books India Pvt Ltd, 11 Community Centre, Panchsheel Park, New Delhi – 110 017, India
Penguin Group (NZ), 67 Apollo Drive, Mairangi Bay, Auckland 1310, New Zealand
(a division of Pearson New Zealand Ltd)

Penguin Books (South Africa) (Pty) Ltd, Registered Offices:
24 Sturdee Avenue, Rosebank, Johannesburg 2196, South Africa

www.penguinbooks.co.za

First published by Grafton Books, a Division of the Collins Publishing Group, as
The Struggle: A History of the African National Congress, 1989
This revised edition published by Penguin Books (South Africa) (Pty) Ltd 2012

ISBN 978-0-14-352879-1

Cover by Michiel Botha
Cover image: Multimedia-Stock
Printed and bound by Interpak Book Printers, Pietermaritzburg

Acknowledgement: The quotation from Oliver Tambo, writing in *No Easy Walk to Freedom* is reproduced on pages 66 to 67 by kind permission of Heinemann Educational Books Ltd.

For

AMINA

CONTENTS

ACKNOWLEDGEMENTS

I would like to thank the people who helped me write this book. Helen Joseph, a remarkable woman who devoted much of her life to the struggle for black liberation in South Africa, gave me insight and wise advice. Thabo Mbeki, chief spokesman for the African National Congress while the organisation was in exile, offered his influential co-operation from the start of the first edition.

Mike McCann, a dear friend and gifted photographer who died tragically in 1988, drove me through rocky mountain tracks in search of Nelson Mandela's relatives in the Transkei. Tom Lodge, an authority on black political movements in South Africa, reviewed the first and second scripts, generously providing informed criticism. The late Tom Sebina of the ANC's information department in Lusaka arranged interviews and corrected factual errors in the first edition. Amina and the late Yusuf Cachalia kindly examined the final proofs of the original version. William Gumede read parts of the manuscript.

My sons Jonah and Niko and my mother Idely supported me by being there and enduring the trying times. My sisters Marion and Sheila, too. Fiona Forde and Alison Grant gave me excellent ideas; Adam Roberts suggested some important changes.

PROLOGUE

When I first thought of writing this book in the mid-1980s, South Africa was in flames. Hardly anybody could imagine the country escaping outright civil war, 'bloodbath' being the most common prediction among pundits.

Although the rest of my family had barely heard of him, I had been an ardent admirer of Nelson Mandela for years. Working as a journalist on the left-wing *Rand Daily Mail* in Johannesburg meant I talked about him and the organisation he symbolised, the African National Congress (ANC), on a daily, if not an hourly, basis. Like all my colleagues, I loathed the politics of apartheid and joined protest marches at every opportunity. Nelson Mandela embodied freedom, courage and integrity. He was the hero of most non-white South Africans – and mine, too.

So I decided to write my first book on Nelson Mandela. He had been in prison for over two decades at that stage, but I believed that he would be released sooner rather than later. Apartheid couldn't last forever and the ANC would eventually compromise, or so I reasoned when setting off to research my subject.

At the University of the Witwatersrand's libraries, the biggest information resource in the country, I was directed to a tiny section of banned books, where a vinegary woman wrote all my details in a black register before reluctantly unlocking a small cupboard. Telling me that she was required to watch me while I read the books – indeed, that I was required to sit in a particular chair, which she pointed out with a vividly painted fingernail – she took the first of my requested titles gingerly from a shelf, handed it to me, locked the cupboard, and sat down opposite with a deep sigh. I had heard that even innocuous books like the classic *Black Beauty* had been banned in South Africa because of its title, so the smallness of the prohibited section was worrying.

Day after day, I sat before the sour librarian searching for information about Nelson Mandela. There was so little that the awful truth began to dawn on me: he had been in prison for such a long time that virtually nothing beyond basic biographical detail was known about him.

For a while, I went in search of people who had known him before his imprisonment, like Yusuf and Amina Cachalia, but most of his ANC colleagues were either in exile or in jail. I was considering a trip to the UK to check out the libraries of the London School of Economics and SOAS when an English friend volunteered to do it for me. But there was nothing much beyond the material I had already seen, he reported. Finally, I realised that I would not be able to accumulate enough knowledge or insight to undertake a book on Nelson Mandela until he was released from prison.

That's when I decided to write about the ANC instead. My research took me to remote parts of South Africa, repeatedly to Lusaka in Zambia – where the organisation had its headquarters – as well as to London. It was a fascinating project conducted under sometimes trying circumstances because the ANC was a banned organisation in South Africa at the time.

On one occasion, after a section of my manuscript was removed from my luggage by security police while I was en route to Lusaka, I was questioned about my contact with the ANC by two South African spooks. Suggesting that we go for lunch at the Sandton Sun hotel, the chatty 'good' cop asked why my hands were shaking when I lifted a glass of Coke stacked with rattling ice. For some reason, his scorn of my fear emboldened me and I started telling deliberately long and tedious tales about my travels. The quiet 'bad' cop became so bored that he almost nodded off.

But the second time they 'invited' me to lunch at the same venue, the two security policemen tried to recruit me to spy on ANC individuals, like military supremos Joe Modise and Chris Hani, with whom I was in contact in Zambia. That was even more scary a prospect than being questioned about who I'd talked to at the ANC's dingy Cairo Road offices in Lusaka. I told them they could yank out my thumb and toe nails one by one but I'd never rat on the organisation I admired. 'You've approached the wrong person. Let's just leave it at that,' I said, trying to keep a steady voice. There was silence at the table for a while before the 'good' cop offered to help with my book research by giving me free flights on South African Airways to London and New York, where ANC heavyweights like Oliver Tambo and Thabo Mbeki spent a lot of time. At that point, I pushed back my chair and told them not to contact me again. To my surprise, the mute spook got up as I was leaving and asked me quietly if I had any journalism colleagues with drug or cash-flow problems to whom they could pitch their espionage overtures. I didn't even answer.

The resultant book, an earlier version of this one, was called *The Struggle: A History of the African National Congress.* Published in London in 1989, when the ANC was still banned, it came out in South Africa during the same week that Nelson Mandela was released from prison in 1990.

I met Mandela in Soweto a few days after his release to hand him a copy of the book, and he quizzed me with great interest on its genesis under apartheid's recently lifted restrictions. Subsequently, I met him on at least a dozen social occasions – mainly at private lunches and dinners arranged by his friends the Cachalias as well as Bram Fischer's family. Observing him at close range both before and during his presidency, I got a sense of the man as opposed to the icon. That's why the Epilogue in this edition is a glimpse of the extraordinary leader I had once hoped to feature as the main subject of the original book.

1

NELSON MANDELA – EARLY DAYS

Only one child in the tiny Transkei village of Qunu could speak English in 1928 and he seldom needed the language. Much of his time was spent herding cattle and goats up and down the rolling valleys surrounding Umtata. He loved animals and would talk quietly to the cows as if they were his friends, addressing each one by name.

Every day after school the boy wandered along grassy hills high above the beehive huts of Qunu, where he had lived with his extended family since his birth in Mvezo on 18 July 1918. He called to his father's herd as he walked, reciting the tables and rhymes he had learnt in the classroom.

His name was Rolihlahla, which means in Xhosa 'one who brings trouble on himself'. It was not a fitting description of the quiet ten-year-old. He was the son along with three daughters and three older half-siblings of a noble man called Gadla Mandela, who had been a chief of the Tembu tribe in the Bashee River district. The boy had learnt from his father that honour begins early in life, and so he examined each animal closely when he found the herd on the hillside, noticing if any were injured or sickening or weary. Then he drove them slowly towards his father's homestead, coaxing with soothing Xhosa words the beasts that laboured.

There were times when English proved useful. Once, after Rolihlahla had seen the cattle safely into their enclosure of mimosa thorn bushes, he heard the sounds of a motorcycle engine revving on the nearby road which runs from Umtata to Port Elizabeth. He listened as the mechanical roar and splutter continued above the lusty winds which often blow through the treeless valleys of the Transkei. Then he called to his sisters and cousins.

They left the game they had been playing in the courtyard formed by a semi-circle of round huts and scrambled up a grassy ridge after Rolihlahla. On top stood a white man with his motorcycle at the side of the road. He was angrily kicking the starter pedal but the engine would not engage for longer than a few seconds. The other barefoot children hung back in a whispering huddle, girls clutching their skirts against the wind. Only Rolihlahla stepped forward and asked in English if he might be of assistance.

The white man glanced up and merely grunted, but Rolihlahla was soon helping him, holding this and pressing that on command, and talking to the stranger. When the man asked his name, Rolihlahla replied 'Nelson'. It was the European name he had been given at school; Gadla Mandela gave his name as Henry if he was dealing with whites.

When daylight had almost gone, the engine finally roared into action. Smiling at Rolihlahla, the white man dug his hand into his pocket and drew something out, giving it to the black boy. Then he sped off.

The other children ran to Rolihlahla's side, begging him to show them what he had been given. Rolihlahla held his clenched hand above their heads, turned away, then drew out three pennies, giving one each to his sisters. The rest he kept himself, explaining that he needed the money to pay his school fees.

Gadla Mandela was a poor man. His ancestors had been much richer, with large herds befitting their status as members of the Xhosa aristocracy. But the arrival after 1652 of white Dutch settlers calling themselves Boers and the mass migration south into the Transkei of black people fleeing the wrath of the crazed Zulu warrior Shaka had brought increasing population pressure. Pastures became overgrazed; or agricultural land was less and less productive. Just over a hundred years before Rolihlahla was born, more white settlers added to the overcrowding of the early 1800s when the Cape was ceded to the British Empire and Englishmen began to claim land on which the Xhosas had formerly grazed their cattle.

Rolihlahla used to listen to his great-uncles talking about those faraway days. He sat in firelight beneath darkening skies on warm summer evenings, a solemn boy among the many descendants of the great Xhosa chief, Ngubengcuka. They recalled how their forefathers had moved southwards down the African continent, seizing land in the Transkei from the indigenous Khoisan and Bushmen; how the Boers had then encroached and how the British had sold large tracts of land to white farmers settling along the corridor which divides the Drakensberg Mountains and the Indian Ocean. When Xhosa cattle strayed on to the annexed land, they were shot by British troops. Herdsmen who dared to take their starving beasts on to white-owned pastures were sentenced to floggings of up to a hundred lashes or given fines for which the black farmers would have to trade precious cattle.

Slowly the Xhosa herds shrank. Turning reluctantly to other agricultural endeavours in the unyielding soil covering the slopes they lived on, the Xhosas invented a sort of spade, two feet long, shaped like the broad end of an oar, which was used from a sitting position because the land was so hard to till. Many had not a single ox left with which to draw a plough.

In 1837 the Boers despaired of British administrators and decided to leave the Cape colony. Abandoning their houses and the land they had cultivated in the Transkei, they loaded their ox wagons and trekked north in search of a new life. British settlers quickly occupied the farms they left behind.

Then an extraordinary event occurred. In 1856 a young Xhosa girl called Nonquase claimed she had seen a vision by a river. She reported omnipotent spirits saying that if the Xhosas killed all their cattle and destroyed all the grain supplies, their ancestors would rise from the dead to drive the white Englishmen into the sea and restore to the Xhosas their former abundance of cattle and grain. Nonquase travelled all over the region to spread the prophecy, announcing 18 February 1857 as the date for the sacrifice. Several thousand cattle were slaughtered on the appointed day and many fields of maize and sorghum were set alight. But the 'blood suns' and the hurricane of her vision did not come. Nonquase blamed the failure on farmers who had not obeyed the ancestor spirits by killing all their cattle and burning all their crops. More animals and fields were destroyed. The sacrifice lasted three months but still her prophecy failed to come true.

Starvation quickly engulfed the Xhosa nation. Over 68 000 people died in a single area west of the Kei River. This marked the beginning of the Xhosas' servitude to whites. Destitute black families staggered into the British colony in the eastern and western Cape in their thousands, begging for food and agreeing to harsh labour terms in exchange.

The Boer War began in 1899. It ended with the Afrikaner republics in the north of South Africa losing their independence and becoming part of the British Empire. Then, eight years later, the British government in London decided it was time for South Africa to become a self-governing dominion, which signalled the beginning of united English and Boer resistance to black advancement.

The Xhosas' hostility towards the British in the Cape continued, especially when the latter began to meddle in tribal politics. There had always been wars between Xhosa families fighting to secure the chieftain paramountcy, but now the British started taking sides and fermenting hostility between rival black groups.

When Xhosa chiefs, known as *inkosis*, complained about British interference, arrogant British governors gave them short shrift. One of them, Sir Harry Smith, used to make the black leaders kiss his feet as a mark of respect. The *inkosis*, including Rolihlahla's grandfather, were outraged that white men thought themselves superior and viewed the Xhosas as savages.

The chiefs returned to their kraals despondent but proud, regaling their fireside audiences with accounts of how, when whites had first arrived in 1652, it was the Xhosas who thought themselves superior. Far from envying the Europeans' pale faces and strange habits, Xhosas thought whites wore peculiar clothing because their bodies were feeble and sickly. At first the blacks coveted the white man's guns and horses but they soon realised their own hunting methods were far better suited to dense bush.

One of Rolihlahla's uncles, who had learnt to speak English while acting as a chief's councillor, often related the story of the hated Sir Harry Smith's encounter with *inkosi* Dyani Tshatshu. Smith said to Dyani: 'Fool! You dared join with the kaffirs against the power of the Queen. Have you anything to say to the Lord Bishop for the furtherance of education among your countrymen?' Dyani replied: 'The Lord Bishop is a great and wise man, and the Great Chief has already remarked that I am a fool. How, therefore, can I give any advice upon this subject?'

Xhosas deeply resented the white Englishman's dictatorial manners. They had never been ruled by autocratic chiefs of the cruel type that periodically rose to power in the Zulu kingdom. Xhosas were accustomed to a democratic tradition in which a chief lost his position if he angered the people. A Xhosa *inkosi* discussed everything thoroughly with his councillors before making a new law. When he announced it to the people he watched keenly for their reaction, immediately withdrawing the decree if it proved unpopular. He would then punish his councillors for advising him badly.

The old Xhosa chiefs particularly resented the British because they scorned co-operation, whereas the early Boer farmers who had settled along the Great Fish River, troublesome though they were to the black farmers, had not only fought but also traded with the Xhosas. A few chiefs who traded peacefully with the Boers for years had eventually seen no reason why the two should not merge; white Africans united with blacks against the common British foe. Indeed, one chief called Nqika hoped to marry a Boer's daughter to cement his alliance with the Dutch.

Young Rolihlahla listened to these stories and thought it mysterious that there had once been a time when his forefathers had contemplated marriage with whites. On the few occasions when he travelled to Umtata to shop with his mother, Rolihlahla was mesmerised by the haughty white ladies of the town, who would sometimes hand oranges out to black children. Though scrambling for their gifts, the children would always be careful not to touch a white lady's crisply starched garments for fear of giving offence.

When he was not absorbing the history of the Xhosa people at the feet of his elders, Rolihlahla thought of little except his education. The boy sometimes played cards and soccer with the other children and he would occasionally challenge a peer to a stick fight. He liked to plough with his father's few remaining oxen in September, when the flowering of the erythrina trees announced it was time to sow. And he helped his mother harvest the maize and pumpkins in January, the sugar cane, melons and beans in March. He helped his father store dried mealies in grain pits dug deep inside the cattle enclosure to await the cold, hungry days of winter. But everyone in Qunu knew that Rolihlahla's real love was learning.

His father knew the child was clever. When Gadla died a painful death from tuberculosis, he left behind a will in which he told Rolihlahla's guardian uncle, the regent Jongintaba, that the ten-year-old boy must be educated no matter how difficult it was to find funds for his schooling. 'God will help you provide for him,' wrote Gadla.

Nelson missed his father. For some months, he took to wearing Gadla's jacket, which was so big on him that it covered his knees. Soon after Gadla's death, Rolihlahla's guardian decided the boy should join him at Mqekezweni, Jongintaba's royal kraal. Nelson said farewell to his mother and his sisters and went to live with his uncle, who had a son of the same age called Justice. The two boys soon became close friends. But Justice was neither quiet like Nelson nor studious. The cousins, always together, began to get into trouble at the mission primary school they attended. One day the headmaster called Jongintaba to his office, telling him Justice had been expelled, though he refused to reveal the student's offence. The father, saddened and shamed, was about to leave the school building when the principal called him back to reassure him that his nephew was still a promising student. After that, Nelson worked harder than ever at his studies.

The primary schools he attended at Qunu, Clarkebury and Qolweni were run by missionaries, and the boy became a God-fearing Christian, always willing to help a neighbour. When he returned to his own family for holidays in Qunu, his devoutly Christian mother and his sisters found Nelson unchanged.

He was still the first to volunteer for a chore when something needed doing; he had not grown lazy in adolescence. If he saw an old man chopping wood he would immediately take the axe himself. He was always ready to help his sisters and cousins with schoolwork they did not understand.

As he and Justice neared the age of thirteen, the two teenagers were sent to their *inkosi* uncle Dalindyebo's kraal. There, in preparation for their traditional Xhosa circumcision rites, they were taught the basic arts of warfare while continuing to attend school. When Dalindyebo's son nearest in age to Nelson and Justice reached maturity the two boys, along with others now living at the chief's Great Place, decorated their bodies with ochre and white dust ground from a rare stone. Wearing hide loincloths and carrying shields and spears, they followed the age-old custom of leaving the chief's kraal for fourteen days of complete freedom before assuming the responsibilities of manhood.

Some of the boys went on daring journeys, carrying fermented milk in leather pouches and fortifying themselves with charms and herbs. They followed footpaths through dense forests of mimosa and yellowwood trees. If they came upon sneezewood, they hacked off branches, hardening them in fire until they formed weapons as strong as iron. They listened for the calls of hammerheads and hornbills, which warned them of danger ahead. They followed the song of the honeybird to beehives and sucked the combs dry. If they failed to spear game, they ate young mimosa roots instead. If they tore their skin, they searched for blue-flowered plumbago to seal the wounds. When a river was too full to cross, they made a raft from reeds. And when walking through long stretches of tall tambooki grass, so high that they were hidden from each other, a code call or whistle was agreed in advance in case they lost one another.

When their time was up they returned to the chief's kraal to be circumcised. It was an intensely painful experience, requiring months of recovery in a special dormitory known as the circumcision lodge, where they remained from seed time to harvest. Then a grand feast was held in their honour. A huge fire was lit and all who lived within sight of the smoke considered themselves invited to the celebration.

Afterwards, the novice adults returned to their family kraals, where final marriage arrangements were being made for them in the prolonged negotiations between families. As Nelson was determined to further his education he was allowed to postpone plans for his nuptials.

He remained at school in Healdtown until he and Justice passed their 'matric', the examination required for admission to university, at the end of 1937. Overjoyed at their success, and relieved that Justice had finally proved worthy of his illustrious parentage, Jongintaba took the two nineteen-year-olds to a tailor, who made each a three-piece suit. They left the kraal together early the following year to enrol at the University of Fort Hare, which was one of the few South African universities open to full-time black students in 1938.

Nelson wanted to be a lawyer but he had to obtain a Bachelor of Arts degree before qualifying as a law student. Six years of study lay ahead, during which there would be barely enough money from Jongintaba to pay his fees. But Nelson was well motivated. During his last years at school he had become interested in politics and the rights of black people in South Africa. Law offered him the best chance of advancing those interests.

Nelson studied diligently at Fort Hare but he and Justice joined the Students' Representative Council (SRC) and became involved in campus protests. Most of their clashes with the university authorities revolved around the poor living conditions at Fort Hare, particularly the unappetising food. When attempts were made to curb the increasingly strident SRC's powers, Nelson and Justice were suspended abruptly, leaving the university at the end of 1940.

Jongintaba was dismayed to hear of their challenge to the Fort Hare authorities. He insisted they return to university and apologise before they lost their hard-won places. Both refused, saying they would never apologise for exercising their legitimate rights. Jongintaba persisted, but when Nelson was on the verge of agreeing to go back to Fort Hare his uncle raised another issue which deeply offended his principles. 'My guardian felt it was time for me to get married. He loved me very much and looked after me as diligently as my father had. But he was no democrat and did not think it worthwhile to consult me about a wife. He selected a girl, fat and dignified: *lobola* was paid, and arrangements were made for the wedding.'

Nelson realised he would have to run away from the Transkei if he was to avoid the tribal marriage. He and Justice decided to go to Johannesburg. Needing money to finance the long journey, they sold two of Jongintaba's oxen to a white trader. On the way, they stopped at their cousin chief Kaiser Matanzima's Great Place. Matanzima, who had been at Fort Hare with Nelson and Justice the previous year, slaughtered a sheep and held a feast to celebrate their visit.

Kaiser, or 'KD' as everyone called him, was fond of Nelson. He admired Nelson's kindness, especially towards his family, and he found the young Mandela agreeably thoughtful company, unlike his frivolous cousin Justice. 'Whatever Nelson said was well considered and worth hearing,' KD once remarked.

Matanzima and Mandela were often seen together in the Transkei during the years before Nelson went to Johannesburg: distinctively tall young men who shared the features of their common *inkosi* grandfather. They were both Xhosa aristocrats, dignified by straight backs and proud heads. Both were destined to be leaders in the struggle for South Africa, though in opposing camps.

2

COLD, COLD CITY OF GOLD

Far away from the boulder-strewn valleys of the Transkei lay eGoli, the city named Johannesburg, which shimmered invitingly in every country youth's dreams. Built on hills six thousand feet above the sea, atop the world's richest gold seams, it could have been an enchanting city. But it was no more than a harsh place of work for most of its inhabitants.

Not that young men returning from Johannesburg to the rural kraals admitted their disappointment. Most were too proud to describe the painful period of transition to eGoli, groping for European standards in bewildering conditions. Instead, they told tales of flamboyant adventure and, since they often came home dressed for sartorial effect in tight trousers, flowing neckties and wide-brimmed hats, the country cousin was suitably dazzled. He too wanted to become a man of the city, looking down on the kraals as retarded and old-fashioned.

As soon as he could hoard enough money for his train ticket, virtually every able-bodied young man set forth to sweeten his life with a taste of the urban experience. Some never saw the gleaming lights of Johannesburg because there were wild men on the trains, young gangsters called *tsotsis*, armed with flick knives and sharpened bicycle spokes, who would kill for a handful of coins.

One country boy of scant schooling, who died in this way before his sixteenth birthday, had nothing in his pockets except a job-seeking letter written for him by his relatively well-educated older brother. 'Dear Sir,' it read. 'Good wishes to you. I wonder, How do you do, Sir, all God knows about. Well, Sir, I am after for a job, Lovely Sir. I am fit as a fidly in delivering for Bicycle all around the Town. Thanks Sir. I am Phineas.'

The city slickers who turned the heads of country youths were often touts employed by mining companies to wander from village to village painting glowing pictures of life in eGoli. European traders were also used as recruiting agents. Some of them encouraged penniless youths to run up debts in their tempting stores and then, when demanding payment, insisted upon pain of police intervention that they sign on with a mining house in order to repay the money owed.

Each recruit signed a contract or, if he could neither read nor write, simply stamped his thumb print on the legal document. Around six thousand youths annually took their glittering dreams to Johannesburg, where most found themselves trapped in a grotesque nightmare. The muscle-wrenching hacking at rock thousands of feet underground was physically exhausting. Adjusting to the sounds of machinery instead of lowing cattle – the mechanical whine of shaft-lifts rushing men a mile deep into the earth, screaming power drills and yelled commands – was psychologically devastating. Those who could not cope deserted, either returning to their kraals or searching for less arduous jobs in towns along the Reef. If caught, a deserter usually went to prison, where he might well find himself back in mining service as convict labour.

On completion of their contracts, black miners usually made the long journey back to their tribal homes for a rest. They travelled by train or relied on chance lifts in order to save the fare, which was around half a month's wages. This sum might be spent instead on a pair of American shoes, tied together and hung around their necks to preserve the leather while trudging barefoot along the road from Port Elizabeth to the Transkei.

Many, encouraged by a small bonus if they came back to the mines within six months, returned to earn more money. The labour demands of the mines varied from month to month according to the opening of new shafts or the price of gold, and the availability of labour fluctuated in ratio to poverty in the kraals. September and October were peak supply 'hunger months' in rural areas, when the usual number of five or six labour trains reaching Johannesburg each week increased to ten or eleven, their coaches of underfed human cargo packed to capacity.

The passengers were almost exclusively male adults. Mining magnates gave no thought to the creation of decent villages where the men might bring their wives and families. Instead, black miners were herded into men-only barracks with scant recreational facilities beyond soccer fields. Most spent their spare time and money in illicit liquor houses or on prostitutes. Some mines operated a token system under which blacks pledged their wages in advance to a concessionary storekeeper who was present on payday to collect his debts, often the entire pay packet. Many plunged deeply into debt, becoming economically chained to the mines.

Workers outside mining lived with families in townships referred to by whites as 'reservoirs of labour' or 'locations'. Both terms betrayed the impermanence with which whites viewed the entire urban black population at a time when the labour supply from the kraals seemed inexhaustible. Streets in the 'locations' had no names. Houses were simply numbered from one to ten thousand. Overcrowding was so acute that a two-roomed house usually accommodated between twelve and eighteen people. Typically, a man, his wife, his mother, his teenage siblings and his own children slept together in a ten-square-metre room, performing all their most intimate human functions in that crowded space. The wardrobe often lay under a raised bed because it would not fit anywhere else. When he dressed before cycling up to fourteen miles to an office or factory in the chilly hours of daybreak, the breadwinner would make a curtain of privacy by holding a blanket between his teeth.

A single tap often served over a hundred houses. Many women had to walk a mile or more to do their washing and fetch water for household needs, carrying it back in drums balanced on their heads. Sewerage was primitive or non-existent. The wind tossed stinking refuse about, spreading diseases and contributing to the high rate of infant mortality. Life expectancy for blacks was at least twenty years less than for whites.

The ruling race saw no need to plan a more conformable urban future for blacks, regarding them simply as migrant workers who would ultimately return to the tribal kraals where they belonged. Those who objected to the conditions in the townships were free to leave the cities, whites contended: there were many more job-seekers to replace the disaffected. But contrary to white opinion, tribal life no longer offered blacks a viable alternative. It had virtually collapsed as a cohesive system in the decades after whites annexed most of the land formerly held by tribal Africans, forcing them to find work in the cities.

Once in the townships, new city dwellers grappled anxiously with complex adjustments. They had somehow to make an indefinite compromise between three societies: the tribal society to which they were expected to return, the black urban society in which they lived, and the white society in which they worked. Clinging to the old dignities of their heritage, young men in homburg hats and girls wearing lipstick danced their old dances on moonlit nights in the townships, facing one another in separate groups, their bodies rigid and quivering, stamping the earth with their hard feet until a dust cloud rose around them. The songs to which they danced blared from the horns of wind-up gramophones, sung by faceless crooners in unimaginably distant lands.

Few whites were sympathetic to the conditions in which blacks lived. Though they knew that the meagre wages they paid could not buy clothing as well as adequate food for a family, white employers nevertheless expected blacks who worked in shops and offices to be neatly dressed at all times. Realising that appearance governed their prospects in the white man's world, Africans saved on food to buy clothes and respectability. As a result, malnutrition grew steadily worse, and was a major cause of the inertia which whites regarded as an inborn racial characteristic.

Thousands of humbly submissive black men and women worked as servants in spacious white homes, daily confronting the fact that wealth was white and poverty was black in South Africa. Men served as gardeners and cooks while women minded children or washed and ironed. They were known in the white households as 'girls' and 'boys', even when they had passed middle age. Most of them knew and despised the nagging voices of white women, who complained constantly about the dirtiness of their servants without stopping to consider whether, in the conditions prevailing in the townships, anything else was to be expected. Though viewing Africans as a lower order, whites continued to expect them to perform their tasks immaculately.

Acute dislike of social or physical contact with blacks was waived only in the case of nannies who, though regarded as potential thieves the minute they walked through the door, were permitted to bath, cuddle and often sleep with cherished white wards cradled in their arms while the parents were otherwise engaged. Most families had a black nanny, yet whites seemed incapable of registering their own hypocrisy. Physical contact in the form of mixed marriage remained the strongest of all colour prejudices, a subject guaranteed to make the white community's flesh creep.

There were a few kind and generous white employers, who became the stuff of legend in the townships. One old white spinster, living alone in a tumbledown house far from neighbours, reputedly treated her servants as her own kin. She had suffered a lifelong dread of thunderstorms and lightning. One of her servants, discovering this fear in the early years of their association, had ever since gone to her room when storm clouds gathered and sat at her feet until the weather cleared.

The white community was capable of great generosity towards Africans on rare occasions when its heart was touched. Once, when a tornado hit a makeshift squatter compound at Albertynville on the perimeter of Johannesburg, ripping off roofs and carrying away walls made from hessian, flattened tins and cardboard, the white conscience was stirred into action. Responding to a wireless announcement calling for relief assistance, cars began streaming out of white suburbs, bringing money, clothes and provisions on a scale few blacks had imagined possible.

It was in this environment that a stocky, aggressive eighteen-year-old named Walter Sisulu sought his first job when he arrived in eGoli in 1930. He came from Engcobo in the Transkei, where he had been raised by his mother, his aunts and an uncle, all staunch Anglicans. His father was white, a foreman who had come to Engcobo briefly in order to supervise black road workers. Walter never met him because none but the most eccentric white South African would commit social suicide by claiming a dusky boy as a son. His pale skin, being lighter than that of his peers, embarrassed Walter throughout his childhood and led to a bitter resentment of whites.

His favourite activities at school were singing and Bible studies. He particularly loved the story of Daniel in the lion's den, and was most interested in David since 'here was a small person who defeated a great enemy because he was able to plan. He killed a giant with a sling, the same kind of sling that we small boys would use to kill birds in the forest. I was usually the youngest and smallest boy in my group so I could identify with David.'

He was in a rebellious mood when he left home, having quarrelled with his aunts because they had constantly spoken highly and gratefully of the few whites who had occasionally been kind to them. In protest, Walter had behaved so rudely in front of white visitors who came to call on his uncle, a tribal headman, that one of his aunts took him aside and issued a stern warning, saying he would never find a job in the city because he was not man enough to be able to serve. Walter was determined to prove her wrong and to demonstrate his manhood by earning enough money to pay *lobola* for a bride.

His first awesome image of eGoli was the city's railway system. The train he had travelled in was itself a marvel to Walter, speeding like a giant steel tube through the countryside, but the platforms and connecting tracks at central station left him truly impressed. It was impossible for Walter to admit the white man's technological genius at the time, but journalist Anthony Sampson later recorded his impression of the railway: 'I couldn't just find out how it was done,' confessed Walter.

He was mesmerised by the restless vitality of the crowds and the variety of motor cars speeding down Main Reef Road; by the shops offering endless choices, and the tall buildings rising out of the veld. To sophisticated outsiders, Johannesburg seemed an infant and vaguely pretentious mimic of New York, but to black country folk who had never seen anything remotely like it, the city was a miracle.

Walter first worked as a labourer in a Johannesburg dairy but he was sacked for insubordination. He then signed a four-month contract with a gold mine called Rose Deep, where he found the work intolerably hard and despised the life he led. Especially hateful were his sour Afrikaner supervisor and a bad-tempered white compound manager: both seemed to enjoy cracking whips which Walter was sullenly obliged to heed.

He decided to return to the Cape, taking a job as a kitchen hand in a white household in East London, an experience that sharpened his insight into white prejudices. He found he could study his white employers closely from a vantage point of virtual invisibility because most of the family members did not even know his name. Watching his employers' children issuing rude instructions to the servants, he realised that whites absorbed their conviction of racial superiority very early in life. Woken each morning by a black hand bearing a cup of tea, they were served by menial Africans throughout the rest of the day and throughout the rest of their lives.

Despondent and broke, Walter went back to Johannesburg and found a job in a bakery. While he was packing loaves of bread, an elderly colleague there told him about trade unions. He was immediately excited by the concept of collective bargaining and began to organise his fellow workers, leading them on a strike for higher wages. The white employer took stock of the situation, speaking to each employee in turn and persuading them to return to work. Then he sacked Sisulu.

Taking jobs in a variety of factories, Walter lost one after another because he protested against unfair labour practices. For a time, he suppressed his frustration by studying Xhosa history and English grammar at home after work. Having advanced his Standard Four education, he began writing articles about Xhosa leaders for a newspaper called *Bantu World*.

One evening, sitting in a train on his way home to the house he shared with relatives in Orlando, Walter watched a white official confiscate a black man's expensive season ticket. Enraged by the victim's helplessness, he intervened and argued with the collector, who eventually punched him. Walter returned a hail of blows until he was arrested by a security guard and later given a prison sentence.

The months in jail further embittered Sisulu, who intensified his search for a political method of retaliation. When war was declared in 1939 he helped campaign to stop Africans volunteering for the army. He became an admirer of the Japanese, hoping they might someday invade South Africa. His closest confidante, later his wife, was Albertina Totiwe, a woman who respected his opinions and gave him confidence, coaxing him to abandon his sensitivity about his racially mixed parentage. 'I'm black enough for both of us,' she used to say of his light skin.

Always kind-hearted, Walter never forgot the cold nights he had spent on the floor of the servants' quarters in East London. During winter Albertina complained constantly about the number of jerseys and coats he peeled off his own body to hand to shivering friends or strangers. His driving force became the desire to help victimised blacks, and his assistance to them came in many guises. At one time he turned his attention to a fight against crime, deciding to do his bit to combat the banditry which unemployed *tsotsis* inflicted on innocent residents. For a week, he patrolled the streets at night, holding a knife under a furled umbrella. When he spotted a menacing group, he would hide ahead of them and spring out, brandishing his knife the minute they accosted a passer-by. He soon acquired a reputation as a street vigilante, and was said to own a magic umbrella capable of making *tsotsis* flee for their lives.

After joining the Orlando Brotherly Society, a group which met to discuss Xhosa traditions but inevitably spent more time on contemporary politics, Walter was at last able to express his beliefs openly, without being made to feel different or contemptible. Friends in the Society advised him to escape obnoxious contact with whites by becoming economically independent – a tall order but one which Walter soon fulfilled. Setting up a modest estate agency in central Johannesburg, he began selling the small plots of suburban land which were still available to blacks.

In 1940 he finally found his ideological home in a black political movement formed twenty-eight years earlier, the African National Congress.

When Nelson Mandela arrived in Johannesburg in 1941 he went to the address of his only contact in the city, an elderly family friend from Umtata who worked as a supervisor at Crown Mines. He arranged for Nelson, a powerfully built man, to work as a mine policeman with a promise of promotion to clerk if he proved himself worthy. He was given a whistle and a *knobkerrie*, a heavy stick carved into a ball at the clubbing end. Thus armed, he stood guard at the entrance to the mine compound, where he discovered that the profitable roar of gold digging had deafened whites to the human misery accumulating inside bleak dormitories at the base of the pyramids of crushed rock.

The miners slept on concrete shelves, often clutching all their belongings under the blankets for fear of being robbed by desperate men stretched out alongside them. Nelson was lonely, hating the life of the miner, and he left as soon as he had enough money to tide him over to the next job, his guardian having sent a telegram requesting his release to the mine management.

He found a room in a location called Alexandra, north of Johannesburg, where living conditions were no better but the human environment was warmer than the all-male mining compound. Children chattered in the dusty streets and young women smiled their shy smiles. Crowing roosters scuttled away to clear a path for Nelson in the hour before sunrise when, as a budding boxer, he jogged around the houses in his daily fitness routine.

The house he lived in was one of a long row made of breeze blocks and tin roofs held down by stones. It leaked through innumerable holes in the rainy season and grew as steamy as a pressure cooker beneath the summer sun. Helped by a small allowance from Jongintaba, he began studying by correspondence to complete his interrupted BA degree course. But he found it difficult to concentrate on his work in the house which, being home to streams of people, was perpetually noisy. There was no electricity so he had to study by candlelight in the evenings. A young neighbour who befriended

Nelson and felt he needed help adapting to city life decided to introduce him to the hospitable Sisulu family. Walter immediately liked Nelson, inviting him to move into the house he shared with his fiancée Albertina, his mother and numerous itinerant relatives, and offering him a job in his estate agency at £2 a month plus commission. Though far from rich, Sisulu was an unusually generous man who loved to see blacks bettering themselves. When he learnt of Nelson's ambition to study law, he offered to pay the remaining fees for his BA studies.

In 1942 Nelson borrowed money from Walter to buy a suit and a graduation gown before meeting his mother, his sisters and his cousin, KD Matanzima, at the solemn Fort Hare ceremony where he received his Bachelor of Arts certificate. KD drove Mrs Mandela and her daughters to the university town of Alice in the eastern Cape for a brief, nostalgic reunion. Nelson longed to return with them to the beloved hills of Qunu but he had to hurry back to work in Sisulu's office.

Through Sisulu, Nelson met a senior partner in a firm of white lawyers, who agreed to employ him as an articled clerk while he studied law part-time at Wits, the University of the Witwatersrand. He later accepted a higher salary at another law firm, where a white partner named Harry Brigish was particularly encouraging, considering him 'a fine and decent young fellow'. But Brigish realised his increasingly politically conscious black clerk might someday fall foul of the law, so he warned Nelson against politics in general and the African National Congress in particular.

Attending lectures each evening at the Johannesburg Public Library or at Wits, Nelson sat with Duma Nokwe, the only other black on the course apart from Seretse Khama, future premier of Botswana, who came to the university for a few months after completing his first degree at Fort Hare. One of their lecturers, Professor Hahlo, an eminent jurist and author, repeatedly warned the students that blacks and women were incapable of becoming good lawyers, though he said Indians could expect to do well in the profession. When Nelson failed several exams there was little doubt among his fellow Indian students that Professor Hahlo's prejudice was largely to blame, although another of their lecturers, a respected advocate named Bram Fischer, was outspokenly committed to black advancement.

Nelson was compelled to halt his legal studies at Wits after failing exams in 1949 – despite his appeals for readmission. He would eventually qualify as an attorney through taking the professional exams in 1952. As one of only a couple of dozen articled clerks, modest though the appointment was, he had joined the new African elite.

Nelson's first brush with the police occurred during his student days when he and three Indian friends boarded an empty tram travelling from Wits down Market Street in central Johannesburg. As Nelson sat down, the white conductor yelled at the Indians, demanding to know why they had 'carried' a 'kaffir' on to his tram. They bellowed back, saying Nelson was no 'kaffir' but a law student, as entitled to sit in the tram as anyone else.

The conductor stopped the vehicle and called a policeman, who arrested the three Indians for obstructing a transport official in the course of his duty. All four were escorted to Marshall Square police station, where Nelson was told to make a statement against the others for allegedly 'carrying' him on to the tram. He refused.

One of the group telephoned Wits in the hope of finding Bram Fischer, who had fortunately lingered in his office after giving them the last lecture of the evening shortly before the incident. Fischer, the son of the judge president of the Orange Free State, hurried to Marshall Square and arranged for their release. He also offered to represent them in court the following day, when the magistrate greeted Fischer warmly, saying he had just returned from the Free State and a meeting with his esteemed friend, the judge president. The accused were quickly acquitted.

The year 1944 was an important one in Nelson Mandela's life: he joined the African National Congress and chose a bride named Eveline. She was a pretty nurse from Engcobo, one of the Sisulu relatives who shared Walter's home, where she and Nelson met and fell in love. After the wedding they moved into a room in Eveline's sister's home, where their first son Tembi was born a year later. Eveline worked in a nearby hospital, supplementing Nelson's salary while he pursued his studies. Finally, in 1946, the authorities granted the couple a two-bedroom house of their own in Orlando, which was soon crammed with needy relations only too happy to sleep on the floor.

Nelson's youngest sister Leaby was the first to arrive from Qunu to attend high school in Orlando. Others came and went, including Nelson's mother. KD Matanzima was a regular visitor who, like Nelson's white employer, continually cautioned him against the African National Congress. KD argued that the black people's best hope of advancement lay in co-operation with the whites, while Nelson, strongly influenced by Sisulu, believed change would not come until black people formed a united front against white oppression.

3

AFRICAN NATIONALISM IS BORN

Bloemfontein is the city in the heart of the Free State where opposing white political forces traditionally met to shape South African history. Eight years after the Boer War, the city hosted a conference resulting in the two Boer republics and the two British colonies forming the Union of South Africa.

The Act of Union signed in Bloemfontein in 1910 absolved Britain of any further responsibility for the country's future, dashing black hopes that England would eventually extend her liberal tradition in the Cape Colony – where blacks and mixed-race people known as coloureds were able to vote – to the other three provinces. Under the Union constitution, blacks in the Cape could lose their franchise if a two-thirds majority of both houses of parliament sitting in joint session ruled against it.

The few educated, politically conscious Africans in the country were appalled at the Union constitution. They immediately formed a delegation which sailed to England to protest against their exclusion from South Africa's parliament. But after pleading passionately for a rethink in London they realised that their long journey had been in vain: the British government's only concern was to secure white unity in South Africa. Historian D D T Jabavu, the country's first black professor, noted: 'The colour-bar clause struck the death-knell of native confidence in what used to be called British fair play. That cow of Great Britain had gone dry, and they must look to themselves for salvation.'

In the same year, 1910, a young Zulu relative of the Swazi royal family, Dr Pixley ka Izaka Seme, returned to Johannesburg from London. Seme was a newly qualified advocate, called to the bar at the Middle Temple after studying at Columbia and Oxford universities. He was energetic, proud and a little snobbish, a descendant of the Zulu warrior kings who had been defeated by whites thirty years earlier.

Seme had already distinguished himself as a speaker, delivering a prize-winning address on his hopes for African liberation when he graduated from Columbia University in 1906: 'The giant is awakening,' he told a startled New York audience. 'From the four corners of the earth, Africa's sons are marching up to the future's golden door, bearing the record of deeds of valour done ... The brighter day is rising upon Africa. Already I seem to see her chains dissolve, her desert plains red with harvest, her Abyssinia and her Zululand the seats of science and religion, reflecting the glory of the rising sun from the spires of their churches and universities ... Yes, the generation of Africa belongs to this new and powerful period ...'

Donning his top hat, morning coat and spats, Dr Seme set forth to establish a legal practice in Johannesburg, but he soon discovered how few opportunities were open to him as a black lawyer. The fact that Africans were not allowed to walk on pavements and were expected to raise their hats to whites infuriated Seme, who put away his dreams of rebuilding the Zulu nation and decided to unite blacks in defence of their rights. He began by summoning a meeting with three lawyers from different tribal origins, who together wrote a manifesto for publication in an African journal called *Imvo*. 'The demon of racialism, the aberrations of the Xhosa-Fingo feud, animosity that exists between the Zulus and the Tongas, between the Basuthu and every other native must be buried and forgotten,' Seme and his colleagues concluded. 'We are one people.'

In 1912 he called for a conference of African leaders. Many blacks harboured ancient grievances from wars fought among themselves half a century earlier, yet several hundred from all four provinces responded enthusiastically to Seme's call. They met in a dilapidated shed in Bloemfontein, some wearing Edwardian frock coats, others in the leopard skins that marked their status as chiefs. They were teachers, clergymen and clerks, businessmen, journalists and builders, all educated in missionary schools in the nineteenth century.

'Chiefs of royal blood and gentlemen of our race,' bellowed Dr Seme in his opening address. 'The white people of this country have formed what is known as the Union of South Africa – a union in which we have no voice in the making of the laws and no part in the administration. We have called you, therefore, to this conference so that we can together devise ways and means of forming our national union for the purpose of creating national unity and defending our rights and privileges.'

The conference ended with the formation of the South African Native National Congress, later renamed the African National Congress (ANC), which aimed to agitate for the removal of racial discrimination in parliament and in the public administration, schools and factories of South Africa. To further the interests of what it called 'the dark races of the subcontinent', the ANC planned to use 'peaceful propaganda' in the first instance and then 'passive action' or 'continued movement' along the lines advocated by Mahatma Gandhi, who had lived in South Africa since 1893.

Dr Seme was elected treasurer. Dr John Dube, a cautious Zulu headmaster from Natal and recipient of an honorary University of South Africa doctorate for his efforts towards establishing the first industrial school for blacks, won the presidential vote. The secretary was Solomon Plaatje, an interpreter from Kimberley who, despite a Standard Three education, had translated five Shakespearian plays into Setswana and was the first African to have written a novel in English.

The following year brought confirmation of the Union government's resolve to halt the advancement of blacks and exploit their labour. Included in a barrage of repressive laws was the Natives' Land Act, stripping blacks of their right to own or lease land in 'white' areas. It left the black population in possession of only about eight per cent of the entire country, forcing it into wage labour. Sol Plaatje wrote: 'Awakening on Friday morning, June 29, 1913, the South African native found himself not actually a slave, but a pariah in the land of his birth.' Black families were evicted from white farms in their thousands. Loading their belongings on to their heads, they trudged for days and nights in the middle of winter, driving small herds and carrying children from one white farm to the next as they begged for shelter. 'It looks as if these people are so many fugitives escaping from a war,' said Plaatje.

The ANC decided to send a petition protesting against the Natives' Land Act and other legislation to the prime minister, General Louis Botha, in Cape Town, and to appeal once again to the British. President Dube, who sported a sweeping walrus moustache, led his hopeful delegation across the seas shortly before the declaration of war in Europe. But their journey again proved fruitless.

When the war began in 1914, the ANC put aside its disillusionment with the British and voted unanimously to support London's war effort. Offering his government the services of five thousand black soldiers, Dube received a stinging rejection from the defence minister. 'Apart from other considerations,' the minister wrote, 'the present war is one which has its origins among the white people of Europe, and the government is anxious to avoid the employment of coloured citizens in warfare against whites.' Though not allowed to carry arms, thousands of blacks were to be recruited to dig trenches and perform menial tasks for white soldiers, a humiliation which the ANC received in stunned disbelief.

Africans had continued to hope that English-speaking whites in South Africa would prevail politically over Afrikaners, who were a largely uneducated, backward race, more threatened by black advancement than the English population. But the extent of the prejudice blacks faced in their struggle for equality was brought home when Jan Smuts, an internationally respected former Boer commander in Louis Botha's cabinet and a man who identified with English speakers in the Union, declared himself in favour of a racially divided society. Addressing a conference at the plush Savoy Hotel in London, Smuts announced: 'It has been our ideal to make South Africa a white man's country, but it is not a white man's country yet. It is still a black man's country.' He was warmly applauded in the British capital.

Shocked by Smuts' statement, Dube sent a reply to London: 'The natives of this continent are loyal subjects of His Majesty King George V, and most emphatically deny that either General Smuts or the Union government have any right to rob the natives of their human rights and guarantees of liberty and freedom under the Pax Britannica.'

When the war ended, Sol Plaatje led another ANC delegation to London, where he was warmly received by Britain's premier Lloyd George and the Archbishop of Canterbury. But his pleas for British intervention on behalf of black South Africans came to nothing: the British officials assured him that they could not interfere in the affairs of a self-governing country. Plaatje went on to the peace conference at Versailles, where he encountered another South African delegation led by one of Botha's ministers, General Barry Hertzog, who was busy trying to lobby support for an Afrikaner republic.

For several years after the war, drought ravaged the kraals in South Africa and thousands of blacks streamed into the cities in search of work. The ANC, with fewer than three thousand paid-up members, continued meeting annually to arrange polite deputations and petitions. Then, as the black urban population's prospects steadily deteriorated, a new militancy began to surface in its dignified deliberations. Sol Plaatje, who had turned down an offer of the presidency the previous year, first noticed the change after an executive committee meeting in 1918. Describing it in a letter to the mining company De Beers, he wrote: 'The ten Transvaal delegates came to the Congress with a concord and a determination that was perfectly astounding to our customary native demeanour at conferences. They spoke almost in unison, in short sentences, nearly all of which began and ended with the word "strike".'

Encouraged by these early trade union rumblings, the ANC organised its first public protest in 1919 to condemn the restrictive pass laws that had been used to regulate the lives of blacks since the nineteenth century. Gathering in their thousands behind the central pass office in Johannesburg, the demonstrators sang 'God Save the King' and raised cheers to the British Crown. They planned to surrender the pass documents that blacks in the city were obliged to carry by law, but squads of police arrived to baton-charge the crowd and arrest those who had already relinquished their passes. Rioting broke out and seven hundred demonstrators were taken to prison.

The ANC recoiled. The government was clearly in no mood to tolerate protest, however peacefully expressed. Two years later, blacks were again horrified to hear that an army of white soldiers had been deployed to shift black members of a religious sect after they refused to vacate white land at Bulhoek in the eastern Cape. The soldiers massacred 163 of the worshippers.

By 1922 protest was coming from a different racial sector: white workers. Simmering animosity between white miners and their employers broke into outright confrontation after a steep decline in the gold price persuaded mining magnates to replace semi-skilled whites with cheaper black labour. Thousands of impoverished white miners, facing unemployment once they had to compete with blacks earning far less, decided to stage a strike. Helped by the newly formed Communist Party of South Africa (CPSA) and by Afrikaner commandos from rural areas, the strikers marched through the streets of Johannesburg beneath a banner proclaiming 'Workers of the World, Fight and Unite for a White South Africa'. General Smuts, who was by then prime minister, summoned the army and air force to quell the spreading riots. As a result, 153 strikers were killed, over 500 injured, and key leaders of the revolt were hanged.

The strike marked a turning point, persuading Afrikaners and poor English-speaking whites to unite behind a leader who would protect them from black advancement. In a general election two years later, Smuts was denounced as a stooge of the mining magnates and ousted from power. In his place came a coalition government of the English-speaking Labour Party and the Afrikaner National Party, led by Afrikaner fanatic, General J B M Hertzog.

It was an ominous development for black hopes of eventual political accommodation with the English community. But Hertzog introduced a succession of minor reforms, such as the provision of first-class railway accommodation for blacks who could afford it. The leaders of the ANC, mostly educated, middle-class men with a greater interest in their own social position than that of the humbler black masses, began to hope that the new government might at least satisfy their appeal for 'some differentiation of treatment ... between those who were educated and civilised and those who had yet to reach that stage'.

The ANC's influence plunged during the 1920s after a large proportion of its supporters deserted to join a rival movement that showed more concern for the interests of black workers than for those of the small black elite. Led by a school teacher and impressive orator from Nyasaland, Clements Kadalie, the Industrial and Commercial Workers' Union had first attracted support in 1919 when it organised a successful dock strike. Its membership, chanting the slogan 'Awaken, O Africa, for the morning is at hand', grew rapidly to a quarter of a million. Initially helped in the organisation of his union by the Communist Party, Kadalie then travelled abroad and adopted the more moderate strategies advocated by British trade union leaders, thereby alienating the communists at home and, eventually, his mass following.

After Kadalie expelled the disapproving communists, they turned their attention to the formation of a trade union movement within the African National Congress. They were well received, mainly because their white members treated blacks as genuine equals, an entirely new experience for many Congressmen. Over the next three decades the Communist Party, working with the ANC and recruiting black members to its ranks, was the only significant multiracial political body in the country. It popularised the term 'African' instead of 'native', encouraging blacks to press for full equality rather than the piecemeal advances many had previously accepted as their only plausible hope.

By 1928 the ANC had taken a sharp left turn under the influence of the Communist Party and the leadership of Josiah Gumede, a teacher who toured the Soviet Union and was so impressed at having been treated 'as though I was the prime minister of South Africa' that he came home declaring he had found 'the key to freedom' in communism. He called for 'the right of self-determination through the complete overthrow of capitalism and imperialist domination ... the principle of Africa for the Africans'. But he fell out with the conservative chiefs, alienating the ANC's valued rural support.

In 1930 the organisation chose a new leader, the man responsible for founding the ANC, Dr Pixley Seme. He had become so moderate in his middle age that the ANC virtually stopped its protests altogether. Seme was so intimidated by the Riotous Assemblies Amendment Act, giving the government power to bypass the law courts and banish from any district any person who might cause 'feelings of hostility', that the ANC failed even to support pass-burning demonstrations organised by communists in Johannesburg. Instead, Seme exhorted Africans to pursue modest aspirations. 'I wish to urge our educated young men and women not to lose contact with your own chiefs,' he said. 'You should make your chiefs and your tribal councils feel that education is a really good thing. It does not spoil people nor detribalise them. Most of the misery which our people suffer in the towns and country today is due to this one factor, no confidence between the educated classes and the uneducated people ...'

Hertzog's repressive legislation was meanwhile accumulating. Pass laws were tightened by successive clauses; new labour policies excluded blacks from skilled and semi-skilled trades; the Native Taxation Act made Africans pay for their schooling. The Native Administration Act brought tribal chiefs under government control as virtual civil servants who could be dismissed for displeasing white authorities. On his way to a conference in Brussels, former ANC president John Dube remarked: 'If the government persists in its present attitude, we can only think that it desires to exterminate us. The Bantu is suspicious of the whole attitude of the white population.'

For several years under Seme's leadership, the ANC was content to leave public protests to the small but energetic Communist Party which, despite its militant efforts on their behalf, failed to attract blacks in significant numbers: traditional veneration of the chiefs and the church continued to favour order and obedience.

The relationship between the Communist Party of South Africa and the ANC was both complicated and unstable during the 1930s. At times the CPSA considered the ANC an ally, at other points viewing it as potentially reactionary.

Seme's leadership was not the only factor in the ANC's apathy during the 1930s. Severe economic depression had hit South Africa, accelerating hunger and unemployment among blacks and distracting them from political goals. The ravages of the Great Depression steadily weakened the government too, persuading Hertzog to join forces with Smuts, who became his deputy in a new coalition, the United Party. It was a union heralding white solidarity against black advancement, giving Hertzog a two-thirds majority in parliament and enabling him to alter entrenched clauses in the Act of Union. Most crucial among these was the Cape franchise, and Hertzog lost no time in campaigning for the removal from the common roll of the eleven thousand black voters.

The ANC was at last stirred into action. Seme called a conference in Bloemfontein at the end of 1935 at which a new movement, the All-African Convention (AAC), was formed to unite black opposition against the proposed legislation. A thirty-man AAC delegation immediately left for Cape Town to meet General Hertzog. Arriving in a belligerent mood at the imposing Assembly buildings, the delegates were entirely unprepared for the warm charm of their hated prime minister. 'I was so confused and dumbfounded by the courteous and dignified way in which he addressed us that I was speechless for a moment,' Dr Albert Xuma said afterwards.

But their mission proved a disaster. Two members of the AAC delegation, including its president, Professor Jabavu, remained in Cape Town after their colleagues had left, holding talks with white members of parliament who persuaded them to support an amended bill allowing blacks to elect seven white parliamentary representatives on a separate roll, and twelve black representatives to a government advisory body called the Native Representative Council (NRC). The other members of the delegation, unaware of Jabavu's agreement, were summoned back to Cape Town for a further meeting with Hertzog, who shook their hands enthusiastically, thanking each in turn for his 'statesmanlike compromise'. White farmers in the Free State were meanwhile lighting bonfires to celebrate the end of the black vote, unwittingly surrendered by the All-African Convention.

When the next AAC meeting took place in 1936 Jabavu's agreement had already become law. The group erupted in quarrels and split into two factions, one wanting to boycott the Native Representative Council (NRC) and the election of whites; the other opting to voice black aspirations and grievances through the two channels. Twelve AAC men were eventually elected to sit on the NRC but it became increasingly obvious, as the boycott lobby had warned, that their recommendations carried no political weight.

When the Second World War broke out in Europe in 1939, many blacks argued bitterly against their enlistment in the army. 'Why should we fight for you?' one NRC councillor asked an Englishman who was serving as a native representative in parliament. 'We fought for you in the Boer War and you betrayed us to the Dutch. We fought for you in the last war. We died in France, in East Africa ... and when it was over, did anyone care about us? What have we to fight for? ... Shall we get back the rights we have lost? Shall we get back the franchise? Shall we get back the right to buy land?' Yet when the ANC met at the end of 1939 and proposed a resolution that blacks support the war effort only on condition they bore arms, it was defeated by conservatives who continued to dominate the movement.

Wartime industries created boom conditions in South Africa's white cities, attracting mass migration from rural areas. Black industrial workers began to be recruited in large numbers to replace the whites who had joined the army. Realising it needed a stable wartime labour force, the government brought in pension plans for selected black workers, introduced feeding schemes in black schools and increased expenditure on African education. But because black urban dwellers multiplied by over fifty per cent during the war years, relatively few found jobs. As staple food costs soared, poverty steadily worsened in the locations, with six out of every ten babies in Port Elizabeth dying of starvation in the first year of life.

A dark mood of discontent started spreading through the locations. Africans employed in commerce and industry joined trade unions in large numbers, organising strikes for higher wages. The conditions were ripe for political exploitation but the ANC, preoccupied with the All-African Convention's attempt to establish itself as a permanent political force, failed to grasp the opportunity. While the two movements quarrelled over their respective claims to popularity, neither bothered to secure the support of the politically aroused but leaderless urban masses.

The ANC had elected a new president in 1940, Dr Albert Xuma, formerly deputy leader of the AAC but a relative newcomer to politics and, at forty-seven, younger than his predecessors. Xuma was a stocky, autocratic man with a dynamic personality and a rags-to-riches history: from Xhosa herdboy to fourteen years at universities in Britain, Hungary and the United States, where he married a vivacious black American called Madie Hall and returned with her to establish a thriving medical practice in Johannesburg's western location, Sophiatown. Having been away from Africa for many years and having chosen a socially ambitious wife, Xuma had difficulty mixing with unsophisticated blacks and chose a circle of mainly white friends. He was never able to identify sincerely with black aspirations although he was a kindly man, sympathising with the grievances of the masses as an outsider overlooking their plight.

What he lacked in the common touch, Dr Xuma made up in reshaping the ANC's chaotic administration. In nine years as president, he brought respectability and efficiency to the organisation, expelling corrupt officials and often digging into his own pocket to pay the salaries of full-time organisers. The post-war breed of black clerks and salesmen admired his social status, answering his call to unite behind the ANC at such a rate that it became known as 'Xuma's hire-purchase Congress'.

But Xuma, like Dr Seme before him, neglected to apply political pressure, the essential purpose of the ANC. While he was busy with office administration, spontaneous demonstrations arose in locations around the country, notably a bus boycott in 1943 by ten thousand blacks protesting in Alexandra against fare increases. The spreading political agitation inspired the birth of the African Democratic Party, led by two former Native Representative councillors. After a promising start, it failed to attract significant support because blacks distrusted its anti-white sentiments.

The ANC responded to the threat of a rival movement by attempting to revive itself. Xuma formed a committee of leading blacks who, inspired by the Atlantic Charter drawn up by Churchill and Roosevelt in 1941, drafted a similar document, called 'African Claims', for presentation to the government. Containing a bill of rights demanding the 'freedom of the African people from all discriminatory laws whatsoever', it achieved no more than an official letter of receipt. In 1944 Dr Xuma chaired a joint conference with the Communist

Party to plan a campaign of protest against intensification of pass law arrests. Calling for a million signatures, Xuma settled for several thousand, forwarding them in a petition to the prime minister. Although officially acknowledged, it was again ignored by the government.

Xuma became aware of the growing dissatisfaction among young members who had for some time advised the ANC to explore more radical resolutions. He summoned another conference, this time deciding on firmer action: a 'mass struggle' to burn passes. His critics at first applauded, but the ANC was unable to agree on the exact form its mass struggle would take and Xuma's bold initiative eventually fizzled out.

The patience of aspirant reformists ran out in 1943. A group of young professionals went to see Xuma, telling him they planned to organise a Congress Youth League and a campaign of action designed to mobilise mass support. In some ways Xuma liked having the young intellectuals engaging with the ANC leadership but he was alarmed by their ideas and tried to discourage them. His secretary, recording the meeting, wrote: '... The delegation went on to say that the erratic policy of the ANC was shown by the fact there was no programme of action; no passive resistance or some such action. Dr Xuma replied that the Africans as a group were unorganised and undisciplined, and that a programme of action such as envisaged by the Youth League would be rash at this stage. The ANC lacked people who were concerned about the movement and who knew what they wanted. Action would merely lead to exposure ...'

Unable to tolerate Xuma's cautious attitude any longer, the new generation resolved to chart its own course.

4

IMPATIENT YOUNG VOICES PREVAIL

The two men occupying an office adjacent to the African National Congress's headquarters off Market Street looked like father and son as they strolled arm-in-arm to and from Johannesburg's law courts in 1943. They worked together in a legal practice, argued a lot about the generation gap and shared a mutual passion for politics. One was Dr Pixley Seme, the founder of the ANC; the other was Anton Lembede, a tall, handsome young man whose philosophies, though scorned by Seme, were soon to revolutionise the politics of the older man's era.

Lembede was born in 1914 in a village near Durban. His parents were share-croppers on a white farm where children as well as adults were expected to work in the fields. His semi-literate mother taught Anton as best she could at home until he entered his teens, when the family moved on in search of schooling. They settled in a nearby town called Isabelo, enrolling the boy at a Roman Catholic mission. He was thin and almost always hungry, but his mother's deep respect for education made him feel grateful for his place in a proper school, preventing self-pity and the lethargy usually accompanying malnutrition.

His academic talent was immediately evident, and in 1933 he was awarded a scholarship to train as a teacher at Adams College in Natal. The bursary covered only a three-year basic course but Lembede was undeterred, setting his sights on the higher university entrance qualification offered at Adams. Leading an austere life of intense study and regular prayer, he became an exemplary student, praised by one of his senior tutors, Albert Luthuli, as a brilliant scholar.

After passing his final examination with a distinction in Latin, Lembede began to study by correspondence for a BA degree while working as a teacher in Natal. He became fascinated by Afrikaners, mainly because they had become urbanised at around the same time as blacks yet had gained strength from the experience, whereas blacks 'gained only their inferiority complexes'. Deciding to explore the subject first-hand, Lembede moved to Heilbron in the Orange Free State, the heartland of Afrikanerdom, where he concluded that the key to the Boers' urban success lay in their cultural pride and solidarity. While teaching there and later in a town called Parys, he completed his BA course, became fluent in Afrikaans and learnt the local African tongue, Sesotho. Then he decided to quit teaching and study law.

Arriving in Johannesburg, Lembede was delighted to find blacks discussing politics on virtually every street corner, a far cry from the sullen but silent resentment he had encountered in the Free State. He was overjoyed when Dr Seme, an able lawyer and a revered figure among blacks, offered him a job as an articled clerk. But Seme's ideas, though suitably conservative for the law courts, seemed hopelessly dated to Lembede. The old man continued to believe blacks would eventually be permitted to share power with their white oppressors. If blacks remained patient, said Seme, the freedom-loving nations of the world would eventually exert moral pressure on Africa's white rulers. Lembede scoffed at Seme's faith in the ultimate triumph of fair play, arguing that blacks had nothing to show for their moral indignation or for the petitions put out by the ANC over the past thirty-five years. It was time for the black masses to confront white authority, he declared.

At night, returning to the room he shared with Peter Mda – a friend from Mariazell, a Catholic school in the Transkei – Lembede complained that black political elitists like Seme and Xuma offered their British and American educations as evidence of their fitness to plead the cause of ordinary blacks when, in reality, their foreign manners and expectations had estranged them from the masses. The two younger men talked interminably about the mistaken strategies pursued by the ANC, to which 'AP', as Mda was known, had belonged since the mid-1930s.

Both were clever men, seizing every chance to exercise their sharp minds. They shared not only a common teaching background but a deep understanding of the poverty, stagnation and growing despair of the African people. Mda's father had been a shoemaker and a Xhosa tribal headman in the Herschel district of the eastern Cape. His mother was an elementary school teacher. Although these were relatively elitist credentials in black rural society, AP travelled from village to village throughout his boyhood on horseback with his father, listening to the people's grievances and his father's counsels. By the time he was a teenager he had developed an active social conscience, trying hard, as a practising Christian, to understand why blacks were despised and ill-treated by whites. 'At first, I thought maybe blacks were backward because they were lazy. But then I realised the whites were the conquerors who made the laws in such a way that blacks remained the underdogs. I stopped blaming the people themselves and began to get quite anti-white ideas.'

Lembede was also hostile towards whites, despising the eagerness with which blacks tried to emulate them. He was not himself prey to the temptations of smart clothing and material status symbols, which he identified as the root cause of the black people's sense of inadequacy. His earnest Catholicism and the lifelong poverty he had endured while feeding on the fruits of his mind left him free to warn that 'Moral degeneration is assuming alarming dimensions … [and] manifests itself in such abnormal and pathological phenomena as loss of self-confidence, inferiority complex, a feeling of frustration, the worship and idolisation of white men, foreign leaders and ideologies'.

Lembede and Mda, often joined by Jordan Ngubane, a journalist friend from Natal, met regularly for months to discuss a new political formula for blacks. Lembede's imaginative views, encompassing formative and destructive forces throughout human history, left AP in 'a state of high exhilaration'. Lembede loved to describe the Renaissance period in Europe or the social injustices which had given rise to the Russian Revolution in 1917. 'That chap had very, very clear ideas, so clear. He had read more widely than anybody I ever met,' said Mda. 'I knew he was no ordinary thinker. You could tell he was going to do something important with his ideas.'

Lembede particularly wanted blacks to be proud of their blackness. 'Look at my skin,' he would say. 'It is black like the soil of Mother Africa. It is the black man's duty not to allow himself to be swamped by the doctrines of inferiority.'

Equally intolerant of ethnic divisions among blacks, Lembede longed for the day when African nationalism might be 'pursued with the fanaticism and bigotry of religion, for it is the only creed that will dispel and disperse the inferiority complex which blurs our sight and darkens our horizons'. He was suspicious of the communist influences which had gained currency in the ANC, emphasising self-reliance and declaring that Africanism, as he had labelled his philosophy, could 'realise itself through, and be interpreted by, Africans only. Foreigners of whatever brand or hue can never properly and correctly interpret this spirit owing to its uniqueness, peculiarity and particularity.' He often quoted an Afrikaner columnist, Dr H F Verwoerd, to illustrate his belief that blacks had much to learn about unity and exclusivity from Afrikanerdom.

Lembede continued studying law, deciding to read simultaneously for a master's degree in philosophy, but nothing was closer to his heart than his new concept of Africanism. He and Mda agreed blacks could hope to secure their liberation only through mass mobilisation, and both began to feel Lembede's Africanism might provide the creed behind which black people could rally, united and finally powerful enough to challenge white rule.

Mda suggested they call a meeting of some of the young rebels known to be discontented with the ANC's leadership. If the new doctrine of Africanism stood the test of debate among a wider circle of like-minded reformists, he told Lembede, they might be able to forge an alliance within the ANC in order to change the course of African nationalism.

Mda had been a member of the African National Congress for many years.

Having watched the growing impatience of its younger members, he knew who to approach for discussions aimed at rejuvenating Dr Xuma's cautious leadership. At an Orlando house marked 7372, he was welcomed by Walter Sisulu's mother and invited to share a meal with her extended family and her lodger, Nelson Mandela. All of them were well known to Mda, whose wife was a nursing trainee with Walter's fiancée Albertina and Nelson's girlfriend Eveline. When Mda outlined Lembede's philosophy of Africanism, Mandela and Sisulu were immediately eager to meet for further discussions.

They were joined at the kitchen table conference by an equally enthusiastic ANC reformist, Oliver Tambo, a man with wispy chin whiskers and tribal scarifications on his cheeks, known among his friends as 'The Christian'. Tambo was a teacher of science and mathematics at St Peter's School in Johannesburg and a student of law, who had spent his childhood in a village called Bizana in the Transkei. Both his parents had been illiterate and Oliver had given little thought to education until a priest from an Anglican mission at Holy Cross visited Bizana. On seeing the Tambo family's dire poverty, he suggested taking Oliver back to the mission's boarding school.

Arriving at Holy Cross at Easter time just as the mass was being sung, Oliver was so impressed by the sweet smell of incense and the rich vestments of the priests that he resolved not only to work hard and achieve a good education but to become a priest himself. By the time he reached the mission's top class, he was considered intellectually gifted, but he knew his family was too poor to further his education. Luck intervened, again in the form of a priest, who offered to send him to an advanced Anglican school, St Peter's, where he excelled and won a scholarship to Fort Hare.

However, while studying for his final Bachelor of Science examinations, Oliver fell out with the Fort Hare authorities over the playing of sport on Sundays. As secretary of the Students' Representative Council, he was told to submit a written pledge about the students' spiritual life and religious duties. 'I asked the warden for time to pray about this, and I went to the chapel for half an hour,' Tambo later told Father Trevor Huddleston. 'I knew I could not sign that pledge. It demanded something from me that I could not give. It would have killed my religion stone dead: an agreement with God, written and signed! I could not do it.'

He told the warden of his decision and was immediately expelled. Wandering around the university town in despair, he '... decided, anyhow, to go back to the chapel and pray ... It was completely dark, completely empty, absolutely silent. But at the far end, near the Blessed Sacrament, there was a glow of light from the lamp which always burned there. I took that as a sign: that somewhere, however dark, there is light ...'

While searching for a teaching job in Durban, Tambo heard of an unexpected vacancy in the science department at St Peter's, his old school, which welcomed him back. Though a quiet, modest man still intent on becoming a priest, Tambo could fly into a rage of indignation if his principles were compromised. He had stunned a group of black and white teachers at St Peter's when they tried to persuade him it was wrong for a teacher to be actively involved in politics. 'The call of destiny throughout history is the challenge for the individual to rise to higher levels of achievement,' Tambo retorted. 'Where men cannot help themselves, they must be helped by others who are able. I want to help lead the struggle for African liberation. How can you claim that this is not the role of the teacher? I refuse to be diverted from it.'

Tambo had a big influence on his students at St Peter's. His interactive teaching style was way ahead of its time, and he inspired many in his classes to take up teaching. Explaining his Africanist philosophy to his senior students, he encouraged some of them to join the growing youth movement.

Mda summoned the first meeting of the reformers, attended by Lembede, Mandela, Sisulu, Tambo, Ngubane and a medical student named William Nkomo, an articulate member of the Communist Party who was noted for his impressive contributions to ANC debates (and his distinctive pink Cadillac). In his opening address, Mda attacked the ANC's leadership, describing it as a 'dying order of pseudo-liberalism and conservatism, of appeasement and compromises'. AP had earlier asked Lembede to outline his concepts only briefly at the outset, in order to give the young Congressmen a chance to express their own ideas before being offered his bold vision of self-reliant Africanism as a means of rescuing the ANC from the mortal dangers of white rule.

Their discussions ranged from Ngubane's moral ideas on the right of all citizens to a full share in the total life of the state, to Mandela's belief that popular protest should be pursued in a spirit of urgency. The war years had produced an industrial boom, dramatically increasing the number of blacks in the national workforce, he said. There had never been a more favourable time to launch an appeal to the malcontented urbanised masses. The question was: how to mobilise those masses? Nkomo favoured the growth of organised trade unions. Lembede contributed to the debate with restraint, saying, like Mda, that a sense of black nationhood was the necessary prelude to mass action. Sisulu warned against any new initiative based on wishful thinking and half-truths, saying it was vital to make a clear analysis of black people's socio-economic position and the real nature of the power they were trying to challenge.

Towards the end of a long evening they were unanimous in their belief that black advancement could be won only by extra-parliamentary methods. It was no longer possible for a remote, foreign-educated leadership to speak through government-sponsored bodies like the Native Representative Council on behalf of the black masses. Amid laughter, somebody illustrated the similarity between white fears of mob rule and ANC leaders' traditional distaste for mass protest by quoting the organisation's first president John Dube's warning that 'unless there is a radical change soon, herein lies a fertile breeding ground for hot-headed agitators among us Natives, who might prove to be a far bigger menace to this country than is generally realised today. Let us all labour to forestall them.'

The meeting resolved that those present should individually consult friends and acquaintances about the possibility of forming a youth movement to act as a 'think-tank' for the 'old guard', the ANC's conservative leaders. They would tentatively and discreetly call themselves the Congress Youth League (CYL). 'We do not want to anger and alienate Dr Xuma,' explained Mda, 'because without his blessing we will be unable to influence Congress.'

Over the next few months, they met to draft a Youth League manifesto. When it was ready, Mda, Lembede and Ngubane took it to Dr Xuma's home in Sophiatown to seek the ANC president's approval. Xuma's bustling black American wife Madie Hall, who had been elected president of the ANC's newly formed women's section the previous year, met them at the door of the doctor's house, a large building among the surrounding hovels. While waiting for Dr Xuma's arrival, she outlined her own political philosophy. Although she was a social worker, daily exposed to the hardships suffered by ordinary blacks, Madie Hall remained unshaken in her belief that the experience of black Americans would be repeated in Africa: liberation would finally come after decades of patient conduct and economic self-help. Dr Xuma seemed more sympathetic to their cause, reading their document of broad intent carefully and approving its contents.

On Easter Sunday 1944 the Congress Youth League was formally founded at a meeting held in the Bantu Men's Social Centre in Eloff Street, Johannesburg. About two hundred attended, mainly Fort Hare graduates from humble backgrounds, to hear a captivating lecture on the history of nations by Anton Lembede. Despite a speech stammer, he was a natural orator, leading his audience on a vivid tour through the ages: from the spread of civilisation in ancient Greece and the Roman Empire to the philosophies of the East; the birth of modern Europe and the expansion to America; the decades of colonisation. Humanity owed a great debt to the heritage of both East and West, he said, but it was a heritage that belonged to everyone. Blacks should take what was worthwhile from their global inheritance and add it to their own cultural traditions, instead of feeling inferior and trying to emulate the white person's lifestyle. 'The fault is not in our stars, but in ourselves that we are underlings,' Lembede declared.

William Nkomo was elected leader of the CYL at a subsequent meeting but his ideas proved too far to the left of most members, and Lembede was chosen to replace him. Around sixty members regularly attended the meetings, including Mandela and Sisulu, who were the firmest of friends and invariably sat together, though they could not have been less alike in appearance. Nelson's sleek frame, immaculately groomed and suited, with a white silk scarf around his neck and shoes that shone like mirrors, towered above bespectacled, jovial

Walter, who wore an old lumber jacket and sturdy boots, his ready smile revealing a wide gap in his front teeth.

Lembede's Africanism was a philosophy of racial exclusivity. 'Africa is a black man's country,' he said. 'Africans are the natives of Africa, and they have inhabited Africa, their Motherland, from time immemorial: Africa belongs to them.' It was a philosophy with which many in the CYL disagreed, arguing instead for a broadly based nationalism open to all who abhorred white domination. The issue bred increasing friction, with the Youth League's first basic policy draft being rejected because whites were referred to as 'foreigners'.

For months they debated the relative virtues of Africanism versus nationalism. Oliver Tambo, viewing Africanism as a reverse form of racial discrimination, believed nationalism was less risky. This was partly because it left the way open to whites who might eventually be persuaded to accept blacks as allies and partly because he feared many mission-educated blacks would reject a vindictive policy towards whites on the grounds that it offended their Christianity. He continually reminded Youth Leaguers that the urge among blacks to win acceptance by whites was in many cases as strong as the competing urge to strip whites of their privileges.

Lembede, Mandela and Sisulu disagreed, claiming it was precisely these opposing aspirations which weakened the black man's resolve, rendering him vulnerable to moderating influences. They argued that liberal whites had for years hampered the growth of effective black opposition because, fearing mass black protest, they had constantly advocated moderation. Africanism was the surest way to awaken black self-respect; to revive the pride in the past and confidence in the future that had been damaged by the demeaning urban experience of living on the fringes of a white world. If they were offered a multiracial form of nationalism, blacks would remain beguiled by white culture. The single-minded concern of the Youth League ought to be to spread a philosophy that was persuasive enough to rally the black masses.

Jordan Ngubane, who had returned to Natal to edit a newspaper called *Inkundla* and thereby spread the words of the CYL beyond the Transvaal, echoed the movement's dominant sentiments when he wrote: 'As long as the

African people are not welded into a compact, organised group they will never realise their national aspirations. When they meet other non-European groups, they will be an unwieldy encumbrance, serving the purpose of being stepping stones for the better organised groups.'

Ngubane's words were directed at those in the Youth League who felt Indians might profitably be invited to lend their organisational skills to the struggle, and at ANC members who were simultaneously members of the Communist Party. Most Youth Leaguers resented the communists' influence on the 'old guard' in the ANC, distrusting their predominantly white policy makers, their emphasis on class rather than racial conflict, and their hopes of an eventual socialist revolution.

In 1945 three men who had been active communists for twenty years were elected to sit on the ANC's national executive, following a communist-inspired increase in the size of the ruling body from eleven to twenty-two members. They were Communist Party secretary Moses Kotane, who had received part of his education in Moscow, John 'JB' Marks, a forceful orator, and Dan Tloome. Also included for the first time on the national executive was the Congress Youth League, represented by Anton Lembede and AP Mda.

Marks' election came four months after he had organised a spectacularly successful mine strike, when 70 000 men refused to work. Some Youth Leaguers, watching his dramatic mass mobilisation with envy and reluctant admiration, began to feel that an alliance with the communists might be more beneficial than they had realised. Others began to tolerate the idea of co-operation with Indians, following the increasingly defiant Indian Congress's successful passive resistance campaign in Natal in 1946, which led to an Indian leader accompanying Dr Xuma on a trip overseas to address the United Nations in New York. Even Lembede, the champion of racial exclusivity, began to hold informal discussions with Indians, telling them: 'We must not only sit together and talk together: we must struggle together.'

Youth Leaguers were conscious of other changes too. The mood of township dwellers had never been more aggressive. Black living conditions had declined sharply under the impact of inflation, wages scarcely rose, and no housing had been erected since before the war. Spontaneous protests were springing up more frequently in townships and on factory floors. Realising the ANC should have been in the forefront of these popular struggles, most Youth Leaguers began to press for an end to their ideological quarrels and a move into action.

Relations between the CYL and the 'old guard' had steadily deteriorated after Youth Leaguers promoted an ANC boycott of the Native Representative Council while Dr Xuma was addressing the United Nations. On his return, Xuma angrily tried to modify the resolution, and a head-on collision between senior and junior members of the ANC became imminent. Early in 1947 Lembede told a meeting of the ANC national executive that blacks were ready to act. Their only problem, he said, was that their leaders lacked the courage to lead.

Xuma was horrified when Lembede called for a boycott of a royal visit to South Africa by the King and Queen of England, a decision made by the CYL at a meeting in Mandela's house, when Lembede argued hotly against paying homage to the head of a government that had failed to honour its moral duty to the African people. Mda described the royal visit as 'an idle picnic for people who discarded us and threw us to the mercy of white wolves when the Union was formed'. Mandela, though not opposing the boycott, cautioned against emotional excesses, saying the English monarchy was among the great and enduring institutions of mankind. The King and Queen and their daughters were coming to Africa as a dignified family, not only as representatives of the British government, he said. 'We mustn't be cowards and go for the weak – the individuals who come to us as human beings.'

The discussion on the royal tour was typical of the open debating tradition that had developed in the CYL under the influence of Lembede's agile mind. Both Lembede and Mda abhorred the dominance of personalities over the exchange of ideas: it was among their chief criticisms of the 'old guard' in the ANC. Though he could be stubborn in the promotion of his favourite themes, Lembede loved the mental stimulation of defending his position against intellectual attack.

A few months later, tragedy struck. Anton Lembede died, aged thirty-three, from an undiagnosed stomach disorder. Walter Sisulu, who had grown particularly fond of the flamboyant Lembede during their four years together in the Youth League, was so grief-stricken he could barely stand unaided at the graveside while AP Mda, pausing frequently to summon his composure, delivered a eulogy. JB Marks and Dr Yusuf Dadoo, leader of the South African Indian Congress, a prominent communist who had devoted his entire life to confronting oppression through resistance, wept throughout the service. A newspaper editorial published on the day of the funeral hailed Lembede as 'a wonderful bird in the garden of life, who sang from the highest tree and then soared away'. Paying tribute to Lembede's great contribution to the struggle, Dadoo told the assembled Youth Leaguers that their president's hostility towards communism had begun to soften in the last months of his life. He urged them to consider a tactical alliance with communists and Indians.

———————

AP Mda succeeded Lembede, immediately establishing a branch of the CYL at Fort Hare under the joint guidance of Godfrey Pitje, an anthropology lecturer, and Professor Zachariah Matthews, the most distinguished black academic in the country and a long-standing member of the ANC. They launched a recruitment drive on campus, bringing fresh talent into the Youth League, notably Matthews' able son, Joe, and another exceptional student, Robert Sobukwe, who was a brilliant orator.

In 1948 the CYL finally formulated its policy. 'The starting point of African Nationalism is the historical or even pre-historical position,' it declared. 'Africa was, has been and still is a Black man's continent. The Europeans ... have carved up and divided Africa among themselves, dispossessed, by force of arms, the rightful owners of the land ... Although conquered and subjugated, the Africans have not given up, and they will never give up their claim and title to Africa.'

It went on to outline the Youth League's vision of 'true democracy' as 'the removal of discriminatory laws and colour bars and the admission of the African into the full citizenship of the country so that he has direct representation in parliament on a democratic basis.

'... The majority of Europeans share the spoils of white domination in this country. They have a vested interest in the exploitative caste society of South Africa. A few of them love Justice and condemn racial oppression, but their voice is negligible, and in the last analysis counts for nothing. In their struggle for freedom the Africans will be wasting their time and deflecting their forces if they look up to the Europeans either for inspiration or for help.' The only basis on which 'Africans could admit Europeans to a share of the fruits of Africa' was upon white agreement to 'completely abandon their domination of Africa ... agree to an equitable and proportionate re-division of the land ... [and] assist in establishing a free people's democracy in South Africa in particular and Africa in general.'

On sensitive internal divisions between the concepts of nationalism and Africanism, the statement read: 'Now it must be noted there are two streams of African nationalism. One centres round [the] slogan "Africa for the Africans". It is based on the "Quit Africa" slogan and on the cry "Hurl the white man to the sea". This type of African nationalism is extreme and ultra-revolutionary.

'There is another stream ... which is moderate, and which the Congress Youth League professes. We of the Youth League take account of the concrete situation in South Africa and realise that the different racial groups have come to stay. But we insist that a condition for inter-racial peace and progress is the abandonment of white domination, and such a change in the basic structure of South African society that those relations which breed exploitation and human misery disappear.'

The Youth League was not the only agency pushing the ANC towards mass action in the second half of the 1940s. Powerful branches of the organisation under the leadership of African members of the Communist Party of South Africa, working in tandem with local trade unions, gave the ANC a militant, organised base.

On 26 May 1948 the white electorate voted in a general election that drastically changed the future of South Africa. Following a campaign against 'the encroaching black peril', featuring slogans like *'Kaffer op sy plek'* ('Kaffir in his place') and *'Koelies uit die land uit'* ('Coolies out of the country'), Dr Daniel Malan's National Party ousted General Jan Smuts' ruling United Party. Though defeated by a narrow margin, Smuts realised Afrikanerdom was in the ascendancy. Describing the National Party's new policy of apartheid as 'a crazy concept, born of prejudice and fear', he warned that it 'may create and inflame native communism and even end in a totally black South Africa'.

For the first time in the country's history, an exclusively Afrikaner party led the government. 'Today South Africa belongs to us once more,' said Malan in his victory speech. 'For the first time since Union, South Africa is our own, and may God grant that it will always remain our own.'

Malan immediately set about a programme designed to replace English-speaking officials in public bodies with Afrikaners. Then he tackled the *'swart gevaar'* ('black danger'). He introduced the Prohibition of Mixed Marriages Act in 1949, which was followed by the Immorality Act, banning sexual intercourse between blacks and whites, and the Population Registration Act, a national roll labelling all South Africans by their race. After appointing advisers to investigate means of ending the coloured vote in the Cape, he introduced the Group Areas Act, demarcating separate residential areas for each racial group, which he described as 'the very essence of apartheid'. Determined to keep black homes as far away from white residential areas as possible, he announced that 'black spots' – locations lying within white urban districts – were to be removed in a slum clearance programme. Top of his list was Sophiatown, a vibrant community housing 60 000 people, which was one of the oldest black settlements in Johannesburg. Although containing numerous tumbledown shacks, Sophiatown had developed schools, churches, cinemas and shops, and was renowned all over the country for its jazz clubs. 'Whatever else Sophiatown was, it was home,' wrote one of its residents, Bloke Modisane. 'We made the desert bloom; made alterations; converted half-verandas into kitchens, decorated the houses and filled them with music ... We took the ugliness of life in a slum and wove a kind of beauty.'

Malan's mounting repression sent shock waves through the ANC. Never before had there been a more urgent need for unity among blacks; Youth Leaguers no longer had to convince the 'old guard' of that glaring fact. Many ANC members were calling for 'one man, one vote' and the CYL's policies seemed assured of an easy passage through the ANC at its annual general conference.

In December 1949, while Afrikaners were celebrating the defeat of the Zulus at Blood River over a hundred years earlier, the ANC's Youth League ousted Dr Xuma and elected another medical man, Dr James Moroka, in his place. Not an obvious choice to lead a reformed and militant ANC, Moroka was one of the wealthiest black men in the country, owning large farms in Thaba 'Nchu, an African reserve in the Orange Free State. He had a history of close co-operation with whites, helping to fund a school for poor Afrikaner children in the Free State and opening a medical practice for white patients. But Dr Moroka willingly accepted the job whereas Professor Matthews, the CYL's first choice, had declined it. Walter Sisulu, whose refusal to work for whites had won him prestige among ANC members, was elected secretary-general. Xuma was furious, launching himself into a campaign aimed at discrediting the new leaders. It was a 'takeover by half-castes', he claimed, referring to Moroka, Sisulu and JB Marks, all of whom were mixed-race men.

Malan's repression continued. In 1950 he delivered a law which his supporters hailed as a peace panacea: the Suppression of Communism Act. It outlawed not only the Communist Party but anyone who attempted to bring about social, economic or political change in the country. Malan's justice minister was given such far-reaching powers that he was absolved from the need to prove a person was a communist. All he had to do was 'name' opponents: simply calling them communists was enough to ban them from public life.

The ANC convened hastily to discuss its response. Although the old antipathy to communism still prevailed among Youth Leaguers, the Suppression of Communism Act was so powerful a weapon against all organised opposition that many began to see sense in uniting against apartheid in general and the

Suppression of Communism Act in particular. Some of the most vehement anti-communists had by now left the CYL. Lembede had died; ill-health and the likelihood of imminent arrest had sent AP Mda into retirement. A new breed of Youth Leaguers had graduated from Fort Hare: young intellectuals who, though dedicated to African nationalism, were nevertheless comfortable with many aspects of Marxism.

Mandela and Tambo, now sitting on the ANC's national executive, remained wary of communists. But Walter Sisulu had begun to strike up new relationships with members of both the disbanded Communist Party and the Indian Congress. When invited by two communist friends to take part in a May Day protest against the Suppression of Communism Act, Sisulu decided to call a meeting in the hope of gaining wider ANC support for the communist initiative.

After a long and at times acrimonious debate, the meeting eventually agreed that the ANC should join black and white communists and Indians in a work stayaway. Mandela, among others, disapproved and tried unsuccessfully to disrupt the strike. When 1 May came, blacks responded enthusiastically, boycotting their jobs in their thousands. But Malan ordered firm action and sent nearly two thousand policemen to disperse the demonstrators. The day ended in bloodshed, with eighteen people shot dead.

Despite continuing opposition from Mandela for its involvement in the tragic May Day strike, the ANC decided to call another protest against both the shootings and the Suppression of Communism Act. Held on 26 June, it was keenly supported by black and white communists and Indians in alliance with the ANC, a partnership that would have been unthinkable only a few months earlier. The well-organised event impressed Mandela, who finally agreed that a broadly based nationalism was preferable to exclusive Africanism. Blacks would need all the help they could muster from anti-apartheid forces in the struggle that lay ahead, he conceded.

Walter Sisulu would eventually join the SACP in 1955 after a protracted apprenticeship in study groups. As such, he became a critical agency through which the newly resurrected ANC could – if it chose to – be influenced by the Communist Party's leadership.

But by the time the ANC's founding father, Dr Pixley Seme, died in the winter of 1951, the ANC was already keen to explore new methods of resistance. Gone were Dr Seme's days of polite protest and the fear of offending white liberal sympathisers. Gone too, though not forever, was much of the dread that outsiders might dominate and subvert the struggle.

Nelson Mandela, Walter Sisulu and Oliver Tambo, now the key leaders of the ANC, interrupted a crucial meeting to attend Dr Seme's funeral. Afterwards, they hurried back to their headquarters to continue planning a mass campaign of civil disobedience.

5

DEFIANCE

Nelson Mandela was well known for his defiance of apartheid. As an attorney, he was offered opportunities through the law courts to challenge whites and their system, and he was always ready to exploit them. Even while still a lowly articled clerk, Mandela made a point of ignoring segregation rules in magistrates' courts. Choosing the 'Europeans Only' entrance, he was ready with a witty answer when reprimanded and told to use the other doorway. Once, a supposedly white clerk, whose features clearly revealed mixed parentage, yelled out: 'What are you doing in here?' Mandela leant over the counter until his face was almost touching that of the alarmed official. Staring straight into the other man's eyes, he asked quietly: 'What are YOU doing in here?'

After qualifying as an attorney, Mandela had quickly developed a reputation for bold courtroom performances. Word of an impending Mandela court case would often spread in the locations, and many blacks, lacking even cinema entertainment in most townships, would arrive to sit in the public gallery, hoping to watch some amusing theatre.

They were seldom disappointed. Nelson, with his fine clothes and polished voice, electrified the court. Well known to white magistrates and public prosecutors too, he was skilled in the art of cross-examination, keeping police witnesses on the stand for hours on end and revelling in the mutually hostile atmosphere. He loved to cultivate racial tension to the hilt in court, determined to show blacks that they did not have to buckle under the pressure of white disapproval.

Time and again, Mandela staged his dramatic play with the authorities, attracting applause from the gallery and infuriating court officials. Once, in Kempton Park, a magistrate began to interrupt Mandela's cross-examination with meaningless interjections. Each time he interrupted, Mandela bowed towards the bench in the customary way; as soon as he tried to proceed, the official spoke again. After a while, when there could be no possible doubt of the magistrate's deliberate intention, the blacks watching began to hiss and stamp their feet. Mandela sat down for a while and then rose slowly. Again he attempted to address the witness; again the magistrate interjected. But this time, instead of bowing courteously towards the bench, Mandela turned his back on the magistrate, bowing instead to the public gallery.

The crowd clapped and whistled with joy, while the red-faced magistrate pounded his gavel for order. Chaos reigned as the prosecutor demanded a charge of contempt. Shouting above the din from the spectators, he protested that the defence attorney had made a rude gesture to the court. It was outrageous, he bellowed. But the magistrate, well aware that his own behaviour could bear no legal scrutiny, let the incident pass.

Not averse to playing to the public gallery, Mandela's own favourite anecdote featured a domestic servant accused of stealing her employer's laundry. Acting for the defendant, Mandela studied the items of clothing laid out on the table of evidence. Then, with the tip of his pencil, he picked up a pair of knickers. Turning to the witness box and brandishing the underwear, he asked the accused's employer, 'Madam, are these yours?' The woman was too embarrassed to answer, and the magistrate subsequently dismissed the case.

Both Mandela and Oliver Tambo worked for firms of white attorneys before establishing a law practice together. Nelson often spent his lunch breaks with Oliver, discussing politics behind the closed door of Tambo's office. A white secretary, Betty Shein, used to study the two black men with interest, noticing that Mandela was much more at ease in white company than Tambo. He would stride into the reception area, glancing around to see whether anyone was going to greet him: then, if met only by the quizzical, faintly indignant stares which usually accompanied a black man's entry into a white office, he would call out, 'Mr Tambo, please,' and take a seat in the whites-only chairs. His conduct caused quite a stir, not least because no one in the firm ever called Oliver 'Mr'. He was simply Tambo, earning little more than the white secretaries who typed his letters, despite his responsible position as head of the thriving black side of his employers' practice.

Betty took to knocking on Tambo's door during his meetings with Mandela, asking the two men if they wanted her to fetch food for them from the café downstairs. 'I sometimes used to chat to them about this and that. Once, when I went to collect their plates to return them to the café, Mr Tambo remarked: "Imagine if the people downstairs knew who had been eating off their nice white plates." We laughed at the thought.'

Many years later, Betty Shein discussed with Tambo a recently published novel about South Africa, Alan Paton's *Cry, the Beloved Country*. Although hailed internationally as a masterpiece and indeed welcomed by blacks as a timely advance on the *Jim Comes to Jo'burg* genre of story which had hitherto been deemed adequate for black readers, Tambo felt the character of Paton's hero, Stephen Kumalo, was misleading. Realistically, Kumalo, no matter how politely and patiently he endured his hardships, would not forgive all in the way that Paton envisaged. Tambo felt the saintly, long-suffering character of Stephen Kumalo reflected wishful thinking on the part of white liberals like Alan Paton, revealing a forlorn hope that whites would not ultimately have to pay for their sins.

In June 1951 Mandela, Tambo and Sisulu began to prepare a mass campaign in defiance of apartheid. Dr Moroka, preoccupied with his medical practice and farming enterprises in the Free State, was content to leave the ANC in the hands of his secretary-general, Sisulu, who helped form a joint planning council of the ANC and the Indian Congress. Its members were the leader and the secretary of the Indian Congress, Dr Yusuf Dadoo and Yusuf Cachalia, and three ANC men: Dr Moroka, JB Marks and Sisulu.

They decided on nationwide civil disobedience as their means of protest, whereby black volunteers would defy apartheid by using whites-only railway compartments, waiting rooms and post office entrances, or by staying in the cities outside curfew hours without permits. A letter signed by Moroka and Sisulu was sent to prime minister Malan, calling his attention to the ANC's forty-year history of patient frustration and pleading for the repeal of six 'unjust laws', including pass regulations, the Group Areas Act and the Suppression of Communism Act. A reply came back from Malan's private secretary, questioning Sisulu's competence to speak for the ANC and complaining that the matter ought to have been addressed to the minister of native affairs. The laws referred to were protective, not oppressive and degrading, the letter stated. Any claim that Bantus were no different from Europeans was self-contradictory, 'especially when it is borne in mind that these differences are permanent and not man-made'.

The government's rebuff marked the beginning of the defiance campaign. At a meeting in Port Elizabeth, Walter Sisulu and Yusuf Cachalia were appointed joint secretaries of the council empowered to prosecute the defiance campaign and to travel throughout South Africa and spread the word: defiance. Mandela, appointed volunteer-in-chief, and Cachalia held hundreds of meetings all over the country, announcing that the time had come for blacks to confront their oppressors. They explained that volunteer corps from every district were to be taught the strict conduct of the campaign by ANC officials and then sent forth in their thousands to commit deliberate acts of civil disobedience. Each group would be small, to prevent the police interpreting their gatherings as demonstrations, which were banned under the Riotous Assemblies Act.

If sufficient numbers came forward to defy, Mandela explained, blacks would make a mockery of the statutory offences which plagued their lives. By deliberately defying the law and going to jail for their defiance, they could give a new significance to petty apartheid regulations. Once imprisonment became an achievement rather than a punishment, it would impart a new message that was proud, brave and dignified instead of criminal and shameful.

Wherever they went, Mandela and Cachalia emphasised the non-violent nature of the campaign. It was imperative that the conduct of volunteers be beyond reproach, they warned. There was to be no drunkenness or rowdiness; no wild individual contributions. Each batch of defiers would have a leader, who would warn the police in advance of the imminent act of disobedience so that arrest could be effected with minimal disturbance. Once arrested, the leader would explain the reasons for the defiance campaign when asked to plead in court. No volunteer would accept an offer of bail or a fine: they would all go to prison and go there happily.

The government reacted to the ANC's campaign preparations by ordering four communists, including JB Marks and Dr Dadoo, to resign from their organisations and stay away from public gatherings. Deciding to act as 'the vanguard of the volunteers', the banned men immediately addressed public meetings and were duly arrested. The government then banned a left-wing newspaper, *The Guardian*, edited by Ruth First, a prominent communist, who simply changed the paper's name to *The Clarion* and resumed production.

On Sunday 22 June, chosen by the ANC as a day of prayer for the safe passage of the defiance campaign, Mandela addressed a packed meeting in Durban: 'We can now say unity between the non-European people in this country has become a reality,' he said.

Four days later, on 26 June 1952, the first batch of volunteers left New Brighton township on the outskirts of Port Elizabeth, marking the start of the defiance campaign. Wearing ANC armbands and singing the song which was to become the cry of thousands of defiers during the following six months, *'Mayibuye! Afrika!'* ('Let Africa return'), they walked through the whites-only entrance to the railway station, where they were immediately arrested by a waiting group of policemen.

In Boksburg, Walter Sisulu and one of Mahatma Gandhi's most ardent followers, Nana Sita, gathered to lead the second batch of defiers into a location without permits. They were arrested and taken to prison.

In Johannesburg, Nelson Mandela and Yusuf Cachalia held a meeting to mark the first day of the campaign. Although they had not intended to be arrested, the meeting continued beyond curfew, eleven o'clock at night, and both were handcuffed and driven to Marshall Square police station. While they were waiting to be taken to the cells, Mandela spoke quietly to the young white officer guarding them. Addressing the Afrikaner as Major, though he was clearly a lower-ranking policeman, Mandela asked if he would use his influence to accommodate the two prisoners in the same cell rather than taking Cachalia to the Indian section of the jail. Obviously flattered, the policeman mumbled about regulations, but when the paperwork in the charge office was complete, he led them to a cell, self-consciously ordering both to enter.

The next morning, when a warder came to deliver breakfast, Mandela was astonished to see that Cachalia's tray contained different food from his own. 'Why do I get mealie pap and water while my friend gets coffee, bread and jam?' he demanded. The warder swung round, staring contemptuously at Mandela. 'Shut up and eat,' he snarled.

They were soon released, and returned to the defiance campaign's headquarters, a flat above Orient House in Commissioner Street. Volunteers were turning out in such great numbers and the campaign was going so well that an atmosphere of celebration prevailed in the crowded flat. On one occasion, when someone brought news of a particularly pleasing act of defiance, Walter Sisulu's high spirits gave rise to an impromptu Xhosa dance. 'He kicked up his leg, clapped and wriggled and jumped,' recalled Yusuf Cachalia. 'I enjoyed it so much that I asked him to do it again.'

Meetings were organised all over the country, partly to mark various stages of the campaign but mainly to secure newspaper reports of the proceedings, particularly in *The Clarion*, which helped to politicise the masses and recruit greater numbers of volunteers. The launching of a batch of defiers often began with a meeting, each speaker's statements being punctuated by the campaign refrain, '*Mayibuye! Afrika!*', and freedom cries, including the plaintive question, '*Senzeni na umnt 'onsundu?*' ('What has the black person done?'). Supporters gathered near the site chosen for an act of defiance and cheered the arrested volunteers, displaying the thumbs up sign which had been adopted as a symbol of solidarity, singing liberation songs and hearing further addresses by ANC or Indian leaders. A similar gathering would again greet volunteers a day or two later when they appeared in court for sentencing.

Few meetings were free from the select attention of policemen, cruising slowly by in unmarked cars or waiting in prison vans. But the fear of going to jail had lost its sting. 'No amount of police presence could dampen the enthusiasm with which the down-trodden masses supported the defiance campaign,' recalled Yusuf Cachalia. 'In the past, when a white kicked a black or sacked him for no reason, he lifted his hat, lowered his eyes and said, *"Ja, dankie, baas."* What he felt in his heart was something quite different. The defiance campaign gave him the courage to say, "Now I'm going to look you straight in the eye. I'm not going to look down and doff my hat. I'm going to face you." It gave blacks the opportunity to manifest their dignity.'

Nearly three-quarters of the volunteers who were arrested came from the politically active eastern Cape.

Among those who drew inspiration from the procession of blacks and Indians volunteering for up to forty days in jail was a slim, middle-aged seamstress, Lilian Ngoyi, who was soon to disclose an exceptional talent for oratory. 'I started following up the papers, and read about the people defying here and there,' she told journalist Anthony Sampson. 'And then one day I went down to the Orlando plantation and saw the cars coming to pick up the people to defy, so calm and brave. And I asked myself, "What is this great thing?" So I went back home and told my mother that I wanted to defy. My daughter was very ill in hospital, under tubes, and my mother did not like the idea of my leaving my daughter. So that night I took her up to the top of the hill and showed her all the lights of Orlando. I said, "Should I serve all these lights, or serve my daughter? This defiance is for the people; my daughter is mine alone." And my mother said I must defy.'

An extraordinary campaigner, Lilian Ngoyi was adept at evading the police, on one occasion faking a large tummy, supposedly pregnant, in order to smuggle masses of pamphlets past a security check.

On 30 July 1952 police raided the homes and offices of Congress and Indian officials in sixteen centres around the country, seizing countless documents. Two weeks later they returned to arrest twenty leaders of the campaign, including Dr Moroka, Nelson Mandela, Walter Sisulu, JB Marks, Dr Dadoo, Yusuf Cachalia and Ahmed Kathrada, president of the Transvaal Indian Youth Congress. After being charged with promoting communism, they were released on bail. Eight weeks later fifteen Cape leaders were arrested and similarly charged.

By late September the number of defiers had escalated to a point where some prisons, particularly in the eastern Cape, were packed to capacity. One evening, after six batches of volunteers had been arrested in the area, ANC office-bearers imprisoned in Port Elizabeth were visited in their cells by a high-powered trio of state officials: the local chief of police accompanied by regional heads of the army and prison service. Admitting they could not accommodate further prisoners and complaining that the defiers refused to go home when offered freedom, Malan's men wanted the ANC to call a temporary halt to the campaign.

Early in October the ANC and the Indian Congress held a conference at Lady Selbourne location in Pretoria to plan the extension of the campaign to rural areas. Journalists covering the event were impressed by the enthusiastic crowd: one correspondent asked if there was 'not some truth in the passionate declaration by Dr Nkomo when welcoming delegates on Friday "that today we witness the turning point in the history of South Africa".' A report in *The Star* newspaper observed: 'All over the township Native children – including those only just old enough to speak – give the [thumbs up] sign and beamingly call out the resistance slogan: "*Mayibuye! Afrika!*".'

However, in the middle of October, tension rose. A white policeman shot two Africans at New Brighton station after they had allegedly stolen a tin of paint and resisted arrest. An angry crowd gathered, shouting abuse, hurling stones and attacking a nearby police station. Four white civilians were killed by the black protesters. The police shot seven Africans dead, soon afterwards issuing bans and tightening curfew hours.

Walter Sisulu rushed to Port Elizabeth. While investigating the tragedy he was informed that a small group of volunteers had broken away from the ANC and was planning to hold meetings in defiance of new police orders. Knowing the authorities were in no mood to tolerate a blatant challenge, and fearing for the lives of ANC supporters attending the meetings, Sisulu was about to go in search of the rebels when a loud cracking sound rang out in the night. Mistakenly thinking it was gunfire from a nearby community hall, Sisulu leapt to his feet and charged out of the room, calling to his colleagues to follow him. Several men rushed to stop him, warning against going to the hall, but Sisulu, shouting in a fury, broke away, saying he would rather be shot himself than stand by as loyal ANC supporters faced danger.

Early the following month a second riot broke out in a Johannesburg hostel, then another in Kimberley five days later. In November the ANC obtained permission to hold a prayer meeting in East London. While it was under way police arrived in troop carriers, claiming that the service was indistinguishable from a political meeting. In the ensuing confusion, shots rang out, the ANC conveners were driven back to the location at gunpoint, and an enraged black crowd ran wild, murdering two white civilians, one of them a nurse whose body was mutilated.

The white population was horrified, as indeed were most blacks. Having scarcely noticed the defiance campaign during the preceding months, whites were informed by the government that defiers had provoked the violence. *Die Burger*, a Cape newspaper, commented: 'For a while primitive Africa ruled, stripped of the varnish of civilisation and free from the taming influence of the white man.' ANC and Indian leaders, eager to reassure whites that their resistance was against unjust laws rather than against white people, invited the white community to a public meeting in Johannesburg; two hundred whites attended, but most were sympathetic trade unionists and former members of the Communist Party. A few days later, however, seven whites identified themselves with the campaign, joining a group of thirty defiers, including Mahatma Gandhi's son Manilal, and illegally entering a Germiston location near Johannesburg. The white volunteers were led by Patrick Duncan, an Oxford graduate whose father had been governor-general in South Africa.

However, the defiance campaign had begun to lose momentum. At its height, the ANC's membership had swelled from 7 000 to over 100 000, but this started to fall away after the government's ban made meetings virtually impossible. The trial of the twenty leaders charged under the Suppression of Communism Act finally took place in the last week of November. All were found guilty of what Mr Justice Rumpff called 'statutory communism' unlike 'what is commonly known as communism'. But he accepted 'the evidence that you have consistently advised your followers to avoid violence in any shape or form', and sentenced them to nine months' imprisonment suspended for two years.

Nelson Mandela and Oliver Tambo decided in December that year to open a legal practice. Like all Africans, they had difficulty finding a landlord willing to rent them offices in Johannesburg. The Group Areas Act reserved the city for white tenants: blacks were told to conduct their businesses from locations or rural reserves.

After numerous refusals they eventually found premises in Chancellor House, near the magistrates' court. But before nailing their brass plate to the door, Nelson had to fight an attempt by the Bar Council to have him disqualified from practising law on the grounds of his arrest during the defiance campaign. Helped by a white lawyer, Walter Pollak, who was the chairman of the council, Mandela successfully cleared his name and the new practice was soon booming. Many blacks travelled great distances to consult the most prestigious black law firm in the country: Mandela & Tambo.

'To reach our desks each morning,' wrote Tambo in the foreword to *No Easy Walk to Freedom*, 'Nelson and I ran the gauntlet of patient queues of people overflowing from the chairs in the waiting room into the corridors. South Africa has the dubious reputation of boasting one of the highest prison populations in the world. Jails are jam-packed with Africans imprisoned for serious offences – and crimes of violence are ever on the increase in apartheid society – but also for petty infringements of statutory law that no really civilised society would punish with imprisonment. To be unemployed is a crime because no black can for long evade arrest if his passbook does not carry the stamp of authorised and approved employment. To be landless can be a crime, and weekly we interviewed the delegations of grizzled, weather-worn peasants from the countryside who came to tell us how many generations their families had worked a little piece of land from which they were now being ejected. To brew African beer, to drink it or to use the proceeds to supplement the meagre family income is a crime, and women who do so face heavy fines and jail terms. To cheek a white man can be a crime. To live in the "wrong" area – an area declared white or Indian or Coloured – can be a crime for Africans. South African apartheid laws turn innumerable innocent people into "criminals".'

Dr Moroka lost his bid for re-election at the ANC's AGM in December. Nelson Mandela won the poll for deputy president and a landslide vote brought in a new president – a grey-haired, deeply religious Zulu tribal leader and former teacher, Chief Albert Luthuli. He had surged to prominence after resisting pressure to retain his position as a state-paid chief in Natal at the expense of renouncing the ANC. Answering the government's ultimatum to make his choice, Luthuli had said: 'Who can deny that thirty years of my life have been spent knocking in vain, patiently, moderately and modestly, at a closed and barred door? What have been the fruits of moderation?

'The past thirty years have seen the greatest number of laws restricting our rights and progress until today we have reached the stage where we have almost no rights at all ... I have joined my people in the new spirit that moves them today, the spirit that revolts openly and boldly against injustice.'

With these brave words, Luthuli had thrown his energy into the defiance campaign, inspiring thousands of blacks to join the volunteers. He was a man of great dignity and kindness, with a real understanding of the problems faced by ordinary black people in their daily lives. Always retaining his optimism about the capacity of whites to undergo a change of heart, he also helped to quell the remaining resentment towards communists in the ANC. 'People ask me why I work with communists,' he once said, 'and my reply is that I have one enemy, the Nationalist government, and I will not fight on two fronts. I shall work with all who are prepared to stand with me in the struggle for the liberation of our country.'

The new president, known as 'The Chief', was greeted by 35 000 ANC members when he visited Port Elizabeth soon after taking office. But within days police had served banning orders on Luthuli, along with more than a hundred Africans, Indians and whites, preventing them from attending public gatherings. Some, like Mandela, were forbidden to leave Johannesburg for the following six months. New laws were passed to toughen the banning orders. Three years' imprisonment, and/or a fine of £300, and/or a whipping of ten strokes now awaited those who committed an offence 'by way of protest or in support of any campaign against any law'. Anyone whose words or actions encouraged another person to commit an offence by way of protest would incur an additional penalty of a £200 fine or two years in jail.

Christmas that year was a time for sombre reflection among ANC members, though an incident on the way to a festive celebration at Walter Sisulu's home gave Yusuf Cachalia, Sisulu, Oliver Tambo, JB Marks, Dr Diliza Mji and Jasmat Nanabhai an unexpected laugh. Travelling in two cars from the city centre along a main road running through a white suburb, they spotted an Indian youth sitting in a horse-drawn cart led by a burly Afrikaner. Suspecting the white man of ill-intent, the drivers of the two cars pulled up and their passengers piled out to investigate. The Afrikaner, outraged at being quizzed by a bunch of 'kaffirs', yelled for help and was quickly joined by heavyweight friends from nearby houses, their fists flying. 'We were all lying on the ground within minutes,' Cachalia remembered. 'I am an absolutely non-violent man: I don't know how to fight physically. Nor did most of the others. If Nelson had been there we would have fared better because he was a boxer. But the only one of us who seemed able to throw a punch was Walter and he didn't acquit himself too well. We all had to run for our lives.'

During Christmas celebrations in Natal, while The Chief was listening to a church choir singing carols and watching candles flickering on a decorated fir tree, he suddenly thought of a way to preserve the memory of the defiance campaign for future generations. When 26 June came the following year, Luthuli decided, he would call on blacks throughout the country to light candles or lamps outside their homes 'as a symbol of the spark of freedom which we are determined to keep alive in our hearts, and as a sign to freedom-lovers that we are keeping a vigil on that night'. He would appeal to older members of every household to tell children 'the story, so far as they know it, of the struggle of the African people in particular, and the non-Europeans in general, for their liberation'.

6

THE FREEDOM CHARTER

The drab Karoo town of Cradock was divided, like all dorps in South Africa, into two racial zones. Houses belonging to the small white community stood in rows behind sagging fences entwined with grenadilla creepers or bougainvillea, their wide verandas shielding the occupants on hot afternoons. Behind each of them stood a very much smaller building, crudely erected, for the two or three resident servants. Nearby in the backyard was an orchard of mango and mulberry trees, situated in what was effectively a neutral racial area where the children of master and servant would squat in the summertime, picking low-hanging fruits and enjoying their sweetness together. The other part of Cradock was its black location. Lying near a dusty road along which whites seldom travelled were the dwellings of most of Cradock's inhabitants: huts made of mud and stone, standing among mealie stalks and parched pumpkin plants.

Despite its humble appearance Cradock had a number of claims to fame. It was the home of one of South Africa's most acclaimed writers, Olive Schreiner, author of *The Story of an African Farm*, which was the first indigenous novel to achieve world recognition. She had lived in a whitewashed bungalow at 9 Cross Street until her father went bankrupt and she was obliged at the age of fifteen to take up a job as governess to a wealthy family in nearby Barkly East.

Cradock was also famous for its black choristers who sang in the Congress Choir of a former ANC president, the Reverend James Calata, with the dual aim of raising party funds and paying the tuition fees of destitute black schoolchildren in the area. The ANC was thus better known in Cradock than in most similar-sized rural towns. The sight of the green, black and gold ANC flag on a tall tree branch was enough to gather a crowd within the hour, eagerly waiting to hear what the organisation had in store for them.

It was in Cradock that Professor Zachariah Matthews first had the idea of forming a popular parliament to draw up a constitution for blacks; a blueprint of hope for the disenfranchised masses to rally behind. As president of the Cape branch of the ANC, he was addressing its annual conference when he said: 'I wonder whether the time has not come for the African National Congress to consider the question of convening a national convention, a Congress of the People, representing all the people of this country irrespective of race or colour, to draw up a Freedom Charter for the democratic South Africa of the future.'

Matthews was not only a major figure in African politics but an internationally admired scholar and exemplary Christian. He had been called Zachariah because his father, a devout storekeeper, believed a 'Christian name' had to come from the Bible if recriminations were to be avoided in the afterlife. As a young man, he became the first black student to take his degree in South Africa, and then the first black principal of a high school, Adams College in Natal. For several years he opposed the boycott strategies favoured by the Youth League, and he incurred scorn among radical blacks for the warm welcome he extended to the King and Queen of England during their visit to Fort Hare in 1947. But after the National Party victory the following year, his moderation turned to militancy. Though he himself was comfortable in his book-lined academic world at Fort Hare, Matthews watched the gathering forces of apartheid with dismay in the days following the Nationalist government's return to office for a second term in April 1953. Knowing the ANC's urgent duty was 'the instilling of political consciousness into the people and the encouraging of political activity', he believed the search for a covenant, a 'Freedom Charter' as he called it, would help to promote the organisation's aims.

Malan's repressive laws were mounting. The Bantu Education Act of 1953 proposed to bring mission schools – hitherto providing the only broad, liberal education for Africans – under government control. Hundreds of churches were ordered to implement government syllabuses and rigid rules of conduct for teachers and students: failure to comply meant forfeiture of state grants, a penalty few of them could afford to contemplate. Africans called it 'education for ignorance', a belief endorsed by Malan's native affairs minister, Dr Hendrik Verwoerd, when he announced: 'There is no place for him [the black man] in the European community above the level of certain forms of labour.'

Prosecutions under the Immorality Act continued. Reports of court cases involving mixed-race couples appeared frequently in the newspapers, often with sordid details gleaned by policemen concealed up trees or underneath beds. The 1950s were also the years of the most zealous enforcement of the pass laws. Convictions exceeded 300 000 annually, about one-tenth of the black urban population. Police harassment late at night was commonplace. Under the Urban Areas Act, a black person could live on white premises only if employed there: neither wives, husbands nor children could legally reside with their working kin unless they could prove legitimate employment. Some whites turned a blind eye, preferring to pay the police fine rather than evict close relatives, but most guarded their servants' quarters against infringements.

Hundreds of black activists had been barred from public life by the Suppression of Communism Act, among them Chief Luthuli, robbed of his livelihood and banished to a remote part of the country on a state allowance of £1 a month. Nelson Mandela, the ANC's Transvaal president and Luthuli's deputy, was confined to Johannesburg and banned from attending or addressing gatherings, though he found ways to combat the restrictions. At the Transvaal annual conference in September 1953 he asked Robert Resha to deliver his presidential address. '... The old methods of bringing about mass action through public mass meetings, press statements, and leaflets calling upon the people to go into action have become extremely dangerous and difficult to use effectively. The authorities will not easily permit a meeting called under the auspices of the ANC; few newspapers will publish statements openly criticising the policies of the government; and there is hardly a single printing press which will agree to print leaflets calling upon workers to embark upon industrial action ... These developments require the evolution of new forms of political struggle which will make it possible for us to strive for action on a higher level than the defiance campaign.'

Mandela's new forms of political struggle centred on a drive to politicise the masses, using the 'M' (for Mandela) Plan, although it actually drew upon an organisational strategy pioneered by local branches in the eastern Cape. It was a branch organisational system designed to combat bans on gatherings, dividing black residential areas into multiple small cells, which comprised a single street under the control of a 'cell steward'. Seven streets made up a zone headed by a 'chief steward', who could quickly relay political messages through the cells to the masses.

That year, at its annual December conference in Bloemfontein, the ANC adopted Professor Matthews' idea: a Congress of the People (COP) to formulate a Freedom Charter as a guide to popular aspirations in a multiracial society of the future. Nelson Mandela and Walter Sisulu were delegated to plan the campaign. Though banned and restricted, Sisulu immediately set about promoting the Congress of the People in his customarily enthusiastic, sometimes incautious way. He spoke so provocatively of alternative forms of government that Professor Matthews' lawyer son Joe, a militant himself, wrote to his father about a 'dangerous statement' Walter had made in Port Elizabeth: 'Now quite clearly no government can tolerate that sort of thing ... I'm scared of these references to our government and our parliament.'

Walter simply ignored warnings to guard his tongue. He was among the ANC's most effective organisers, largely because his humble origins gave him easy rapport with the ordinary people who were increasingly spearheading the struggle. 'Walter would always say "Do you think we ought to do this and that?" or "Shall we do so-and-so?" or "Would you mind helping us with this?", whereas many of the other ANC leaders just issued commands and expected us to jump,' said a veteran ANC activist.

Walter's wife Albertina remembered numerous discussions with Mandela when she and Walter tried to persuade him to adopt a less lofty manner in his public life. 'But he was a Xhosa aristocrat and his training from childhood had made him the way he was, aloof and sometimes a bit arrogant,' said Albertina. 'It didn't matter because the people liked to look up to a leader who was regal and maybe even a bit distant, though Walter's way was sometimes more effective. The two of them made a very good team.'

On occasions, however, Nelson's severity alarmed his colleagues. Robert Matji, one of the ANC's key organisers in the Cape, remembered coming to Johannesburg for a briefing about the Congress of the People. He stayed at Nelson's house, sleeping on a mat on the floor of the living room alongside a number of other visiting Cape officials. The two Mandela sons Tembi and Magatho – the latter named after an early ANC president who chained himself to a pavement hitching post as a gesture of public protest – were playing among the sleeping bodies early one morning before school when Tembi realised a vital textbook was missing from his satchel. The nine-year-old was close to tears when Nelson appeared, joining the search for the book, which was eventually found. Flicking it open, Nelson discovered another boy's name on the flyleaf. 'He then set about cross-examining his son as if he was standing trial in the Supreme Court,' recalled Matji. 'Where did he get the book? Did the owner know he had borrowed it? And so forth. He even started quoting from various laws. We were sitting around listening and feeling very sorry for the little boy because, where we came from, if you had to have a school book, you got it, never mind what the law said about this or that. Nelson's legal training made him very, very conscious of rights and wrongs.'

Mandela and Sisulu began their preparations for the Congress of the People by summoning meetings to train and inspire leaders. Arranged through the 'M-Plan' network, they were usually held on commercial premises, such as the Indian tailor's shop where Walter briefed numerous organisers. Those arriving for forbidden talks were instructed to wander into the shop at prearranged intervals, linger awhile like ordinary customers, fingering bolts of cloth, until they were sure they had not been followed by police, then slip into the back room occupied by ANC colleagues. On one occasion when Walter had to bring important documents from ANC executive member Dan Tloome's office in central Johannesburg, he arrived at the tailor's shop with his small daughter. Once safely in the back room, he lifted the giggling girl's skirt, taking the wad of papers from her knickers.

In March 1954 a national council was formed to mobilise the Congress of the People campaign. It comprised members of the ANC, the Indian Congress, the Cape-based South African Coloured People's Organisation, a small, but influential, group of radical whites called the Congress of Democrats, and Communist Party members. They were jointly known as the Congress Alliance, and the organisers began calling for 'shock brigades' of volunteers, recruiting as leaders men and women who were capable of working on their own initiative and dealing sympathetically with the people at all levels.

Among them were defiance campaign stalwarts like Dorothy Nyembe, one of the first women to go to jail for defiance in 1952. Then aged nineteen, she had pleaded with sceptical ANC officials who felt she was too young to participate. 'My child,' Luthuli had said to her, 'these people don't believe you will do it. It's not easy.'

Again ignoring the risk of police reprisals, Dorothy Nyembe held Congress of the People meetings in densely populated Cato Manor in Natal, cajoling, berating and inspiring her listeners until they agreed to join the growing army of volunteers. Approaching blacks in their homes, she would announce: 'I am the voice of Chief Luthuli,' which usually guaranteed a welcome.

The volunteers, wearing khaki uniforms designed to become familiar throughout the country, were delegated to canvass support for the Congress of the People. Their task was to distribute copies of an ANC newsletter, *The Call*, and sell the newspaper, *New Age*, which was helping to promote the campaign. They were also asked to collect ideas from the groups they addressed for inclusion in the Freedom Charter, 'a document to guide all our future work ... written by the ordinary people themselves, through the demands that they themselves send in'. To help volunteers, the Congress Alliance distributed regular directives: 'The volunteers should carefully write down the demands and grievances that are voiced. They should guide the discussion so that people do not say only what they suffer but also what changes must be made to set things right. They must encourage people to talk of small things, and not speak generally of "unjust laws" or "oppression". They must ask: what laws are unjust, and what should be done about them; what is oppression, and how can it be abolished?' Once each group understood the concept of the Freedom Charter, it was invited to elect a representative to attend the Congress of the People as a delegate. (The extent to which the Charter became a reflection of the dominant Communist Party's doctrine – an expression of its conception of a 'national democratic' revolution – is an issue that remains unresolved.)

If volunteers struck hostility, they were told to inform Congress Alliance headquarters so that persuasive senior politicians could conduct follow-up discussions with resisters. Roy Naidoo, a veteran activist and adopted son of Mahatma Gandhi, was one of those delegated to convince detractors of the wisdom of the Congress of the People. On one occasion, after talking for days to an Indian who insisted on remaining politically neutral, Naidoo's patience finally expired. Pointing to the photograph of Gandhi that most Indian homeowners displayed on their walls, Naidoo bellowed: 'Take this photo off! What the hell is the matter with you? Why do you want to keep this photo when you talk like that?'

Many of the volunteers were assisted by experienced trade unionists, among them members of the reorganised Communist Party, who offered advice to volunteers approaching factory workers: they should borrow a pair of the overalls worn by employees so that they could slip through the security gates unnoticed in a crowd; they should approach workers during the lunch break when a gathering was normal; they should retreat as soon as white supervisors showed suspicion.

Though Malan's labour minister, Ben Schoeman, had vowed 'to bleed the African trade unions to death', dozens of new worker bodies sprang up during the Congress of the People campaign, led by dynamic men like Billy Nair in Natal, who was in and out of prison for breaching the laws that sought to curb black solidarity. In March 1955, a few months before the Congress of the People was due to take place, the South African Congress of Trade Unions (SACTU) was formed, uniting many small unions that had been established over the years. SACTU's first national project was to collect workers' demands for the Freedom Charter.

In the early months of 1955 a report in *New Age* informed the public that 'for months now the demands have been flooding in to COP headquarters, on sheets torn from school exercise books, on little dog-eared scraps of paper, on slips torn from COP leaflets'. Oliver Tambo issued a press release in April, saying that the Freedom Charter was being compiled by the Congress Alliance action committee 'from thousands of written statements ... gathered at thousands of small meetings'. Once it had been endorsed by the ANC's national executive, the Congress of the People – due to take place on 25 and 26 June – would be ready to present its goals to the nation.

Delays and gremlins intervened: by the time the Freedom Charter was finally presented to the ANC for approval by Rusty Bernstein and the rest of the small groups who had underwritten its compilation, the event was only three days away. Thousands of copies of the document had already been printed and distributed, much to the fury of the Africanists within the ANC who strongly objected to its opening declaration: 'South Africa belongs to all who live in it, black and white.'

The Congress of the People was to be held in Kliptown – a location ten miles southwest of Johannesburg – on a privately owned soccer field, which was decked in bright flags and banners as the day approached. Fires were prepared in advance for the cooking of mountains of food organised by a catering committee led by Ahmed Kathrada. Kathy, as he was known, had spent months collecting utensils, pots and dishes, including a huge consignment of small tin bowls which he thought delegates could buy cheaply to eat from and afterwards keep as mementoes. A few weeks earlier, while he was haggling for a reduced price from the obstinate manufacturer of the bowls, Kathy had grown impatient, finally resorting to a gentle threat: 'Give them to me at a shilling each and I'll make sure the Metal Box Company is left alone when we take over power in South Africa.' The white businessman laughed a little uneasily, then agreed.

In the early hours of 24 June, a Friday, thousands of delegates from all over South Africa began their journey to Kliptown. Many had to travel for days on buses and trucks packed with blankets and food. Dozens of poor delegates were sponsored by the extraordinary energies of John Mtini, a seventy-year-old man in frail health, who had risen early each morning for months, leaving his tiny hut in Elsie's River to trudge all day from door to door collecting money for travel expenses.

The roads approaching Johannesburg swarmed with police: some vehicles full of singing delegates were stopped half a dozen times before reaching Kliptown. As the buses drew up in the early hours of Saturday morning a band struck up, playing freedom songs and marches.

It looked like a massive carnival. Some of the 2 884 delegates and 700 spectators were in tribal costumes of animal skins and bright beads; others wore the green, black and yellow colours of the ANC or khaki volunteers' uniforms. Indian women hurried about in shimmering saris. Old men leant on sticks, yelling to each other; babies screamed beneath blankets tied on to their mothers' backs; teams of shouting youths carried placards and flags; city men in suits and hats watched quietly; half-naked Xhosa elders from Pondoland looked tall and forbidding in patterned blankets, their cheekbones stained with clay. Up on the platform, in front of a giant, four-spoked wheel symbolising their unity, sat key Congress Alliance organisers. 'Perhaps it was the first really representative gathering in the Union's history,' Chief Luthuli wrote. 'Nothing in the history of the liberatory movement in South Africa quite caught the popular imagination as this did, not even the defiance campaign.'

At three in the afternoon, the Congress of the People got under way. Groups of Special Branch policemen stood near the entrance to the football field, their pens and notebooks ready. A cordially worded invitation had been sent by Chief Luthuli to prime minister Malan, who had not bothered to reply: the only representatives he sent to Kliptown were policemen.

Not far away, in a Kliptown house, sat a gathering of banned VIPs. Walter

Sisulu, Dr Dadoo, JB Marks, Maulvi Cachalia and his brother Yusuf didn't plan to miss the great day, even at the risk of imprisonment. Though unable to see what was going on, they could hear the sounds of the crowd and they had arranged for runners to bring them regular reports. Dr Dadoo, Chief Luthuli and Father Trevor Huddleston, an Anglican priest who had thrown himself behind the ANC during the Sophiatown 'black spots' removal campaign, were each due to receive the ANC's highest honour, the 'Isitwalandwe', during the proceedings but only Huddleston was free of bans and able to attend.

One of the ANC's banned members did arrive inside the stadium, his face masked behind a balaclava. He was Gert Sibande, known as the Lion of the East, who suddenly found himself standing next to a white man named Muller, head of the Special Branch. When his turn came to speak, Sibande sprang on to the platform and removed his disguise. Muller shouted, 'It's Sibande,' which immediately sent a cordon of policemen around the stage. But Muller decided not to act, ordering his men to disperse.

The process of ratifying the Freedom Charter began. Each clause was read out and debated, each delegate was entitled to speak on the platform on behalf of those he represented. It was a long, slow process, interspersed with freedom songs. After affirming the right of all citizens to vote, hold office and attain equality before the law, the Freedom Charter went on to offer equal status for all national groups, an end to discriminatory legislation, redistribution of land, and public ownership of mines, banks and monopoly industries. Offering free education, medical care and welfare for the elderly, as well as minimum wages, it lapsed at times into impractical promises: 'Rent and prices shall be lowered, food plentiful and no one shall go hungry.'

Towards the end of the second day's proceedings, when Sunday's agenda was almost complete and the clause calling for universal peace and friendship was about to be discussed, the police suddenly launched a raid. Driving up in trucks, they charged towards the delegates' enclosure and escorted a dozen Special Branch detectives on to the platform. There they presented their search warrants, announcing that they had come to investigate a case of high treason. Several tanks rumbled in. Ida Mtwana remembered a roar rising from the sea of black faces below her as she scrambled to her feet on the platform. 'Comrades, this is the hour! Please do not do a thing,' she implored. 'Let's start singing!' Her high voice led the crowd into the first bars of *Nkosi Sikelel' iAfrika*.

Seizing every document they could find, the police began a massive body search while their colleagues on horseback sealed off the entrances. Officers armed with rifles moved through the crowd. One by one, the delegates and spectators were cleared to leave the field. All the whites present, mostly members of the Congress of Democrats, were photographed for security files. Manilal Gandhi described policemen with 'a wild look on their faces. Some jeered at the delegates and, while the delegates were shouting "Africa" with their thumbs up, some of the police were responding with their thumbs down.'

As darkness descended, the police brought hurricane lamps from their vehicles, and continued the questioning until eight that night. When the football field was finally empty, officers loaded crates of confiscated literature on to their trucks, driving away to study the 'treasonable' evidence. By now in cheerful mood, the police had found what they wanted. Or so they thought.

7

ACTS OF TREASON?

Three months later, in the early hours of 27 September 1955, over a thousand officers launched the biggest police raid in the country's history. Hundreds of search warrants were prepared for the occasion, authorising the seizure of books, letters, notes and diaries – anything that might provide evidence of the Nationalist government's version of treason.

At least five hundred people were body-searched in offices and homes throughout the country, their possessions combed for signs of sedition or violation of the Suppression of Communism Act and the Riotous Assemblies Act. The police carted away piles of impounded documents, adding them to the mountain of papers already collected during the Congress of the People raid in Kliptown. A search of Professor Matthews' home and office at Fort Hare lasted four hours. All the material he had been collecting for a documentary history of the ANC, including his typewriter, was bundled into boxes, never to be returned. A few of the suspects called their lawyers but most, having no telephones in their homes, stood by helplessly as the silent policemen searched. In Roy Naidoo's house, an exhausted white officer was tipped off a dining room chair by one of Naidoo's daughters who informed him that the seats were reserved for friends.

The offices of *New Age* in Johannesburg and Cape Town were stripped of virtually all files and records. Govan Mbeki, editor and chief reporter in the Cape, lost research material covering hundreds of hours of investigation, including a dossier on potato farm workers in Bethal: they wore sacks with holes cut out for their heads and arms, working every day from 4.00am until sunset under the tyrannical watch of white farmers wielding *sjamboks*.

Mbeki, a former member of the original Communist Party of South Africa, now signed up with the SACP, was the most prominent ANC member in the eastern Cape. He had joined Ruth First the previous year on the editorial board of *New Age*, a newspaper that replaced its banned forerunners, *The Clarion* and *Advance*. Born in the Nqamakwe district of the Transkei in 1910, the son of a Xhosa chief, Mbeki's political education began at the age of fifteen when he acted as interpreter for his cousin, a leader of the Industrial and Commercial Workers' Union. As a high school student at Healdtown in the 1920s, Mbeki was angered to see poor Afrikaners as well as blacks suffer the breakdown of subsistence farming in the Transkei. 'Many whites came to our house asking for food and shelter,' he recalled.

After passing matric in the secondary school section of Fort Hare in 1933, Mbeki went on to achieve an honours degree in economics, and became a school teacher. His interest in communism was aroused in the 1930s by Dr Edward Roux, a university lecturer and author of *Time Longer Than Rope*, a history of the black people's quest for liberty in South Africa. His involvement in trade union organisation in Natal during the late 1930s led to dismissal from his teaching post, after which he bought a store in Idutywa in the Transkei, began writing a book about labour exploitation, and served as an elected member of the Transkei administration.

Since his first visit to Johannesburg from the Transkei in 1929, Mbeki had been tormented by policemen thumping on doors in the hours before daybreak. 'Where I lived, in the city and in the suburbs, police raids were always taking place,' he recalled. 'Either they wanted to check our passes, or were looking for illegal drink. No other event up till then had provoked my anger as much as those raids and I decided definitely to join the struggle and put an end to such a system.'

Anti-apartheid protest continued despite the September raids. When the Nationalists decided to extend pass law regulations to women, the move was bitterly denounced by the Federation of South African Women (FEDSAW). Led by a dynamic teacher-turned-social worker, Helen Joseph, who was a prominent member of the Congress of Democrats, and Bertha Mashaba, Transvaal secretary of the ANC's women's league, FEDSAW mobilised two thousand women to march on government headquarters at Pretoria's Union Buildings in October 1955. Each woman strode individually up the steps of the imposing institution to deliver her petition, a strategy which successfully evaded the Pretoria City Council's ban on FEDSAW meetings.

A year later, on 9 August, FEDSAW mounted a second, far bigger protest. Summoning 20 000 women of all races from every corner of the country, the organisers chartered hundreds of vehicles, including a full railway coach in Port Elizabeth, to ferry women demonstrators to Pretoria. Some had trudged for many miles to transport assembly points; some from distant areas had sold scarce possessions in order to afford the fare.

Each carrying a petition against pass laws, the women surged up the steps of the terraced gardens at Union Buildings behind their leaders, Lilian Ngoyi, Helen Joseph, Rahima Moosa and Sophie Williams. Crowding into the stone amphitheatre, they watched as their representatives carried heaps of protest letters to the office of prime minister Johannes Strijdom, Malan's successor, who was said to be away at the time, though many of the demonstrators and one journalist claimed to have seen a person closely resembling Strijdom peeping down at the crowd from behind drapes in the prime minister's suite.

After leaving their protests in Strijdom's office, the leaders returned to the packed forecourt, where Lilian Ngoyi called on the women to stand in silence for thirty minutes, their arms raised in the ANC salute. 'The clock struck three and then a quarter past; it was the only sound,' wrote Helen Joseph. 'I looked at those many faces until they became only one face, the face of the suffering black people of South Africa. I know there were tears in my eyes and I think there were many who wept with me.' When the clock struck half-past three, Lilian Ngoyi began to sing, joined by the 20 000. *Nkosi Sikelel' iAfrika* was followed by a song specially rehearsed for the occasion: *'Wathint' abafazi, wa uthint' imbolodo uzo kufa'*, meaning 'Now you have touched the women, you have struck a rock'. Then they walked quietly away.

Other ANC campaigns in the 1954-1955 period included the Bantu Education Boycott, which was effective on the East Rand, parts of Johannesburg and around Port Elizabeth. Abortive efforts to oppose removals in Sophiatown showed, however, that the ANC did not have the resolve for effective disobedience in that particular campaign.

Sporadic police raids on the offices and homes of opposition political leaders continued throughout 1956. Sometimes the policemen themselves seemed bemused by their senior officers' insatiable appetite for every opposition document they could lay hands on. On one occasion, when the news leaked that a night raid was about to be launched on the Indian Congress's offices in Johannesburg, activists decided to stand vigil outside their building in order to make entry more difficult for the moonlight searchers. Hours passed as the Indians watched police cars cruising past them. Then a squad of plain-clothes officers arrived to keep watch over the Indian vigilantes. 'We sat on one side and they sat on the other,' recalled Suliman Esakjee. 'They watched us and we watched them. Very late that night, a police car drew up bringing flasks of coffee for the policemen. We were eyeing the refreshments longingly when, to our great surprise, a couple of the cops walked across, handed us mugs and began to share their coffee with us.'

Towards the end of 1956 the police finally found the evidence they had been seeking. Through a microphone hidden in the ceiling at an ANC meeting, they recorded Robert Resha, a leading Congressman in the Transvaal, telling branch organisers: 'When you are disciplined and are told by your organisation not to be violent, you must not be violent. If you are a true volunteer and you are called upon to be violent, you must be absolutely violent. You must murder! Murder! That is all.'

At 2.00am on 5 December 1956 hundreds of police officers assembled in their stations all over the country for a final briefing on a massive security swoop code-named 'Operation T'. Three military transport planes from Pretoria revved their engines in the darkness, flying off to collect prisoners in Durban, Cape Town and Port Elizabeth. By daybreak, 140 people had been arrested and brought to Johannesburg's central jail to face charges of high treason, a capital offence. By the end of the week, a total of 156 sat in the crowded cells.

At police headquarters nearby, a stream of detectives drew up with their car sirens wailing, offloading boxes of items seized during the arrests, including a biography of Dr Johnson, an anthology of English verse, and a silk dressing gown with Chinese lettering embroidered on the pocket.

The jailed suspects were men and women of all races: lawyers, doctors, priests, businessmen, social workers and housewives. All 156 were initially held in two cells, jokingly compared with the country's 159-member parliament and dubbed the upper and lower houses. Their collective political experience spanned the ANC's forty-four-year history: one seventy-year-old man had been a founder member in 1912; the Reverend James Calata had been an active Congressman since the 1920s; Professor Matthews and Chief Luthuli had joined after the abolition of the Cape black vote in 1935; Nelson Mandela, Walter Sisulu and Oliver Tambo had been members since the 1940s. They included a highly unlikely suspect, a man called Tshungungwa, who had accepted a government-sponsored job and been expelled from the ANC as a result. Other more likely candidates, like Yusuf Dadoo, a well-known communist and key organiser in both the defiance and Congress of the People campaigns, were neither arrested nor listed in the co-conspirators' indictment.

Preliminary proceedings began two weeks later. Because there were too many accused to fit in any regular courtroom, the Johannesburg Drill Hall in Twist Street was selected as a makeshift venue. Measuring 90 x 120 feet, it proved inadequate to accommodate a dock of 156 prisoners, a bench for the magistrate, a public gallery, as well as tables for a sizeable press contingent. So chaotic were the arrangements which greeted the prisoners as they filed into the Drill Hall that the trial was dubbed the 'Twist Street Affair' by journalists. The prisoners were spaced along ten rows of chairs, the twenty-three members of the Congress of Democrats sitting slightly separate from the blacks, Indians and coloureds.

At lunchtime, when their food was delivered, the hall took on a carnival atmosphere. Eager to exchange views with colleagues, many of whom had been isolated from each other by bans, the prisoners wandered around, chatting and laughing. When it was discovered that the absence of a loudspeaker system left the accused unable to hear the case proceeding against them, the magistrate ordered an adjournment until later in the afternoon, by which time a crowd of five thousand had gathered around the Drill Hall. Shouting and singing, they jostled against the building's railings. Lawyers and journalists wishing to leave the premises were told by police to climb over the railings rather than risk opening the gates in the face of the surging demonstrators.

Next morning, when the accused and their legal representatives arrived at the Drill Hall, they were astonished to find the prisoners' dock enclosed inside a six-feet-high wire-mesh cage. Defence lawyer Maurice Franks, QC, immediately launched a protest. Normally a composed man with an expressionless face, he could scarcely contain his outrage. 'The scene is unprecedented,' he declared. 'The accused are caged. I am most anxious not to allow my indignation to get the better of me ... I mean, caged like wild beasts ... It is a shame on everybody who is responsible ...' Some of the accused, struggling to conceal their amusement, wrote labels and hung them on the wire-mesh: 'Do Not Feed', 'No monkey nuts'. One visiting newsman, astonished at the setting for the historic treason trial, described the Nationalist government as 'a tyranny tempered by inefficiency'.

The defending counsel threatened to withdraw from the proceedings unless the cage was removed. After court officials lowered the mesh, removing it entirely from the front of the dock, they agreed to proceed. The prosecutor began to outline his case, occasionally interrupted by laughter from the dock in response to alleged statements. 'The ANC wants money to buy machine guns' was a claim which particularly amused the defendants.

Then chaos erupted in the street outside, where black supporters had been gathering all morning. Resentful of the small numbers allowed into the Drill Hall, the crowd began to shove against the railings. Police decided on a baton charge to push them back. An answering hail of stones and oranges came flying through the air, and some of the officers panicked. Gunfire rang out: five shots followed by bursts from a dozen rifles. The crowd ran in every direction. Women were screaming, falling beneath stampeding feet. The Anglican bishop of Johannesburg, Ambrose Reeves, shouted, 'They've lost control!' and ran towards the retreating crowd with his hand in the air, appealing for calm. The police, claiming they intended only to fire warning shots over the heads of the crowd, radioed for ambulances to carry twenty-two injured people to hospital.

In August 1958 the main trial began beneath the Star of David in an old synagogue in Pretoria, a venue chosen by police in the hope that the proceedings would attract less public interest there. It meant that most of the accused, who were all granted bail, had to travel up to ninety miles each day from their homes in Johannesburg. Many lost their jobs, being unable to work during office hours. Others, like Nelson Mandela and Helen Joseph, went to their desks around six every morning, returning early in the evening after the journey from Pretoria and working until nine at night.

The prosecution alleged that the accused had been planning the 'overthrow of the existing state by revolutionary methods, involving violence and the establishment of the so-called People's Democracy'. Much of its evidence centred on the Freedom Charter, which the prosecution claimed would lead to communism. Statements recorded by police at various meetings, such as 'organising the people against fascist reactionaries' and promoting a 'programme of political education', were cited as proof of 'a countrywide conspiracy' inspired by international communism. Seemingly unable to summarise its case, the state presented scores of witnesses and introduced around 12 000 documents in the first month alone, while many of the accused dozed or knitted in the dock.

In the politicised community outside the synagogue, protest continued despite the treason trial. Responding to a proposed increase in bus fares, the residents of Alexandra – a large proportion of Johannesburg's labour force – launched a bus boycott in January 1957. Organisers distributed leaflets at night, crying '*Azikwelwa!*' ('We shall not ride!'), and set up pickets at bus stops throughout the township, the 'dark city' as it was known.

Early in the morning, blacks began their journey to the city on foot. By the end of the first week 45 000 people were walking or cycling to work, many covering twenty miles a day. Transport minister Schoeman, who formerly held the labour portfolio, was adamant that the government would never give in to boycotters. He declared that the protest was political, not economic, and said, 'The ANC is testing its strength.' Calling on white motorists not to offer lifts to the boycotters, he told employers to punish those who arrived late. Policemen began to stop cyclists carrying colleagues on their cross-bars, in some cases letting down their tyres.

Africans in Port Elizabeth, though not facing a fare increase, decided to support their Transvaal comrades. The protest began to hit productivity in factories and offices. Six weeks later the Johannesburg Chamber of Commerce, announcing that its members had raised £25 000 to subsidise bus fares, offered a refund of the fare increase at the end of each day's journey to and from work. But the remedy was available to workers only: women and children were excluded. The protest committee consulted the people of Alexandra, who rejected it. '*Azikwelwa!*' yelled the crowd, and the boycott continued.

As the protest entered its third month, some boycotters began to contemplate a general strike: 'When we are tired, we will rest,' warned a slogan. Bishop Ambrose Reeves decided to intervene and he consulted ANC leaders on trial in Pretoria, who drafted a proposal to end the boycott. But when this was put to the weary residents of Alexandra, they roared their disapproval.

Searching for another solution, the ANC's leadership erupted in quarrels. Left-wing Africanists, led by Josias Madzunya, could think of no better outcome than a general strike, while moderates like Chief Luthuli feared the suffering it would bring to black families. Finally the ANC put out a leaflet urging the people to accept the Chamber of Commerce proposal and promising a concerted campaign for wage increases. Footsore residents agreed reluctantly, climbing aboard the buses next day.

By the time the Chamber's funds ran out three months later, the government had decided it could not risk a general strike. Introducing the Native Services Levy, which required employers to subsidise bus fares, the legislators obeyed the will of the black population for the first time in fifty years. In the process blacks learnt a valuable political lesson: they could in fact vote, albeit with their feet, on issues where white profits were at stake.

The 1950s was a time when Africans foresaw imminent reform, believing that increased sympathy from the white community would bring an end to apartheid. Attaching undue significance to the handful of whites facing treason charges alongside them, and encouraged by the success of liberation movements in other parts of Africa, many talked openly of decline in Afrikaner power. 'As far as the Nationalist Party is concerned,' wrote Walter Sisulu in 1957, 'any serious analysis will reveal that it has reached its high-water mark. There is no possibility of the Nationalists growing stronger than they are at present.' Journalist Lewis Nkosi, describing the 1950s, wrote of 'a time of infinite hope and possibility; it seemed not extravagant in the least to predict then that the Nationalist government would soon collapse, if not from the pressure of extra-parliamentary opposition, certainly from the growing volume of unenforceable laws.'

However, Nationalist power was in reality advancing. The government had been busy for several years on a goal long close to Afrikaner hearts: removing coloureds from the common voters' roll. To do this it required a majority of two-thirds in both houses of parliament sitting together. Unable to secure the necessary vote, it introduced the Separate Representation of Voters Act on a simple majority in 1951, a move challenged by the white opposition and declared void by the Appeal Court in Bloemfontein. The following year the government resorted to a blatantly unconstitutional device, 'a high court of parliament', in an attempt to validate the defeated legislation. It was again rejected by the courts.

Deciding to secure a majority by 'packing' the senate, the government then introduced the Senate Act, increasing the body from 48 to 89 members, 77 of them government appointees. This time, when the opposition went to Bloemfontein to challenge the legislation, it discovered that the Appeal Court had also been enlarged for the occasion, from six to eleven judges. Enraged liberal politicians and newspapers warned of illegal, undemocratic tricks. The prime minister said the act had been passed in order to end a constitutional deadlock. When the verdict was handed down, ten judges found in favour of the government. Only Justice Schreiner dissented, insisting that the law must operate within the bounds of morality.

The battle was over; the Nationalists had won. Coloureds had lost the Cape vote. 'We are taking this step,' declared a triumphant MP, 'because we are Calvinists who believe God is sovereign and that sovereignty is delegated to the lawful rulers of the land.'

The treason trial dragged on for more than four years, watched from the public gallery by foreign diplomats and relatives of those in the dock, anxiously waiting to see if the accused would pay the dreaded penalty for treason. Among them was a beautiful young woman from Pondoland, wearing the brilliant garments and turbans of tribal dress, her eyes seldom straying from the elegant figure of Nelson Mandela. Her name was Nomzamo, and she was a social worker whose friends called her Winnie. She was Mandela's new wife; his marriage to Eveline, strained beyond repair by his long absences from home and his alleged affairs with other women, having ended in divorce soon after the birth of their third child, a daughter named Makaziwe.

Mandela's evidence alone occupied 400 pages of the court record. Judge Bekker, a resolute Afrikaner who once recalled that his favourite pastime as a schoolboy was to sit on a kerb in Johannesburg's city centre, picking out *Engelse* (English people) as they walked by, joined the cross-examination. 'Isn't your freedom a direct threat to Europeans?' he asked Mandela.

'No, it is not a direct threat to Europeans,' Mandela replied. 'We are not anti-white; we are against white supremacy, and in struggling against white supremacy we have the support of some sections of the European population ... It is quite clear that the Congress has consistently preached a policy of race harmony, and we have condemned racialism no matter by whom it is professed.'

To illustrate how the accused had 'deliberately created an explosive situation', the prosecution read out the works of Alex La Guma, a coloured Congressman: 'South Africa is littered all over with dry firewood which will soon be kindled into a conflagration. We need only to look at ... the defiance campaign, the strikes of the non-European workers, the Congress of the People, to see that it will not take long for these sparks to become a prairie fire.'

The defence opened its case, declaring it would 'strenuously repudiate' that the terms of the Freedom Charter were treasonable or criminal. 'On the contrary, the defence will contend that the ideas and beliefs which are expressed in this charter, although repugnant to the policy of the present government, are such as are shared by the overwhelming majority of all races and colours, and also by the overwhelming majority of citizens of this country ... We will endeavour to show that what is on trial here are not just 156 individuals, but the ideas which they and thousands of others in our land have openly espoused and expressed.'

The task of defending the Freedom Charter against charges of communist inspiration fell to Jack Simons of the University of Cape Town, a member of the regrouped Communist Party, who seemed almost to consider the allegation an affront to Marxism – though his indignation was disingenuous, given the role the communists had in fact played in drafting it. Using words like 'reactionary', 'meaningless' and 'muddle-headed' in his description of the Freedom Charter, he pointed out that it contained no reference to the abolition of classes and the establishment of public ownership of the means of production. Such nationalisation as was proposed characterised state capitalism rather than communism; to a Marxist, said Simons, the Freedom Charter's omission of specific terms for the transfer of wealth was inexcusable. Also defending the controversial clause calling for the nationalisation of mines, banks and monopoly industries, Chief Luthuli told the court: 'It is certainly not Congress policy to do away with private ownership of the means of production.'

At the end of 1957 the attorney-general suddenly announced that he had decided to suspend charges against sixty-one of the accused. Included among them were Oliver Tambo, accepted by Bishop Reeves as a candidate for ordination shortly before his arrest a year earlier, and Chief Luthuli. 'It is with mixed feelings that I received the news of my release,' said Luthuli. 'The truth is that I would be happier to see the whole thing through with my comrades.' Nearly twelve months later, charges against sixty-four of the remaining ninety-five defendants were suspended, leaving only thirty-one to face the three red-robed judges.

In 1960, a year before the trial ended, the government declared a state of emergency in response to widespread rioting following a massacre at Sharpeville. In nationwide dawn raids, police arrested 1 800 activists, including the remaining treason trialists. As a mark of protest, the defendants asked their team of lawyers to withdraw from the trial, contending they could no longer conduct the case efficiently under the state of emergency. The accused then used their own legal team, headed by Duma Nokwe, the country's first black advocate, and including Nelson Mandela, Robert Resha and Ahmed Kathrada. Finally, on 29 March 1961, the court reached its decision. Taking thirty-eight minutes to read the unanimous verdict, Mr Justice Rumpff declared: 'You are found not guilty and discharged. You may go.'

Commenting afterwards on the futility of the marathon trial, a defence attorney noted that twelve of the twenty-nine detectives giving evidence during the first two months had admitted that non-violence was a publicly stated part of ANC policy. Alfred Hutchinson, one of the accused, wrote: 'What treason was there? Is it treason to ask that black and white should live together, as brothers, countrymen, equals? Is it treason to ask for food? Is it treason to ask that passes be abolished? And that we might walk freely in the land of our birth?'

8

SHOOTING AT SHARPEVILLE

A scholarly man with an aloof smile and a love of Milton's *Paradise Lost* spoke for a vociferous minority of Africanists in the ANC when he demanded in 1958 that the movement oust its non-black allies. Accusing white communists of 'speaking in a foreign voice' on behalf of blacks, he went on to condemn the ANC's leadership for following spontaneous protest, instead of directing dissent. His name was Robert Mangaliso Sobukwe, or 'Prof' to his friends.

Born in the Afrikaner town of Graaff Reinet in the Cape in 1924, Sobukwe was the son of a labourer-cum-Methodist lay preacher. His father was a stern disciplinarian who taught his six children to accept austerity as the will of God. From his earliest school years, despite contracting tuberculosis, Sobukwe showed academic excellence, winning a scholarship to Healdtown and then a financial gift from his headmaster in order to pursue his passion for literature at Fort Hare. An active member of the ANC Youth League on campus, he distinguished himself as a public speaker and, unlike the majority of his peers, learnt African languages so that he could address meetings in the vernacular rather than in English. A teacher in the eastern Transvaal and later a language lecturer at the University of the Witwatersrand, he edited a magazine called *The Africanist*.

Echoing the sentiments of his political idol, Anton Lembede, Sobukwe wrote: 'Our contention is that the Africans are the only people who, because of their material position, can be interested in the complete overhaul of the present structure of society. We have admitted that there are Europeans who are intellectual converts to the Africans' cause but, because they benefit materially from the present set-up, they cannot completely identify themselves with that cause.'

High on Sobukwe's list of grievances against the ANC was the Freedom Charter, particularly its reference to blacks and whites as 'brothers'.

Most blacks still hungered for acceptance by whites, though they had learnt to recognise the bogus overtures of half-hearted liberals intent on taming rather than liberating them. Often, when whites made honest attempts towards sharing equally with blacks, they were rewarded with an almost embarrassing gratitude, as author Alan Paton described in a passage about a student Christian conference at Fort Hare: 'Though white and black slept separately at the conference, they ate together ... On the Sunday morning there was a joint communion service ... To some it was the deepest experience of their lives; they could hardly control the tumult of emotions that threatened to overwhelm them. Spiritual and invisible unity is very fine, but visible unity stabs at the heart and takes away the breath and fills one with unspeakable and painful joy; unspeakable because glory is unspeakable, painful because it is all a dream, and who knows how many years must pass and how many lives be spent and how much suffering undergone before it all comes true.'

ANC leaders believed their policy of co-operation with anti-apartheid whites helped blacks to resolve the contradiction between their dreams of unity and the realities of a racially divided country. Sisulu explained: 'Most Africans come into political activity because of their indignation against whites, and it is only through their education in Congress and their experience of the genuine comradeship in the struggle of such organisations as the Congress of Democrats that they rise to the broad, non-racial humanism of our Congress movement.'

Joe Matthews, who had shared Sobukwe's Africanist stand during his years at Fort Hare, described his conversion to non-racialism as 'an awakening':

'You start meeting ... people whom you'd never thought you'd meet. You meet white people who say they entirely support you ... and you feel, well, I don't think there can be such whites, but anyway, here they are. And then you see them being arrested, you see things happening to them, you see them banned ...'

In April 1959 Robert Sobukwe led an Africanist breakaway from the ANC into a new organisation named the Pan-Africanist Congress (PAC), of which he was elected president. Touring the country for the rest of the year and the early months of 1960, he called on blacks to galvanise themselves in resistance against pass laws, 'the symbol of white domination'.

Assured of anti-pass support, the PAC planned its first protest to take place on Monday 21 March 1960. During the preceding weekend thousands of leaflets were distributed in townships nationwide, instructing residents to stay away from work and hand in their passes at administration offices. Early on the Monday, PAC activists ran through township streets, knocking on doors and telling the occupants to leave their passes at home and join processions outside. Launching the campaign, Sobukwe walked solemnly in front of a team of PAC colleagues to Soweto's police headquarters in Orlando, announced themselves as the leaders of the work stayaway, and were promptly arrested for incitement.

What happened afterwards in a township called Sharpeville, thirty miles south of Johannesburg, was to prove a tragic endorsement of Sobukwe's prophecy a few days earlier, when he had said: 'The tree of freedom is watered with blood.'

Answering the PAC's call to assemble in the streets, Sharpeville residents milled around during the morning, most not knowing exactly what was expected of them. They drifted to the township superintendent's office and to the school square, finally converging on the police station. Word began to spread that a statement was to be made about pass laws by an important government official from Pretoria. Circulating for hours, the rumour became embellished to the point where some standing outside the police station expected an announcement scrapping passes forever.

By midday the crowd had swelled to 20 000, according to police estimates, though blacks denied their number ever exceeded 5 000. Reports reaching Johannesburg newspapers claimed the demonstrators were in a hostile mood, and two cars carrying journalists were stoned as they approached the police station. In Evaton, a nearby township, thousands of demonstrators were readily dispersed by jets swooping overhead, but similar tactics failed to shift the Sharpeville crowd. A squadron of planes repeatedly diving towards them brought cheers from children and had the opposite of its intended effect, bringing more people to the area to see what was happening.

As the crowd swelled, local police discovered their telephone was out of order. Calling the town of Vereeniging – three miles away – by radio, they waited for reinforcements. Five Saracen armoured cars arrived, inching their way through the demonstrators and bringing the total number of police from twelve in the early morning to two hundred by lunchtime.

The head of the Special Branch, Colonel Spengler, arrived at 1.00pm, followed soon afterwards by Lieutenant-Colonel Pienaar, a senior officer from Witwatersrand police headquarters. Spengler tried to address the demonstrators but his voice was drowned. The crowd jostled and the fence around the police station began to sway. Pienaar ordered his armed men to line up facing the demonstrators. Then Spengler became entangled in a brief scuffle at the station gates. Seeing his colleague stumbling back from the crowd, Pienaar told the police to load five rounds, not realising that some had already loaded their weapons fully.

Deciding to arrest the ringleaders, Pienaar and Spengler hauled three PAC men over the fence into the station yard. But when the gate was opened to bring in a fourth organiser, dozens of demonstrators surged through it. The police staggered back amid a shower of stones. A black constable yelled: 'Run! They are going to shoot!' Two shots rang out, followed by a deafening burst of gunfire. Stopped by the frantic shouting and arm-waving of Spengler and Pienaar, the shooting lasted twenty seconds. But by then 743 bullets had been fired.

Sixty-nine bodies lay dead on the ground outside the police station; 178 more were wounded. Over half the victims had been hit in the back while running away.

Ten minutes later a photographer took a picture of the scene, which appeared the next day in virtually every newspaper in the world. Showing a field full of corpses and two policemen armed with rifles looking on, it was the first image of South Africa to capture international attention; a repulsive impression of apartheid which was to remain in the collective conscience of the world for many years to come.

While international attention was spotlighted on South Africa in the immediate aftermath of Sharpeville, the police committed another blunder which was to earn the country yet more shame abroad. The wounded men, women and children from Sharpeville were still being rushed to Soweto's Baragwanath Hospital in a cavalcade of shrieking ambulances when a police colonel and a team of junior officers moved uninvited into the superintendent's office. Dr Isidore Frack, frantically clearing wards and operating theatres for the emergency intake, dashed into his office to find the policeman sitting at his desk. Infuriated, he demanded an explanation. The colonel replied: 'I want you to understand that the wounded coming in here are all under arrest.'

Frack protested. The colonel repeated his statement. Turning to a sergeant carrying ink-pads, he instructed him to proceed to the wards to take fingerprints from the Sharpeville victims, and then ordered another officer to station two policemen beside each bed. Frack was horrified. 'Have some pity, please!' he appealed. 'There are some people out there who are dying. Others are going to lose an arm or a leg. How can we carry on treatment in the wards if there are two policemen standing at each bed?'

Frack was at the hospital late into the night, organising operating lists, touring wards, and comforting the shocked patients. Deciding to call in a priest, he telephoned Bishop Ambrose Reeves, who swept into Baragwanath the next morning. Aware of the bishop's reputation as a champion of black rights, the colonel asked Frack to order Reeves out of the hospital. He refused. By the weekend, Frack had been dismissed from his post on orders from Pretoria. He immediately informed the international media, telling the world he seemed to have lost his job as a result of his concern for the victims of police violence. In the ensuing media outcry the government realised it had blundered. Frack was summoned to Pretoria and reinstated.

On the evening of the Sharpeville massacre police had shot six demonstrators in the Cape township of Langa. A disciplined crowd of 30 000 marched into Cape Town four days later, causing panic among whites. Liberal Party member Patrick Duncan played a critical role in negotiating a suspension of the pass laws on that occasion. Another demonstration on 30 March, again led by Philip Kgosana, regional secretary of the PAC, was met by Colonel Ignatius Terblanche. Ignoring orders from his headquarters to fire on the crowd, Terblanche negotiated with Kgosana, persuading him to disperse the demonstrators in exchange for a meeting with the minister of police. But when Kgosana returned to the city for the promised talks he was arrested, spending nine months in detention. Terblanche also paid for the attempt at conciliation. Due for promotion to the rank of brigadier the following year, he remained a colonel for the rest of his career.

The police were publicly commended by government officials for their actions at Sharpeville and Langa. Nevertheless, the days following the shootings were anxious ones for the police commissioner, Major-General Rademeyer, as he monitored the tense mood in the townships. Expecting further disturbances after Chief Luthuli joined the PAC in calling for a day of mourning for the victims, General Rademeyer negotiated with the PAC, making a surprise announcement that pass laws were to be temporarily relaxed. A sensible gesture in the circumstances, it cost Rademeyer his job. Not long afterwards, he unexpectedly announced his early retirement.

The government set up a judicial commission to inquire into the shooting at Sharpeville. Bishop Reeves instructed counsel and attorneys to cross-examine witnesses on behalf of dependants of the dead and injured.

Colonel Pienaar, attempting to explain why he had failed to order the crowd to go home, said his voice had been drowned when he tried to address them. Counsel asked: 'You could have climbed on to a Saracen in your striking uniform and held up your hand for silence – and perhaps they would have been silent. And then you could have said, "Now go home or you are going to be shot." You could have done that, couldn't you?'

Pienaar replied: 'The only explanation I can give is that time did not permit that.' Counsel insisted: 'You could have done that, couldn't you?' Pienaar finally agreed: 'I could, yes.'

The only plausible, though inadequate, explanation given for the shooting was the anxiety of some of the policemen on duty at Sharpeville (especially the younger constables who were thought to have started the firing) following an event at Cato Manor in Natal a few weeks earlier when an angry crowd of blacks had murdered nine policemen.

Overall, the testimonies damned the police, yet Colonel Pienaar showed no remorse. When asked: 'Do you think you have learnt any useful lesson from the evidence in Sharpeville?' he replied: 'Well, we may get better equipment.'

The lesson prime minister Dr Hendrik Verwoerd drew from township upheavals following Sharpeville was unequivocal: black political activity must cease forthwith.

Verwoerd had taken over as National Party prime minister two years earlier, having been native affairs minister since 1950 and the dominant influence behind the government's race policies. An able leader, he had a photographic memory, a brilliant analytical mind, and an immense capacity for hard work. Also a formidable bigot, he hated English-speaking people as fervently as he despised blacks. Editing the influential Afrikaans newspaper *Die Transvaler* in the years before the Nationalists gained power, he publicly supported Hitler, protesting against South Africa's pro-British participation in World War II. The only reference *Die Transvaler* made to the South African visit of the British monarch in 1947 was a note warning readers to avoid traffic jams in certain Johannesburg streets because 'some foreign visitors' were in town.

Verwoerd's master plan for apartheid, described by Alan Paton as 'the finest blend of cruelty and idealism ever devised by man', was to turn black tribal reserves into eight separate 'bantustans', eventually to be granted independence as nations. The first region to be thus transformed was the Transkei, where Verwoerd succeeded in buying the loyalty of Chief KD Matanzima, one of Nelson Mandela's cousins. By the time it was considered ready for semi-autonomy the Transkei was anything but independent of South Africa, which supplied most of its civil servants and most of its budget. It was virtually devoid of industry, its soil was barren and eroded, and most of its roads remained tracks designed for ox carts.

Playing a skilful diplomatic game in neighbouring territories, Verwoerd sent generous technical assistance to the British protectorates of Bechuanaland, Basutoland and Swaziland, knowing that once they gained their independence all three countries would be reliant on South Africa for economic survival. Untempered by white opposition, the once-powerful United Party having been reduced to what he called 'nothingness – both topless and bottomless', Verwoerd was supremely confident of his own instincts. 'I do not have the nagging doubt of ever wondering whether, perhaps, I am wrong,' he once declared.

Making a rapid decision after the Sharpeville shootings, Verwoerd introduced the most oppressive legislation ever seen in South Africa: a state of emergency prohibiting all gatherings except those held for religious worship. Magistrates and policemen were empowered to arrest and detain any person who was considered a risk to public safety. Such detainees could be held in prison without trial and without charges preferred against them for 180 days or until the termination of the emergency.

Verwoerd's next move was to declare the African National Congress and the Pan-Africanist Congress banned organisations. This was followed by the arrest of 1 800 activists, including two of the attorneys who had acted for Bishop Reeves in the Sharpeville inquiry.

Oliver Tambo was attending a meeting in the Cape Town offices of a trade union when there was a sharp knock at the door and a black woman burst in, warning him that police were searching a nearby office. Accompanied by a journalist sympathiser, Ronald Segal, Tambo tiptoed on to the landing and down a flight of stairs. Hearing no ominous sounds, he bolted into the street outside. On the pavement was a billboard proclaiming the news in the late edition of the evening paper: Verwoerd had outlawed the ANC.

At the nearby home of a friend, Tambo outlined a long-standing ANC directive selecting him as the leader who was to slip out of the country in the event of his party being banned in South Africa. Segal offered to drive him to the border and, wrapping a blanket around the telephone as a precaution against police bugging devices, they began to plot their getaway.

Taking his mother's car because his own was well known to the Special Branch, Segal packed sandwiches and they set out into the night on the first leg of their journey. Tambo wore a white dust-coat so as to look like Segal's driver: police suspicions would have been aroused by the sight of a black and white sitting together without evidence of a master and servant relationship between them.

After driving a thousand miles they reached Johannesburg in the early morning. Tambo went to consult ANC colleagues while Segal slept, preparing himself for a further long drive that night. Tambo returned at 11.00pm, accompanied by his wife Adelaide. Not knowing how many months or years would pass before they met again, the couple clung to each other sadly. Segal started the car and they began their journey to the Bechuanaland frontier.

Undecided whether to abandon the car and illegally enter the neighbouring territory on foot or to risk an open crossing, they eventually agreed to take the legitimate route. To their intense relief, only one sleepy black immigration official was on duty at the border post. At 3.30am they entered Bechuanaland. Pulling up outside the deserted hotel in Lobatsi, five miles from the border, they stretched their exhausted bodies and fell asleep in the car.

At dawn they went to the office of the local district commissioner and informed him that Oliver Tambo, deputy president-general of the African National Congress, intended seeking political asylum. Back at Lobatsi's hotel, feeling safe after registering his presence in the British-administered country, Tambo was astonished to find himself still controlled by racist rules: no blacks were permitted accommodation at the hotel.

After getting permission to stay in a state guest house Tambo sent a telegram to the secretary-general of the United Nations, requesting permission to appear before the Security Council. From the post office, he and Segal went to the only restaurant in town, the hotel, for lunch. Minutes after they entered the colonial building, a white man drinking at the bar rushed towards them shouting racial abuse. Segal watched in horror as the man raised his hand and hit Tambo, ordering him off the premises. The hotel manager was embarrassed and apologetic but Tambo, not wishing to pursue the matter, left immediately.

He was still waiting in Lobatsi for travel documents promised by the Indian government when he heard on the radio that Verwoerd had been shot while inspecting an agricultural show at Milner Park in Johannesburg. Eagerly listening for updates, Tambo hardly dared imagine what might become possible should the assassination attempt succeed. To his surprise, he heard that the murder bid had been made not by a black but by a white farmer. Later broadcasts brought the news that the South African prime minister's life was not in danger: he had been hit in the ear and jowl but would soon recover.

9

RISE OF THE SPEAR

'Supremacy means that you have the political power in your hands and that you can be overthrown only by a revolution,' observed transport minister Ben Schoeman during the 1958 general election, not realising that the leaders of the black population were rapidly reaching the same conclusion.

In a final bid to avert violence – the only option blacks saw available to them in the wake of Verwoerd's crushing emergency measures – the ANC, the PAC and the Liberal and Progressive parties formed an 'All-in conference representative of African people'. Its aim, to agitate for a national constitutional convention, was discussed at a meeting in Pietermaritzburg on 25 and 26 March 1961, attended by 1 400 anti-apartheid activists. The highlight of the meeting was the sudden appearance of Nelson Mandela, whose bans had expired the night before and who made his first public speech since his original banning order in 1952. A national action council, led by Mandela, was formed to organise the first phase of the convention campaign: a three-day strike which was to end on 31 May, the day South Africa declared itself a republic.

Still awaiting judgment in the treason trial, Mandela donned a variety of disguises while directing the organisation of the strike from hideouts. Verwoerd responded swiftly to the campaign, introducing unprecedented laws that enabled police to detain people without trial simply on suspicion of involvement in the impending stayaway. Thousands were arrested. On 29 May, the first day of the strike, armoured cars patrolled townships and forced many blacks to go to work. By the third day the strike had collapsed, heralding the end of an era of non-violent protest.

'Of all the observations made on the strike, none has brought forth so much heat and emotion as the stress we put on non-violence,' Mandela said afterwards ... 'The question that is being asked is this: is it politically correct to continue preaching peace and non-violence? ... Have we not closed a chapter on this question?'

Outside the country, Oliver Tambo explained the reluctant decision by many members of the ANC to opt for revolutionary methods of struggle: 'We had sought by every non-violent means at our disposal to realise the liberation of our people ... But true to the traditions of colonialist rule and the ideology of race superiority, the rulers of our country paid no heed to the demands of our people. They drowned our efforts in blood and brutality. The Sharpeville massacre of March 1960 epitomised this reality ... We knew that anger alone would not bring victory.'

Less than a month after the strike, the ANC's national executive met to consider Mandela's proposal in favour of violence. The ANC itself, led by the avowed pacifist Albert Luthuli, refused to change from its non-violent pledge but agreed that those of its members wishing to join a separate organisation pursuing violent tactics were free to do so. Mandela was clearly very much in favour of it.

Unlike the ANC, the Communist Party made a formal policy decision, fiercely contested by some of its members, to help form an armed movement. Among those most in favour of violence was attorney Joe Slovo, husband of Ruth First and long-time ANC ally, who began to plan a revolutionary campaign with Mandela. At an ANC consultative conference in Lobatsi, Botswana, in 1962, the organisation finally endorsed the armed struggle.

Operating secretly in the face of the nationwide police manhunt, Mandela's courage soon became legendary among blacks as well as among white journalists, who compared him to the Scarlet Pimpernel of the French Revolution. Often walking through busy streets dressed in mechanic's overalls, Mandela would keep his face hidden by stooping over a punctured tyre which he wheeled along the pavement. Calling a couple of colleagues to a meeting in a central city park, he arrived disguised as a priest leading a funeral procession comprised of activists. On another occasion he dressed as a tribal healer, hair entwined with beads and his face painted, to attend a meeting in a building not far from Johannesburg's police headquarters. After dark he usually wore the typical attire of night watchmen: a large grey overcoat and a cap pulled over his eyes, with the occasional addition of a pair of outsize earrings.

He sometimes arranged to see his wife and two small daughters, Zeni and Zinzi, and Winnie never knew when to expect a meeting. 'Someone would come and order me to follow him in his car,' she wrote years later. 'We would drive a kilometre or so from the house, we would then meet another car, we would jump from that one into another, and by the time I reached him I had gone through something like ten cars ... His hideouts were all over the country. The people who arranged this were, of course, mostly whites. I don't know to this day who they were.'

After conducting a number of interviews with journalists and warning them to expect dramatic developments, Mandela issued a press release headed 'Letter from Underground'. 'The precise form of the contemplated actions will be announced to you at the appropriate time,' it read. 'At the present moment it is sufficient to say that we plan to make government impossible.'

Mandela was on the run from the police for fifteen months, yet he succeeded not only in arranging recruitment and strategies for the new underground organisation but in making a trip abroad. Much to the chagrin of the South African police, he arrived unannounced at a conference of the Pan-African Freedom Movement in Addis Ababa, where he was warmly welcomed by the emperor of Ethiopia and invited to address the African leaders on their proposed campaign for international economic sanctions against South Africa. 'It would be fatal to create the illusion that external pressures make it unnecessary for us to tackle the enemy from within,' he told them. 'The centre and cornerstone of the struggle ... lies inside South Africa itself ... South Africa is now a land ruled by the gun ... A leadership commits a crime against its own people if it hesitates to sharpen its political weapons which have become less effective.'

From Addis Ababa Mandela travelled to Sudan, Tanganyika, Tunisia, Mali, Senegal, Guinea, Liberia and Uganda, receiving a crash course in military training at premier Ben Bella's army headquarters in Algeria.

In London, where he stayed with Oliver Tambo and Yusuf Dadoo, he held talks with Labour and Liberal party leaders, pausing in Parliament Square to pose for pictures next to Cromwell's statue. Tambo, having spent his first year in exile travelling around the United Kingdom and Europe, related his dismay at the level of ignorance he had found outside Britain's main centres. On one occasion, at a public meeting in Sheffield, his audience had persisted in the only question they wanted Tambo to answer: what did he intend to do about white women who had been sexually violated in the Congo?

On 16 December 1961 a series of explosions interrupted Afrikaners commemorating the defeat of the Zulu chief Dingane at the Battle of Blood River in 1838. Rushing to investigate, the police discovered home-made bombs and dynamite had damaged electrical installations and government buildings in Johannesburg, Durban and Port Elizabeth.

In fact, one MK unit had jumped the gun and started the campaign a day earlier. Because the African Resistance Movement (ARM) was already engaged in sabotage, some ANC militants were in a hurry to get going.

Next morning the birth of Umkhonto we Sizwe (MK) – 'Spear of the Nation', the armed wing of the ANC – led by its absent commander-in-chief, Nelson Mandela, was formally announced from an underground hideout. 'The time comes in the life of any nation when there remain only two choices – submit or fight. That time has now come in South Africa. We shall not submit, and we have no choice but to hit back by all means in our power, in defence of our people, our future and our freedom.'

Ironically, Chief Luthuli had just returned from Oslo after accepting the Nobel Peace Prize. While Umkhonto we Sizwe was preparing its bombs,

Luthuli had been telling the world of the ANC's success in averting racial warfare: 'How easy it would have been in South Africa for the natural feelings of resentment at white domination to have been turned into feelings of hatred and a desire for revenge against the white community ... That [this has not happened] is no accident. It is because, deliberately and advisedly, African leadership for the past fifty years, with the inspiration of the African National Congress ... has set itself steadfastly against racial vaingloriousness ... Our vision has always been that of a non-racial democratic South Africa which upholds the rights of all who live in our country.'

Describing Umkhonto we Sizwe's early days, one of its chief strategists, Joe Slovo, wrote: 'Among the lot of us we did not have a single pistol. No one we knew had ever engaged in urban sabotage with home-made explosives. Some of us had been in the army, but, for all practical purposes, our knowledge of the techniques required for this early stage of the struggle was extremely rudimentary.'

The most experienced military man among them was Jack Hodgson, a communist member of MK's Johannesburg Command and a veteran of the Abyssinia campaign in World War II. 'Jack and [his wife] Rica's flat became our Johannesburg bomb factory,' recalled Slovo. 'Sacks of permanganate of potash were bought and we spent days with mortars and pestles grinding this substance to a fine powder. After 16 December most of our houses were raided in search of clues. By a stroke of enormous luck, the Hodgson flat was not among the targets. Had the police gone there, they would have found that permanganate of potash permeated walls, curtains, carpets and every crevice.'

Long hours of experimentation in Hodgson's kitchen produced a timing device made of thin tubing from a particular type of ballpoint pen, bought in large quantities from Johannesburg shops. Hodgson used acid in a small bottle to improvise an incendiary device, its outlet covered by a specified thickness of cardboard and the bottle having to be turned upside down immediately before it was placed in a target area.

'It was with this rather primitive device that I set out to burn down the Johannesburg Drill Hall which had housed the preliminary examination of the treason trial in 1956,' wrote Slovo in an Umkhonto publication. 'I had reconnoitred it carefully on more than one occasion and had chosen the spot ... but when the moment came, I found ... myself in the presence of about fifty black cleaners ... 'I wandered through the complex in an attempt to locate another suitable spot. It was past five in the afternoon and the administrative offices seemed empty of staff. I chose an office with huge wooden cupboards, turned the bottle upside down and was about to place the carrier bag behind one of the cupboards when a clipped military voice came from behind me: "Can I do anything for you, sir?" '

Fearing the bomb might explode while he was talking to the sergeant-major, Slovo quickly said his brother had received call-up papers but needed an exemption. 'The sergeant-major, who obviously had no inkling of my real intentions, politely asked me to follow him. I did so with racing pulse, knowing that the acid in that small bottle had begun to eat away at the flimsy cardboard ... Fortunately for both of us, the officer dealing with exemptions had already left and I was politely advised to come back another day. I gave him a sweaty hand and walked briskly away. As soon as I decently could, I opened the tennis ball cylinder box which housed all the ingredients and snatched the bottle.'

Umkhonto's first Molotov cocktails, also made in Hodgson's kitchen, were tested by Mandela at a disused brickworking site near Johannesburg. 'We had arrived at the scene of operations and hidden the car when a man emerged out of a galvanised iron building and strode menacingly towards our group,' recalled a colleague accompanying Mandela that night. 'He was the watchman of the place. This spelt danger for us and it seemed that this unforeseen circumstance would prevent us from continuing with our plan. But we had calculated without the persuasive qualities of our commander-in-chief ... He signalled to us to bring the equipment forward while he took aside this man ... Soon the two of them were in deep conversation, with one arm of comrade Nelson around the shoulder of his newly acquired friend. We noticed that the watchman was nodding his head vigorously, and then he walked away from the scene. Comrade Nelson explained that he'd persuaded the man to accept our presence there.'

Volunteers for Umkhonto we Sizwe's operations were usually recruited by leaders in the organisation's high command, using carefully selected contacts to summon small gatherings of ANC activists with a proven track record in the struggle and an expressed inclination towards the new tactics of violence. In a typical recruitment approach, a few militants from the Indian Congress were told to gather in a house in Fordsburg, Johannesburg at 7.55pm. Sitting together expectantly at the appointed time, they watched an unknown man walk in, search the house and, without a word, walk out again. He reappeared seconds later with a big man in dirty Caltex overalls walking close behind him. At first, the group did not recognise Mandela: the characteristic centre-parting in his hair was gone and he'd grown a moustache. 'But when he said, "Sit down, comrades," I realised who he was and my heart leapt,' said Indres Naidoo, one of MK's first saboteurs. 'He said he'd come to talk to us about the armed struggle and told us about his trip outside the country. After about an hour, he stood up and said goodbye. We all rushed forward to grab his hands.'

Those clearly wanting to join Umkhonto were later approached again and then enrolled in an induction ceremony. Standing with the balled fists of their right hands upraised in the MK salute, the recruits swore an oath of secrecy, repeated the words 'Amandla Ngawethu' (Strength is Ours') and sang 'Mayibuye! Afrika!' They were told that they could thereafter never refuse an assignment, and were warned that refusal to carry out the orders of the high command might end in execution.

Many in MK's junior-ranking 'struggle groups' had difficulty adapting to the code of secrecy. The fact that the identities of Umkhonto's leaders were supposed to be known only to the central command corps meant that many organisers of the armed struggle continued to live openly in the community, their underground roles remaining undetected even by those who knew them well. Not long after his induction, Indres Naidoo began to feel aggrieved with an Indian Congress colleague, Mac Maharaj, who had preached militancy for years but seemed unaware of MK's existence. Discussing his suspicion of cowardice with two MK friends, Naidoo decided to confront Maharaj and, if necessary, beat him until he agreed to join Umkhonto. Luckily for Naidoo, the confrontation never took place: Mac Maharaj was in fact a member of Umkhonto's regional command.

Umkhonto's headquarters were at Lilliesleaf Farm in the outlying Johannesburg suburb of Rivonia, accessible only to the most trusted comrades through a complex system of contacts. The high command consisted of Nelson Mandela, Walter Sisulu, Govan Mbeki, Joe Slovo, and two Congress stalwarts, Andrew Mlangeni and Raymond Mhlaba. Kathy Kathrada, Arthur Goldreich and Dennis Goldberg, were involved as auxiliaries in the Johannesburg regional command, as were Jack Hodgson, Mac Maharaj and a long-standing member of the ANC, trade unionist Elias Motsoaledi. All of them were communists, though some pretended otherwise. (Mandela, then in prison, seemed to have joined the Communist Party in the 1950s and become a member of its central committee by 1961, according to internationally respected scholar Dr Stephen Ellis of Vrije University in Leiden, Netherlands, after he had scrutinised the ANC's archives when they became available.)

Adopting pseudonyms and disguises, Ahmed Kathrada made himself look more Portuguese than Indian, calling himself 'Pedro' and later dyeing his hair ginger. Walter Sisulu became known as 'Allah'; Govan Mbeki was 'Dhlamini'; Dennis Goldberg had two names, 'Williams' and 'Barnard'.

To allay suspicions among neighbours, the high command undertook a genuine though small-scale farming operation at Lilliesleaf, selling produce on the road outside its entrance, on occasions to policemen stationed nearby. The farm was a twenty-eight-acre property bought through Arthur Goldreich and equipped with a radio receiver, a transmitter and typing and duplicating machines. It had a secret entry road, known only to members of the high command and the few men acting as conduits through which orders were sent out and reports brought back. A second Umkhonto house, called Trevallyn and intended to function as an arms factory, was bought on a seven-acre stand in Krugersdorp; another in the Johannesburg suburb of Mountain View was rented as a hideout. Money for the properties came from the Communist Party.

Though security was tight at Lilliesleaf, the traffic flow into the farm was steady enough to invite suspicion. 'Rivonia ... was bound to be discovered and destroyed,' Slovo admitted years later. 'People like me were in Rivonia three times every day, moving from my chambers. Same with Bram Fischer and others.'

Apart from the problems of maintaining secrecy at MK's headquarters, security was threatened by police informers and by those among the captured combatants who succumbed to police torture, betraying their colleagues. 'When it came to how one should deal with the police in the event of arrest, the slogan was "die alone",' recalled Steve Tshwete, a young recruit from the eastern Cape. But this ideal inevitably proved too great a sacrifice for some of the arrested men, who were offered police protection and immunity from prosecution in exchange for information.

In addition, informers were recruited at an unprecedented rate during the early 1960s. The police went so far as to issue a public appeal for spies through a black newspaper, *World*. 'Any reliable informer can be assured of making a comfortable living by giving information,' it promised. 'A man with attentive ears can easily net something in the neighbourhood of R250 per month as an informer ... We treat all information confidentially and protect the identity of informants. It is essential for the men who volunteer information to deal only with the white staff.' Since the average township dweller earned between R24 and R42 for a month's work it was not surprising that they came forward in droves to assist the police.

Attempts were also made to recruit white informers. One young journalist claiming to be a communist sympathiser aroused suspicion when he persisted in taking notes at a secret meeting. Walter Sisulu, informed of his behaviour, decided to set a trap. The journalist was given a sealed letter of 'the utmost importance' and told to deliver it immediately. Tailed by Sisulu's men, he was seen giving the letter, which he had steamed open, to a police contact. On his way to the addressee he was apprehended and warned never to set foot near a political gathering again.

Some informers successfully infiltrated MK struggle groups. Indres Naidoo and two loyal comrades were caught red-handed during an act of sabotage because the fourth member of their unit was a police spy. Nevertheless, it took the police two years of collating bits and pieces of information before they knew enough of Umkhonto's underground activities to identify its leadership.

Nelson Mandela's time ran out sooner. In August 1962 he was betrayed by a suspected CIA agent. Dressed as theatre director Cecil Williams' chauffeur in a knee-length white dust coat and black peaked cap, he was stopped and arrested at a roadblock on the way from Durban to Johannesburg, where police had been tipped to expect 'someone special'.

While Mandela sat in prison awaiting trial on charges of inciting workers to strike and leaving the country without a passport, Umkhonto's sabotage campaign continued under the direction of Raymond Mhlaba. Working closely with Mhlaba was Joe Modise, who had resigned his job as a truck driver in order to devote all his time to Umkhonto operations. He was among MK's most successful saboteurs, active night after night with his unit, severing telephone and power lines. 'We had pliers and cutters with which we ripped the wires off completely,' he said of one incident. 'On our way home, we felt that not enough work had been done ... We decided to go for the overhead telephone lines. We cut off some barbed wire from a fence next to the road, tied it to a stone and threw it over the telephone lines, then tied the wire to the back of the car and pulled it ... The following day, it was reported in the newspaper that saboteurs destroyed the main communication as well as the overhead telephone lines linking the Vaal Triangle and Johannesburg.'

In Durban, Modise confronted members of the Natal regional command at a meeting held in a sugar cane field. Ronnie Kasrils remembered the encounter: ' "You're not doing enough," the burly figure of Joe Modise snapped at us ... In the Transvaal, there had been some spectacular actions with dynamite smuggled out of the mines. One of our number proffered the excuse: "If only we had dynamite like you comrades on the Reef ... Modise cut in: "We're getting small quantities from sympathetic mine workers. You've got quarries in Natal ... Get your own supplies and get on with it." '

Thus challenged, the Natal command went in search of dynamite. Finding a road construction camp using explosives outside Pinetown and discovering that the camp gate was locked with a standard padlock, they bought a replica in a hardware store and waited for a dark night. 'We skulked up to the gate and quite a band of desperadoes we must have looked,' recalled Kasrils. 'I fiddled with the padlock and engaged the key. It fitted easily enough. One turn and the lock clicked open. What a gratifying sound that was! We were in!

'We went quickly to work as though we were professional safe crackers. Sparks cut the night air as we jemmied the magazine doors open. We began emptying the contents. Box upon box of explosives piled up. We had not anticipated that there would be such a quantity and realised we should have come in a truck.'

Once they had loaded their station wagon, Mannie Isaacs drove off at high speed. Kasrils and Eric Mtshali lay on top of the boxes of dynamite as they careered along a bumpy gravel road. Next morning the Durban newspapers carried the sensational headline: 'Half a ton of dynamite stolen near Pinetown.' Driving to work, Isaacs was so startled at seeing the news posters that he drove through a red traffic light, colliding with a car ahead.

'We knew next to nothing about using dynamite, let alone storing it,' recalled Kasrils. 'I was dispatched to the Durban library to consult books on mining and explosives. To my horror, I read the safety regulations: "Never drive in excess of 15 M.P.H. when transporting dynamite" was one rule. "It is forbidden to strike a match or make sparks where dynamite is stored" was another. "Dynamite must be stored under cool, well-ventilated conditions" was yet one more chilling rule.

'What alarmed me far more than the recollection of the violent way we had cracked open the magazines and our rapid getaway was the horrific thought of our explosives sweating miserably in the small stuffy storeroom of a school … We soon installed an electric fan in the storeroom and proceeded to construct caches around the outskirts of Durban.'

On 22 October 1962 Nelson Mandela was brought to trial. Although he had not been charged with violence, the police being unaware of his involvement in Umkhonto, Mandela made open reference to the armed struggle. 'Government violence can only do one thing and that is to breed counter-violence,' he said. '... if there is no dawning of sanity on the part of the government ... the dispute between the government and my people will finish up being settled in violence and by force.'

Describing his own circumstances, Mandela told the court: 'It has not been easy for me during the past period to separate myself from my wife and children, to say goodbye to the old days when, at the end of a strenuous day at the office, I could look forward to joining my family at the dinner table; and, instead, to take up the life of a man hunted continuously by the police, living separated from those who are closest to me, in my own country, facing continuously the hazards of detection and arrest. But there comes a time, as it came in my life, when a man is denied the right to live a normal life, when he can only live the life of an outlaw because the government has so decreed to use the law to impose a state of outlawry upon him. I was driven to this situation, and I do not regret having taken the decisions that I did take. Other people will be driven in the same way in this country ...'

Met by supporters when he arrived at the court each morning and cheered by them when he climbed into a prison van after the day's proceedings, Mandela raised his clenched fist: '*Amandla!*' he shouted. '*Ngawethu!*' roared the crowd.

Ending his testimony with words that were to ring in the ears of ANC supporters for decades afterwards, he declared: 'Whatever sentence Your Worship sees fit to impose upon me for the crime for which I have been convicted before this court, may it rest assured that when my sentence has been completed I will still be moved, as men are always moved by their consciences; I will still be moved to dislike of the race discrimination against my people ... to take up again, as best I can, the struggle for the removal of these injustices until they are finally abolished once and for all.'

Sentenced to five years' hard labour he was taken to an isolation cell in Pretoria Central Prison and ordered to sew mailbags.

Umkhonto we Sizwe's campaign continued. Among its most daring acts of sabotage was the destruction of three pylons in Natal, plunging virtually the whole city of Durban into darkness. Some newspapers reporting the event the following day speculated on the possibility of a Cuban and Algerian conspiracy. One of the MK culprits, Ebrahim Ismail Ebrahim, was working for *New Age* at the time. Unaware of Ebrahim's involvement in the sabotage, his editor sent him to record the scene. 'I took my camera and went to the area in the afternoon to photograph the pylon that was blown up. I went to the local population to enquire where the pylon was so that nobody would think I knew the place.'

Umkhonto's leaders at Lilliesleaf were meanwhile preparing for a more ambitious war. 'When it became clear towards the middle of that campaign that it was necessary to prepare for a long-term build-up of a real people's army, a large part of the energy of the high command and its structures was then devoted to sending out of the country a contingent of many hundreds of experienced political cadres at all levels who were subsequently trained in the art of guerrilla warfare and military struggle,' explained Slovo.

The first group sent out of the country for military training consisted of eastern Cape stalwarts Wilton Mkwayi, Raymond Mhlaba, Joe Gqabi and Andrew Mlangeni. Subsequent units came from Natal, the western Cape and the Transvaal. Assembling in Johannesburg, they were housed in the homes of township sympathisers until driven by truck either to the Rhodesian border near Plumtree or through Bechuanaland to Kazungula. From there, they went to Lusaka in Zambia and on to Tanzania. The Rhodesian route proved too risky after a group of students, including Govan Mbeki's son Thabo, were arrested and deported to Bechuanaland.

Trainee guerrillas were drawn from several sources other than traditional ANC branches. A number of offshoots of the banned ANC had been created, including a youth club movement called Olutja and various labour bodies such as the General Workers' Union. Transporting men to military bases in Algeria and the Soviet Union was so costly that the high command, attempting to ensure that only superior calibre recruits went for training abroad, set up preliminary training camps to select the best candidates in South Africa.

One of the first such camps, gathering in dense bush near Mamre in the western Cape, began its programme the day after Christmas in 1962. Under the leadership of Dennis Goldberg, who spoke through an interpreter and was assisted by an MK organiser, Looksmart Solwandle, the agenda included lectures on politics, economics and first aid; Che Guevara's theories on guerrilla warfare; and the use of field telephones, radio and mimeograph machines. An internal combustion engine, hauled into the bush camp under cover of darkness, was demonstrated to those with little experience of motor vehicles. An arduous programme, conducted in the heat of summer, it sometimes sent trainees to sleep. 'Looksmart Solwandle had a thin branch in his hand and every time someone's eyes closed, he would flick the branch on the person's arm to wake him up,' recalled Albie Sachs, a lawyer and one of the camp's lecturers.

Adopting military discipline, Goldberg told the recruits to stand at attention and address him as 'Comrade Commandant'. However, the camp's life was cut short after three days, when the police heard about it and launched a raid. Goldberg and his communist colleague Sachs were taken away for questioning. A coloured recruit, asked by Goldberg to claim he had been the leader of the camp, resisted police pressure for a time but eventually disclaimed responsibility. Looksmart Solwandle, interrogated in the hope that he would give evidence against Umkhonto, died in police custody.

One of the aims of the internal training camps was to uncover leadership talent, and the organisers of the ill-fated Mamre exercise were well rewarded in this respect. Among those selected for training abroad was a young intellectual known as Martin, who was immediately notable for his qualities of courage and reliability, despite Sachs' view that he might prove 'a little soft for the city, having spent most of his life in educational institutions in the Transkei'. An exemplary soldier in later years, he adopted a different name, Chris Hani, and rose rapidly in the ranks of MK's exiled army.

In preparation for the return of guerrillas trained abroad, the high command at Rivonia produced a plan called Operation Mayibuye (Comeback). A veteran

member of the Communist Party and the ANC, 'Uncle' JB Marks, and Joe
Slovo were delegated to take the plan to Oliver Tambo's external mission for
discussions with African governments. On their way from Francistown in
Bechuanaland to Dar es Salaam, Slovo and Marks ran into Samora Machel,
leader of Mozambique's guerrilla army, Frelimo, who was stranded without
transport but also bound for Tanzania. About to take off in a chartered Dakota,
the Umkhonto team left a colleague behind in order to make space for Machel.

Operation Mayibuye, a nine-page document, called for extension of
sabotage and guerrilla warfare and the eventual invasion of South Africa by
foreign forces. '[The government] has presented the people with only one
choice, and that is its overthrow by force and violence,' read the preamble.
The priority was to train people in rural areas, teaching them to support the
guerrillas. A 'massive onslaught on selected targets' in Port Elizabeth, Port
Shepstone, the north-western Transvaal and the north-western Cape was to
take place in order to create 'maximum havoc and confusion'. In each of the
areas 2 000 men would be deployed, except in the Cape, where there would
be 1 000. Once the plan was under way, it was envisaged that the ranks of
insurgents would swell to around 7 000 men in each of the main regions. With
the increased success of the guerrilla operation would come the invasion by
foreign troops. The two forces would then combine to overthrow the South
African government.

Transport requirements detailed in Operation Mayibuye included a
submarine to bring trained guerrillas home from Algeria and Russia. 'We had
a rather euphoric expectation of what the African states would be prepared to
do for us,' said Slovo. 'We thought they might even provide aeroplanes to drop
our personnel. We were a little naive.'

Apart from the logistical problems of an underground movement
attempting to reach beyond the country's borders, and the ever-present
threat of treachery from various sources, one of Umkhonto's chief concerns
was a policeman with extraordinary detective skills: Sergeant Donald Card.
Stationed in East London, but regularly transferred to police posts around the
country in hot pursuit of MK's men, Card proved a formidable opponent and

was responsible for the arrests of scores of saboteurs. He never relented once he found a trail, such as the wood chips on Andrew Masondo's jersey, which he matched to a sawed-down telephone pole.

One of Umkhonto's most courageous men, Vuyisile Mini, was an energetic member of its eastern Cape regional command until Sergeant Card was dispatched to find him. After a long chase Mini was arrested and sent to trial, having spurned Card's offer of a reduced penalty if he agreed to give evidence against Wilton Mkwayi. Sentenced to death for murdering an informer, Mini secured a place of honour in Umkhonto's history when he marched to the gallows singing freedom songs, his balled fist held high.

Another of Umkhonto's early heroes was a fearless young man called Wellington Bongco who attempted to get even with Donald Card. Telling the wily sergeant he had decided to work for the police instead of MK, Bongco tried to set up a remote assignation with Card, insisting he arrived there alone. Card demanded that Bongco surrender his pass book at the police station and sign a statement accepting responsibility for anything untoward which might happen. On the appointed day Bongco and a friend lay in wait, planning to ambush Card and kill him. But the sergeant failed to arrive.

Later arrested and sentenced to die on the gallows, Wellington Bongco joined Vuyisile Mini in Umkhonto we Sizwe's roll of honour when he quietly told the judge: 'You are going to hang Bongco but you will never hang freedom.'

10

THE RIVONIA TRIAL

The police strongly suspected a direct link between clandestine ANC activities and the spate of sabotage attacks throughout South Africa. But they lacked proof, until a series of breaks turned the situation to their advantage.

After arresting a number of men attempting to cross illegally into Bechuanaland in the early months of 1963, they discovered through interrogation that the prisoners had been on their way to receive military training abroad. Armed with this knowledge they gave the hunt for Umkhonto's leadership red-alert priority. Soon afterwards, Walter Sisulu broke his R6 000 bail order and disappeared while awaiting an appeal against a six-year sentence for furthering the aims of a banned organisation. Police suspected he had left the country, until a second lead brought them closer to unmasking the mysterious men behind the bombings. Reading the contents of an envelope delivered to the South African Press Association and passed on to the police, they discovered that Sisulu was still in the country. The typed document headed 'Full Text of Inaugural Broadcast by Radio Liberation' began: 'This is the radio of the African National Congress, calling you from underground in South Africa. Our radio talks to you for the first time today, 26 June, but not for the last time ...

'The government imposed a 24-hour house arrest order on Walter Sisulu.

We could not accept this ... Our Congress decided that Walter Sisulu should leave his home ... Today he continues to lead our organisation and the people. He leads from underground. Here, from underground, is Walter Sisulu to speak to you.'

Excited policemen pored over text indicating that Sisulu's voice then came over the air. 'Sons and daughters of Africa! I speak to you from somewhere in South Africa. I have not left the country. I do not plan to leave. Many of our leaders of the African National Congress have gone underground. This is to keep the organisation in action; to preserve the leadership; to keep the freedom fight going. The struggle must never waver. We of the African National Congress will lead with new methods of struggle ... In the face of violence, many strugglers for freedom have had to meet violence with violence. How can it be otherwise in South Africa?'

The police were jubilant, and sent an urgent command countrywide: find Walter Sisulu. Offering rewards for information, they soon received a vital tip-off. While one of the Special Branch's most able detectives, Lieutenant Willem van Wyk, was leafing through files marked Top Secret, he received a phone call from a black informer. Claiming to have been to MK's headquarters in Johannesburg and to have seen Sisulu there, he offered to show Van Wyk the way.

That night, Van Wyk collected the informer, an ANC member, in an unmarked police car and followed the man's directions northwards towards Pretoria. So scared of being recognised that he wore sunglasses in the darkness, the informer pulled the brim of his hat over his eyes and wound a long scarf over the lower part of his face. They drove repeatedly along the Rivonia Road, up and down tree-lined side streets, searching in vain for landmarks that never appeared.

Insisting he had seen a sign reading IVON near the entrance to Umkhonto's headquarters, the black man said he remembered it being close to a church. But neither sign nor church appeared. After several hours, Van Wyk called off the search and drove his companion home.

Though he had virtually lost confidence in the informer, Van Wyk decided to try again the next night. And the night after. Having travelled the Rivonia Road countless times on the third occasion he looked at his watch and saw it was past midnight. About to call off the search, he was startled by a sudden cry from the huddled figure beside him: 'That's it, Lieutenant!' Van Wyk stared ahead in disbelief, realising that the church they had been looking for was in fact a gabled house. The sign IVON was actually a battered board proclaiming RIVONIA before the paint of the R and the IA wore off, leaving only IVON.

Around the next bend was the gate leading to Lilliesleaf Farm. Van Wyk's pulse was racing but he was careful not to slow down for fear of attracting attention. Noting that a caravan park lay opposite, he sped back to town, dizzy with excitement. In the early morning hours he sat alone at home, making plans for a raid.

By 2.00pm the next day, 11 July 1963, Van Wyk had conferred with his superiors, revealing how he intended to invade Umkhonto's headquarters. Discreetly interviewing a white couple living next door to Lilliesleaf, he discovered that the farm belonged to a Mr Goldreich, who had a lot of well-dressed black friends. Van Wyk looked up Goldreich's number in the telephone directory, then asked the wife of a colleague to dial it and enquire after a fictional Mrs Brown, a ploy to confirm someone was home at Lilliesleaf. Then his plan went into action.

He summoned the policemen selected for the raid: an expert on radios; two men with long experience of political documents; a dog handler with his tracker Alsatian; a skilled driver; a canny officer whose comical nature and gift of the gab had often proved useful as a foil during investigations. A total team of sixteen men crowded into Van Wyk's office for the briefing. They were all to arrive at Lilliesleaf in a dry-cleaning van, two sitting in front and the rest in the back with Van Wyk and the dog, Cheetah. They would pretend, if stopped by guards, to have lost their way while looking for Sleepy Hollow Hotel. To buy time, they would ask if they could offer their dry-cleaning service to the occupants of the house.

At three o'clock that afternoon the dry-cleaning van drove through the gate to Lilliesleaf Farm, dense bush virtually concealing the road in parts. Suddenly a black man dressed as a domestic servant stepped out of the undergrowth, blocking the driveway and informing the driver there was nobody at home. Sweating nervously in the back of the crowded vehicle, Van Wyk made a swift decision. As the driver reversed, his voice rang out from behind: 'We're closing in! Raid the place!'

The van swung round and shot forward, bouncing to a halt in front of Lilliesleaf's homestead and spilling sprinting policemen in every direction. Within a few minutes all exits from the house were blocked and detectives had blocked the doorways of the outbuildings.

Van Wyk ran to the back door of the main house and flung it open. A startled servant almost dropped the dish of ice cream he was carrying. The sweet was for Pedro Perreira, he replied to Van Wyk's barked question, pointing toward a thatched cottage nearby. Only one person besides the servant occupied the house: Dennis Goldberg, a bearded man in thick-lensed glasses, who had a fixed half-smile on his trembling lips when the police burst into the sitting room. Jumping up from his chair, he started putting on his hat and coat. A detective told Van Wyk afterwards: 'He looked like a man who knows that he has to go somewhere in a hurry but can't for the life of him remember where.'

Meanwhile the most dramatic events of the raid were under way in the cottage. A policeman sprinting towards the open entrance saw a hand reach out to pull the door shut from inside. The officer kicked the door open, revealing three startled men within: two whites and a black. As his glance flew around the room, the policeman spotted a fleeing red-haired figure outside and two others speeding towards the bush. Having escaped through a window in the cottage, the three ran into a group of detectives charging round a corner of the house. Ordered to freeze, they continued running until they spotted the snarling Alsatian straining on its leash and policemen pointing their weapons. One of the runners called out a warning to his colleagues and they all stopped and walked slowly back to their captors.

As they approached, Van Wyk realised they were disguised. Scrutinising their features, he barely recognised Kathy Kathrada beneath his mop of red hair. Kathrada, alias Pedro Perreira, grinned when Van Wyk finally identified him. Pointing theatrically to the absurdly long jacket hanging around his knees, he asked the policemen if they liked his outfit. Van Wyk turned to examine the light-skinned man standing beside Kathrada. Despite a small Hitlerian moustache and hair dyed blacker than its natural colour, he quickly recognised the man staring back at him: the slight deprecatory smile had been a feature he noticed in the file photographs at Special Branch headquarters. It was Walter Sisulu, the most wanted man in South Africa. Next to Sisulu stood the tall, dignified ANC leader from the eastern Cape, Govan Mbeki.

The three men arrested inside the cottage were architect and Communist Party member Lionel Bernstein, known as Rusty; an ANC activist from the eastern Cape, Raymond Mhlaba; and Bob Hepple, a Johannesburg lawyer. They had all been engrossed in a discussion about Operation Mayibuye, a copy of which lay on the cottage table. Seized by detectives along with many other papers, its importance only became apparent some time later when the attorney-general's office announced the plan was damning enough to convict Umkhonto's leaders on documentary evidence alone.

Arthur Goldreich, a communist and well-known artist, was arrested an hour later when he drove up to his home. Seeing what was by then obvious police activity, he tried to reverse his car but found himself staring into the barrel of a revolver. Known in Umkhonto as 'The Caretaker', he had been an army commander in the 1948 Israeli war. Though he was one of the principal planners of Operation Mayibuye, he was unable to maintain his dignity in the face of defeat. Lieutenant Van Wyk reported that unlike the other captives he displayed plain and inglorious terror.

The police rounded up the occupants of Lilliesleaf, including servants and farm labourers, then drove them to Special Branch headquarters, known as 'The Grays', for questioning. There were eighteen altogether, including most of Umkhonto's key leaders. Nelson Mandela was already in prison; Oliver Tambo was in exile; Joe Slovo was on a mission to promote Operation Mayibuye abroad, but virtually all the other members of MK's high command were now in police custody, soon to be joined in jail by most of the leaders of Umkhonto's regional command structures.

Crates of documents, six typewriters and over a hundred maps were loaded into the back of a police van, together with a radio transmitter and aerial masts. Finding a duplicating machine in one of the outbuildings, police also discovered a small tin revealing clear fingerprints: they belonged to Harold Wolpe, a lawyer and member of the Communist Party, who was immediately arrested. Other documents led the police to two further suspects: Elias Motsoaledi and Andrew Mlangeni.

Dr Percy Yutar, deputy attorney-general of the Transvaal, was appointed to conduct the state's case. Moving his team of lawyers into offices at The Grays, he joined police experts sifting through the mounds of documents confiscated in the Rivonia raid. To Yutar's delight, a vital witness came forward, volunteering his services and making the state's task a great deal easier. Named Bruno Mtolo, he was referred to as Mr X during the trial. He was among a group of Umkhonto saboteurs arrested in Natal, and he decided to betray his leaders by giving evidence against them in exchange for his own immunity from prosecution.

Drawing up a long list of potential witnesses to give evidence in the impending prosecution, which was to become known internationally as the Rivonia trial, Van Wyk travelled all over South Africa taking statements from 270 people. While going through witnesses' statements in his office one day in August, Van Wyk received a phone call which was to provide yet another lucky break for the state. The call, from Rosebank police station, reported the discovery of political papers in a house on a smallholding in Krugersdorp, which was let to a bearded man calling himself Charles Barnard. The owner of the house discovered the documents when he went to see why the rent was overdue. Including files, circulars, lists of names and addresses and a number of political reports, the papers gave Van Wyk clues leading to the discovery of a further Umkhonto hideout: a house in Terrace Road in the suburb of Mountain View, which was duly raided.

Exactly a month after the arrests at Lilliesleaf police were dismayed to learn that two of their sabotage suspects, Arthur Goldreich and Harold Wolpe, accompanied by two Indian prisoners, had bribed a nineteen-year-old prison warder and escaped from cells at Marshall Square police station. Setting up one of the biggest manhunts in South African history, the police were unable to catch Goldreich and Wolpe, who initially travelled to Swaziland dressed as priests, then flew by light aircraft to Bechuanaland.

Due to board a Dakota bound for Algeria, Goldreich and Wolpe found their plans going awry in Francistown. A mysterious explosion destroyed the plane on the eve of their scheduled departure, and public opinion in the town grew daily more hostile towards them as rumours began to spread of a massive South African police reward for their capture. Asking the Bechuanaland police for protection against bounty hunters, they were relieved to accept accommodation in a prison cell. But their bad luck continued. A second aircraft dispatched by the ANC to rescue them crashed at Mbeya in southern Tanganyika. Finally, late one night in September, they flew to Dar es Salaam in a single-engined plane.

The Rivonia trial opened on 8 December 1963 and lasted eleven months, during which the state called 173 of the people from whom statements had been taken. Nelson Mandela, already in jail, was brought to court in a prison van. He, Walter Sisulu, Govan Mbeki and their six co-accused, admitting they were guilty of sabotage and preparation for guerrilla war, denied that they had taken a decision to begin guerrilla warfare. But Operation Mayibuye was incriminating evidence against them, as was the testimony of the trainee guerrillas captured en route for military camps abroad and the detailed evidence given by Mr X, Bruno Mtolo.

Defending counsel Bram Fischer, fearing his clients would be sentenced to death, concentrated his energies on securing life imprisonment instead. Privately exasperated by the fanciful schemes outlined in Operation Mayibuye, Bram Fischer revealed his opinion of the naive war plan some months later. It was, he said, 'an entirely unrealistic brainchild of some youthful and adventurous imagination . . . If ever there was a plan which a Marxist could not approve in the then prevailing circumstances, this was such a one . . . if any part of it at all could be put into operation, it could achieve nothing but disaster.'

Dr Yutar described the trial as 'a classical case of high treason par excellence', but the accused were not facing treason allegations in terms of the common law, under which most of them had been charged seven years earlier. Common law had proved impossible for the state's case in 1956 because it required two witnesses to every overt act and proof beyond a reasonable doubt. Consequently, it was rejected by the Rivonia prosecution in favour of the Sabotage Act, which carried the death penalty and shifted much of the onus of proof from the state to the defendants.

Most of the men in the dock had come to terms with the likelihood of the death sentence, though others in the courtroom worked feverishly to avert it. Among them were Dean Rusk, the American secretary of state, and Rab Butler, Britain's foreign secretary. Both held private meetings with the South African prime minister urging him to grant clemency in the event of the death sentence being passed.

Each day when Mandela and his co-accused entered the court they turned to the packed black sector of the public gallery and raised their fists in the ANC salute. '*Amandla!*' they called, and '*Ngawethu!*' rang back around the hallowed chamber. Special Branch detectives, noting the names of those in the public gallery, photographed every one of them as they left the building at the end of each day's proceedings.

Addressing the court on behalf of all the accused, Mandela gave a speech which journalist Anthony Sampson had helped to write, saying: 'I do not deny that I planned sabotage. I did not do this in a spirit of recklessness. I planned it as a result of calm and sober assessment of the situation after many years of oppression and tyranny of my people by whites.

'We of the ANC shrank from any action which might drive the races further apart. But the facts were that fifty years of non-violence had brought the African people more repressive legislation and even fewer rights.'

Mandela told the court that strict instructions to Umkhonto's members had forbidden injury to people, and he repudiated charges that the sabotage campaign was communist inspired. Close co-operation had developed between the ANC and South African communists because they had been for many years the only whites prepared to join blacks in their struggle to attain political rights and an equal stake in society, he said.

'Above all,' Mandela went on, 'we want equal political rights because without them our disability will be permanent. I know this sounds revolutionary to whites in the country, because the majority of voters will be Africans. This makes the white man fear democracy. But this fear cannot be allowed to stand in the way of the only solution which will guarantee racial harmony and freedom for all. It is not true that the enfranchisement of all will result in racial domination. Political division based on colour is entirely artificial and when it disappears, so will the domination of one colour group by another. The ANC has spent half a century fighting against racialism. When it triumphs, it will not change that policy.'

Concluding his testimony, Mandela looked up at the bench, saying: 'During my lifetime I have dedicated myself to this struggle of the African people. I have fought against white domination, and I have fought against black domination. I have cherished the ideal of a democratic and free society in which all persons live together in harmony and with equal opportunities. It is an ideal which I hope to live for and to achieve. But if needs be, it is an ideal for which I am prepared to die.'

His speech left a stunned silence in the courtroom. 'It was so quiet, you could hear a pin drop,' Albertina Sisulu recalled. 'For perhaps thirty seconds, there was silence,' said a defence lawyer. 'One could hear people on the public benches release their breath with a deep sigh as the moment of tension passed. Some women in the gallery burst into tears. We sat like that for perhaps a minute before the tension ebbed.'

Alan Paton later spoke eloquently in mitigation but his pleas for leniency were in vain. Eight of the accused were sentenced to life imprisonment: only Lionel Bernstein was acquitted but police immediately rearrested him on a charge of breaching his banning order.

Commenting on the trial the next day, the British newspaper *The Times* wrote of 'men goaded beyond endurance ... The verdict of history will be that the ultimate guilty party is the government in power – and that already is the verdict of world opinion.'

11

ROBBEN ISLAND

Political prisoners had been incarcerated on Robben Island for centuries before the Rivonia trialists began life sentences there in June 1964. Autshumayo, an early African hero known to whites as 'Harry the Beachcomber', was banished to the rocky isle at the mouth of Table Bay in the Cape after the 1658 war between the Khoi Khoi people and the Dutch settlers. He was the only prisoner ever to escape into the wild green waters of the Atlantic Ocean – in a leaky old boat which took him safely to Saldanha Bay. A number of Xhosa chiefs were subsequently dumped on Robben Island to rot among the large populations of seals and penguins, including resistance leaders like Makana, commander of the Xhosa army in the fourth war against colonisation; Maqoma, who led the fifth rebellion in 1834; and Chief Langalibalele, condemned by a Natal court in 1873 to die there for the crime of high treason.

The island subsequently became a leper colony; then a prison. During the first half of the twentieth century, most of the people making the forty-five-minute journey from Cape Town harbour to its windy shores were common law criminals. By 1960 they had been joined by men of an entirely different character: political prisoners whose purpose was to liberate blacks from the stranglehold of white rule. It was not long before many of the black warders in the island prison took pity on their captured liberators and began to bring them illicit food, cigarettes and newspapers. Once discovered, the warders were shipped back to the mainland and replaced by an exclusively white Afrikaner prison administration.

News of the outside world was thereafter limited. Most of it came from new inmates, who were questioned interminably while pounding hammers in the limestone quarries where they laboured in blistering summer heat and the freezing winter winds blown in by the Benguela current. For a time the news source was a priest, bringing a copy of the *Sunday Times* in his briefcase each week. Criminal prisoners chosen to work as servants in warders' homes sometimes smuggled discarded newspapers into the cells. Invariably written in Afrikaans, they encouraged many political prisoners to learn the language when study facilities were offered. 'Whenever someone managed to read a paper, he'd do so knowing he'd have to relate what he'd learnt to his comrades many times over,' said Indres Naidoo, one of three Umkhonto saboteurs tagged the 'dynamite coolies' by warders when they arrived in chains, their ankles ripped and bleeding, to serve ten-year sentences. Transistor radios occasionally found their way into the cells but the penalty for being caught with a radio was severe: it could add six months to a prisoner's sentence.

ANC men imprisoned on Robben Island for sabotage during Umkhonto's first campaign had heard about the Rivonia raid and the ensuing trial on the prison grapevine. Speculating endlessly about the fate of Nelson Mandela and the men arrested with him at Lilliesleaf, they were given a dramatic version of the trial one night when the voice of a fellow prisoner began to echo from cell to cell. Imagining the court proceedings, the narrator's words rose and fell, impassioned with anguish as he described sten guns at the ready, snarling dogs straining on leashes, wives weeping pitifully. After each climax in his tale, he called out '*Amandla!*' and the prisoners chorused '*Ngawethu!*' Listening in enthralled silence, they envisaged advocate Bram Fischer pushing his way through the crowd, his black gown folded over his arm, as Nelson Mandela rose slowly to his imposing height, wearing an immaculately tailored suit and gleaming Bostonian shoes, to address the judge. The story lasted two hours, ending with the arrival of a Black Maria and a mighty roar from the crowd: '*Amandla!*' Mandela, followed by Sisulu with smiling eyes behind black-rimmed spectacles, then Govan Mbeki, came marching towards the van, fists held high. Behind them were Kathy Kathrada, Andrew Mlangeni, Raymond Mhlaba and Elias Motsoaledi.

When the true story was later told on Robben Island by the Rivonia trialists themselves, only one of the imagined details proved inaccurate: there had been no weeping from wives hearing their husbands condemned to life imprisonment. The women had made a pact: 'We agreed never to shed a tear, from the day of the sentence for the rest of our lives if necessary,' recalled June Mlangeni. Still a learner in the emotional survival game ahead, she was unaware of the constant police harassment meted out to wives, unlike Winnie Mandela and Albertina Sisulu who had already experienced it for years. 'I was not caught unawares,' Albertina said of her feelings on hearing that her husband was to go to prison for life. 'I knew what was going to happen. He used to tell me that he didn't belong to the family and that he would be sent to Robben Island. As early as only a few years after we married, he used to tell me that his time with us was going to be very short.'

The day after the Rivonia trial ended, June Mlangeni went to Pretoria Prison to see her husband. Waiting for several hours at the gate, she suddenly spotted a figure waving to her from a high window in one of the prison buildings. As she watched, the hand released a scrap of paper which came fluttering down to the ground not far from her feet. Scrawled on it was a message saying her husband had been taken to Robben Island at three o'clock that morning. Although she remained at the prison gates for most of the day, no official came to confirm the secret transfer. A box containing the clothes Andrew Mlangeni had been wearing the previous day in court was brought to her for identification but her request to see him was neither granted nor denied. The authorities simply left her standing at the gate until she could bear it no longer, finally making the long journey home to her children in Soweto. Six months later, following numerous abortive visits to the prison, she at last received a letter telling her that Andrew was being held on Robben Island and that she could apply for a permit to visit him there three months hence. 'I felt like crying many times in those early days,' she said, 'but I held the tears back because I had to remain strong for my children, for my husband and for the struggle of my people.'

A week after the Rivonia trial ended, Bram Fischer arrived on Robben Island to discuss an appeal against the life sentences. An Oxford-educated man with faultless manners and immense kindness, he did not tell the prisoners that his wife Molly had died in a car accident the day after the trial ended, for fear the news would distress them. On his return to Johannesburg he was arrested without charge, held in solitary confinement for three days, then released.

Hints of his involvement in the Communist Party and Umkhonto had emerged during the trial, alerting the police, who were determined to prove his complicity in the actions of the men he had defended and saved from the death penalty. In September 1964 he was again arrested, and joined twelve men and women charged under the Suppression of Communism Act. Applying for bail in order to argue a patents case before the Privy Council in London, he told the court: 'I am an Afrikaner. My home is in South Africa. I will not leave my country because my political beliefs conflict with those of the court.' Held in high esteem by fellow lawyers, he was granted bail of £5 000, which he borrowed from a colleague.

When he returned to South Africa to stand trial, Fischer decided to continue the struggle underground and disappeared in January the following year after repaying the friend who put up his bail. Evading a nationwide police dragnet for ten months, he was finally captured in November 1965 and taken to one of the courtrooms in which he had often appeared on the other side of the law. Guarded by forty-five armed policemen, he was charged under the sabotage and anti-communism acts and sentenced to life imprisonment. He described in court the events which led him into the Communist Party. 'Like many young Afrikaners, I grew up on a farm. Between the ages of eight and twelve, my daily companions were two young Africans of my own age ... For four years we were ... always in each other's company. We roamed the farm together, we hunted and played together, we modelled clay oxen and swam. And never can I remember that the colour of our skins affected our fun, or our quarrels or our close friendship in any way.

'Then my family moved to town and I moved back to the normal white South African mode of life where the only relationship with Africans was that of master and servant. I finished my schooling and went to university. There one of my first interests became a study of the theory of segregation ... I became an earnest believer in it ... trying to induce various authorities to provide proper (and separate) amenities for Africans ... I found myself being introduced to leading members of the African community. This, I found, required an enormous effort of will on my part. Could I really, as a white adult, touch the hand of a black man in friendship?

'That night I spent many hours in thought, trying to account for my strange revulsion ... What became abundantly clear was that it was I and not the black man who had changed ... I came to understand that colour prejudice was a wholly irrational phenomenon and that true human friendship could extend across the colour bar once the initial prejudice was overcome. And that I think was lesson number one on my way to the Communist Party, which has always refused to accept any colour bar and has always stood firm in the belief, itself two thousand years old, of the eventual brotherhood of all men ...'

No government institution in South Africa, apart from the police, served to deepen acute feelings of wrong in the hearts of blacks as did the cruel prison service. Warders, as well as many of their superiors, tended to be profoundly prejudiced; a harsh and vindictive breed of men in whose minds many lines of exclusion and denial had been drawn since the earliest years of childhood. Their impoverished spirits made it impossible for them to see that many of the political prisoners condemned to a stagnant, menial existence behind bars were decent, even noble, men.

The worst of the Robben Island bullies were three brothers named Kleynhans, who had been raised in an orphanage and knew nothing about kindness. Sometimes, under Piet Kleynhans' evil supervision, fifty prisoners would be required to push a massive seven-foot-high grass roller weighing several tons round and round the prison grounds. Like his brothers, Piet Kleynhans was tall and powerfully built, his eyes ice-blue and his hair closely cropped in a crew cut. Standing on top of the crossbar of the roller's axle, bellowing obscenities, he would crack a long leather whip, cutting into the flesh on the prisoners' backs and leaving broad gashes on the faces of those who dared look up at him.

Johnson Malambo, a PAC prisoner often among the men ordered to push the roller, angrily confronted Kleynhans one day when he could endure the warder's torture no longer. Kleynhans was outraged. Calling a group of common law criminals to dig a hole nearby, he ordered Malambo into it, telling the criminals to pile soil around him until only his shaven head was exposed.

It was a hot day and the sun beat down on Malambo's bare head, leaving the soil surrounding it stained with perspiration. The interminable roller circuits continued until, hours later, Kleynhans jumped off the crossbar, walking slowly towards Malambo's head. 'Kaffir, do you want water?' he asked in Afrikaans. Malambo did not respond. 'No, I won't give you water, I'll give you whisky of the best kind,' said the warder. Unzipping his trousers, he took out his penis and urinated into Malambo's face while other warders yelled to each other to come closer and enjoy the fun.

The three cruel Kleynhans brothers were later joined by their youngest sibling, who was so contemptible that even some of the warders turned against him. Political prisoners lodged numerous complaints but they were ignored for years, despite word of the notorious brothers having long since reached indignant campaigners in the outside world. Far from feeling ashamed by the accusations made against him, Piet Kleynhans seemed to revel in the attention, boasting to prisoners in the political blocks: 'You think you're important? I'm more important than you; my name is even mentioned at the United Nations.'

It was only after the first of a series of hunger strikes that prison authorities, hitherto deaf to the sufferings of inmates, began to hear complaints and respond to them.

Waiting one evening for their food, prisoners watched a member of the cookhouse squad dishing up on to long rows of tin plates. One row was for Indians and coloureds, who were supposed to get half a loaf of bread, eight ounces of vegetables and four ounces of meat, while the longer rows for blacks were each meant to contain a dollop of maize porridge and two ounces of meat. As often happened, the food ran out, leaving about a hundred plates empty, whereupon a warder told the servers to reduce the rations on the blacks' plates. Muttered protests rose into a swell of anger. Two inmates stepped forward to speak to the warder in charge, who rudely rebuked them, saying they could take the food or leave it. The prisoners glanced at each other, whispers of solidarity spreading through their ranks. When signalled to take up their plates, they filed slowly past the mounds of food. Nobody took it.

The strike lasted six days, by which time a few prisoners had collapsed. Others were showing signs of imminent breakdown, their speech becoming incoherent and their sight blurring. Finally the chief warder capitulated, telling prisoners to nominate six representatives to discuss their grievances with the administrators.

Nelson Mandela and the other Rivonia prisoners, confined to an isolation block especially for them and known as Koeloekoetz, had joined the hunger strike as soon as word of it reached them. When a warder brought the news that the strike was off, Mandela cautioned his colleagues not to accept the claim: they would continue to reject their food until reliably informed that the strike had ended, he said.

Conditions slowly began to improve. In 1965 Piet Kleynhans and his brothers were transferred to other prisons. By 1967 inmates were sometimes invited to watch outdoor movies. Sitting under the night sky, they marvelled at the moon and stars, which many had not seen for years. Some warders began to tolerate the prisoners' home-made cigarettes, known as zols and made from pages torn out of the Gideon Bible which was provided in each prisoner's cell. Matches, among the most cherished possessions on the island, were each split lengthwise into four, giving the briefest of flames.

Although many prisoners were deprived of their Saturday night cinema outings as punishment for misdemeanours, only one man on the island was barred from the treat altogether: PAC leader Robert Sobukwe. Living alone in a stone bungalow surrounded by high barbed wire, he did not have to toil in the quarries like Nelson Mandela, who daily pounded rocks, his hands blistered, his eyes stinging and clogged with the fine white limestone dust. Sobukwe's solitary life was interrupted only by occasional visits from his wife and relatives. Prime Minister Johannes Vorster, who had succeeded Verwoerd, feared Sobukwe's 'magnetic personality'. He introduced the 'Sobukwe clause' in parliament in 1960, which gave the justice minister power to redetain prisoners who had completed their sentences but who, in the minister's opinion, might constitute a security risk if released. Pressed by opposition MPs to say how long he was prepared to detain people without trial, Vorster declared he would keep them in custody for 'this side of eternity'. Though sentenced to a three-year term for incitement, Sobukwe was detained without trial on Robben Island for a further six years.

The Saturday night movie sessions sometimes gave ANC men the chance to consult with their leaders from Koeloekoetz. Discussing the formation of committees to press for various reforms in the prison, they also comforted and counselled prisoners who had received demoralising news from home, such as the dreaded announcement of divorce proceedings from their wives' attorneys. Sisulu was always ready to listen to the heartache of a prisoner struggling to come to terms with a death in the family, the illness of a relative or the ravages inflicted by poverty on a wife and children deprived of a breadwinner. Mandela continued to practise law on Robben Island, giving legal advice to prisoners who needed it. Returning to his cell after listening to prisoners' problems, he drafted legal memos on scraps of paper which were slipped from hand to hand until they reached the men who needed the advice in order to brief attorneys in Johannesburg or Cape Town.

Like Sisulu, Mandela helped fellow prisoners bear their emotional crises. 'In his unobtrusive way, he finds out if anybody has problems and he tries to spend time with them if they do,' wrote Mac Maharaj, who spent twelve years on the island. 'When something is worrying him, he does not come out with it easily. Both his eldest son and his mother died while I was in prison with him;

both deaths were severe blows to him. He was very close to his son. When he returned from hearing the news, he just stayed in his cell and kept out of the way. However, Walter Sisulu noticed that he was quiet and went to his cell and asked him what was wrong. Nelson then confided in him, and Walter stayed with him a long time, talking to him.'

Next day Nelson was back doing what he most enjoyed: tending the small garden of vegetables and flowers which gave him solace in the long, lonely years of imprisonment. Elias Motsoaledi also found peace in gardening and the creative processes of nature, while Wilton Mkwayi made the island's pigeons his hobby and pets. Gathering scraps from the dining room, he threw them from his cell window into the courtyard below. The pigeons knew his routine, and would be flapping and cooing in their hundreds outside Mkwayi's window by the time he opened it and scattered the crumbs. Self-educated Sisulu never tired of playing Scrabble and looking up new words in his well-thumbed dictionary.

Kathrada's passion was collecting a library in his section of the prison. An honours history student for several years, he was fond of describing the joys of learning to his colleagues, urging them to enrol for university courses and use their years in prison for self-improvement. Mandela also encouraged learning whenever he saw an intelligent mind growing stagnant, so much so that Robben Island became known as the University of Mandela.

Study was the privilege most cherished by the majority of political prisoners. Govan Mbeki accumulated three degrees during his years on the island, adding BA, BEcon and BA Hons to his name. Mandela began by studying towards a London law degree until postgraduate studies were suddenly banned, when he read economics, history and Afrikaans instead. The worst punishment Mandela ever suffered, the result of one of his many prison protests, was withdrawal of his study facilities for four years.

Getting academic books was always a problem, and prisoners often suspected that the texts they ordered from libraries and suppliers were deliberately withheld until it was too late to read them for exams. The choice of titles in Kathrada's humble library was severely curtailed after historical volumes like President Eisenhower's *Mandate For Change* were deemed too popular with political prisoners and removed. 'They gave our section thirty new books, twenty-five of which were by Daphne du Maurier,' recalled Maharaj.

Although the quality of prison meals improved in the months after the hunger strike, repeated pleas for fruit were ignored. In the ten years Indres Naidoo spent on the island, he received an orange on two consecutive days but never saw fruit again. Ismail Ayob, Mandela's lawyer, was shocked when given permission to share with Nelson a fruit and sandwich lunch he had brought to the prison. Taking a banana from the picnic box, Ayob noticed a look of astonishment on Nelson's face. 'That's the first banana I've seen in twenty years,' he explained.

Deprivation of food was among the most resented forms of punishment. If prisoners were caught talking after eight o'clock at night, warders often confined them to their cells without meals the following day. If a prisoner was thought not to have worked hard enough breaking stones in the quarry, a warder yelled: '*Jy het nie gewerk nie. Sondag sal jy nie eet nie*', meaning 'You didn't work. On Sunday you won't eat.' Colleagues sometimes managed to smuggle food into the locked cells: Mac Maharaj used to run past, fling a plate to a punished man, then snatch it back as he jogged by again to return it to the kitchen a few minutes later.

As the years passed, warders took note of the successes achieved by hunger strikes. Sometimes they complained to political prisoners about their own unsatisfactory conditions in the prison service, and they were advised by ANC men to act in unison, demanding better food for themselves. Eventually the warders agreed and boycotted their canteen until their demands were met.

In 1967 the prisoners were overjoyed to hear that they were to be given new privileges: soccer, cricket and tennis. Singing was permitted in controlled conditions, leading to the formation of a large choir calling itself The Islanders and including in its repertoire a version of the lilting Irish ballad, 'Galway Bay': 'Have you ever been across the sea to Robben Island? Where the chain gangs break the rocks all through the day ...' An unauthorised band was formed, comprising a tea chest with a stick and a piece of fishing gut for a bass, plastic bags stretched across oil tins for drums, and dried seaweed of varying shapes for wind instruments.

The sports ground provided many hours of enthusiastic play, made especially rewarding by the knowledge that Mandela and other ANC leaders were watching from behind the bars of high windows in Koeloekoetz. But that thrill did not last. One day when soccer players looked for the shadows of their leaders' heads watching the game, they saw blackened squares where the windows had been: thick paint covered the glass.

From time to time, the living conditions of political prisoners improved dramatically, usually signalling a visit from a human rights organisation such as the International Red Cross. Shortly before a United Nations official visited the island on one occasion, prisoners watched in astonishment as all but the most perilously ill patients were summarily discharged from the clinic. Carting in new beds, blankets, sheets and pillows to replace the old mats previously provided for the sick, warders escorted several favoured common law prisoners known as 'trusties' into the clinic. Given freshly starched pyjamas and told to feign sleep when the visitors arrived, they jumped happily into bed for an afternoon of leisure.

Political prisoners were always glad to see the 'trusties' engrossed in activities that took them away from the cells and their customary spying role in the prison. It was a relief to be free, for a few hours at least, from the despised cry of a 'trusty' discovering contraband: 'Chief, chief, look what the kaffir's got.'

A humiliating ritual known as 'tausa', devised by warders to detect contraband, had to be performed each day by prisoners returning to their cells from the quarries. Waiting in line without their clothing, they were required to run naked towards the warders then leap up in the air like ballerinas, twisting their bodies around while clapping their hands above their heads and spreading their legs wide apart, finally landing in a crouched position with their rectums exposed. Far from preventing the flow of contraband into the cells, 'tausa' often provided opportunities for it. A few of the convicts performed the bizarre dance with such entertaining agility and drama, leaping skyward and landing virtually on top of the warders with shouts of 'My king!', that the warders were amused and distracted long enough to allow bundles of tobacco and food to be smuggled past them.

The ANC campaigned continuously for the right to live in prison with the dignity befitting the status of political prisoners rather than as common criminals. Exhorted by their leaders in Koeloekoetz to use civil language no matter how severely they were taunted by warders, ANC men were commended for their good conduct by one of the chief warders in a report to his superiors. An early prison rule, decreeing that inmates could speak only for themselves and never on behalf of other prisoners, was assiduously ignored by the ANC men: whenever a culprit was asked to identify himself, the entire ANC group stepped forward. Their insistence on calling prison staff 'sir' rather than 'baas' enraged warders, but they persisted despite the punches and whippings it provoked. Mandela called junior warders 'boy', which they resented bitterly, but they dared not retaliate once they realised how cautiously the ANC leader was treated by their senior officers. As time passed, Mandela's imperious attitude towards prison personnel and their observation of his dignified conduct brought grudging respect, encouraging a few warders to address him as Mr Mandela instead of by his prison number, 466/64.

Men like Mac Maharaj, Michael Dingake, Stanley Mogoba and Billy Nair, who served their sentences and were released, emerged from Robben Island to speak with pride of the solidarity and sense of community that the ANC retained among its prisoners there. When someone dear to the struggle died, like Albert Luthuli or Bram Fischer's son Paul, they held memorial services. Punctuated by cries of '*Amandla!*' and the answering call '*Ngawethu!*', they ended with the ANC anthem *Nkosi Sikelel' iAfrika* reverberating around the prison.

Many months after Luthuli was crushed to death by a train in 1967, prisoners heard the poem a young white girl, Jennifer Davis, had written in his honour:

Bounded

You gave me knowledge

Of freedom

Silenced

You taught me how

To speak

Some of them felt the verse so well reflected their feelings about Robben Island and particularly about Nelson Mandela's incarceration there that they learnt it by heart.

At times the ANC openly conducted its political business in prison. In the late 1970s, when Mandela's cousin KD Matanzima asked permission to visit the island, Mandela put it to the vote, obtaining clearance from the authorities to hold meetings in the two sections containing ANC men. A traitor in the eyes of the organisation since he accepted Pretoria's appointment as Chief Minister of the Transkei in 1976, Matanzima was told not to come. His rumoured offer to stand down in favour of Mandela being released to become leader of the Transkei was immediately rejected. The offer was never officially made but Ismail Ayob issued a statement on Mandela's behalf saying, 'He will not stay in a homeland under any circumstances. If he is banished there, he would return to Johannesburg immediately.'

Nothing mattered more to the prisoners than keeping in touch with their families. Nelson Mandela worried constantly about his wife Winnie, whose courage in the face of police harassment was becoming legendary.

Each prisoner was permitted only two letters a year, until post-strike reforms in the late 1960s, when two letters could be written and received per month. Whenever an ANC man received a letter from home, an excited sense of expectancy spread through dozens of neighbouring cells. For the first day after its arrival the recipient would be left alone in his cell to enjoy it, savouring every word and dreaming of the remote family images it conjured. But by the next morning the letter was considered public property. Circulating slowly from one prisoner to the next, its contents were discussed down to the last trivial detail for weeks. Some never received letters of their own, usually because their relatives were illiterate, so their only source of family news – apart from what was brought by two visitors a year, subsequently increased to two a month – came from other men's letters. Photographs, even more treasured, were also shared out. Many walls displayed photos of wives or of children who had never met the occupants of the cells in which their portraits hung.

Nobody ever threw a letter or photograph away: it was unthinkable. Then in 1974 the authorities suddenly ordered all prisoners to burn their letters, decreeing that only 'first-degree' relatives would henceforth be allowed to visit prisoners. Visiting requests from in-laws, cousins, aunts and uncles were rejected – a painful blow to Sisulu who was very fond of his son's wife, and to prisoners from the Transvaal whose second- or third-degree relatives in the Cape could more easily make the journey to the island than wives and children living in faraway Johannesburg. Discussing the matter, the ANC decided to fight it. When asked to submit a list of the names of their first-degree relatives they refused, and the ruling was eventually scrapped.

Only family news was permitted in letters, and prison censors scratched out additional information. However, political prisoners continued to receive word of the struggle from newcomers to the island. In 1971 they heard of the arrest of one of Umkhonto's most courageous guerrilla fighters, James April. He was betrayed by a friend to whom he showed an East German watch containing a microphone. Rumoured to have been carrying a Chekhov play when the police caught him, he was said to have had another book, *Pennygreen Street*, which looked like any other novel but contained his instructions from a contact in London. Every page ending in the figure eight had been treated with chemicals, making the contact's handwriting invisible.

Details about the heroism or arrests of ANC men were discussed for hours in the cells at night when warders were out of earshot. On one occasion, a new inmate brought news of a captured guerrilla who had taken a book from his backpack and read a quote from Leo Tolstoy to his police captors: 'I sit on a man's back choking him and making him carry me and yet I assure myself and others that I am sorry for him and wish to lighten his load by all possible means except by getting off his back.' The prisoners loved to hear such tales of men determined to uphold the struggle: they gave light to eyes that had witnessed too many bleak and inhuman deeds.

When justice minister Jimmy Kruger visited Robben Island in 1973 and again in 1978 to hold talks with Mandela, the ANC leader was shocked to discover how ignorant Kruger was about the ANC and the history of the struggle. Kruger insisted that Umkhonto had chosen a violent course without properly investigating non-violent alternatives. 'I think you'd better go back to the prime minister's files and see the letters written by the ANC,' Mandela told him.

'He could not argue on the Freedom Charter of the ANC; he had not read it,' wrote Michael Dingake, who met Kruger during the fifteen years he spent on the island. 'This, of course, did not stop him from condemning it as a communist document.'

Sometimes, when the political mood of South Africa's black population became restive, ANC prisoners experienced a hardening attitude among prison officers. In the winter of 1976 they were accused by the warders of idleness while collecting the seaweed they had been ordered to haul from the icy shores of the Atlantic. 'It was a bitterly cold day and we came back filthy from the seaweed, which dirties your body and clothes, so we rushed into the shower and switched the taps on,' recalls Mac Maharaj. 'They were cold; there was no hot water. We were then taken out to work on days when the weather made it impossible to work because it was too cold ... We tried to negotiate the matter by going to the authorities. They refused to come and we reached a critical point.'

As it turned out, a critical point had been reached in the world outside Robben Island too: the Soweto students' uprising of June 1976 plunged South Africa into chaos and created the conditions for mass recruitment of disillusioned young blacks bound for guerrilla training camps in Angola and Tanzania.

On her visit to Robben Island at the end of 1976, June Mlangeni had to find a way to tell Andrew that their sons Aubrey and William had abandoned their schooling in Soweto in order to join the ANC's fighting force. 'The boys have got lost,' she told him, speaking into the microphone that carried her cryptic words past the listening warders and across the thick glass barrier separating her from her husband. Mlangeni nodded without comment. He knew what the message meant.

12

THE STUDENTS' UPRISING

The first child killed by a police bullet in Soweto on 16 June 1976 was a thirteen-year-old boy named Hector Petersen, hit by a shot fired at him from behind. A couple of his teenage school friends picked him up from the blood-spattered ground where he fell and ran with him out of the huge crowd of children who had gathered to protest against the government's insistence on Afrikaans as a language of instruction in black schools. Bundling his mortally wounded body into a journalist's car, they sped to the nearest clinic, but the journey was in vain. Hector was already dead.

Near the grounds of Orlando West Junior Secondary School, where Hector had been one of thousands of children hoping to convince the authorities of their hatred of Afrikaans, chaos had broken out after the police fired their first shots. Prior to the shooting, the crowd had been excited and good-humoured, some taunting the police with the clenched-fist black power salute but most waiting expectantly. 'We thought they were going to disperse us with loudhailers or a loudspeaker, or maybe talk to us,' said one student.

Instead, the police threw two teargas canisters into the massive gathering, only one of which exploded, making little impression. Although they later claimed they had then ordered the crowd to disperse, no such call was heard by those present at the scene, including a number of journalists. No warning shots were fired before the officers opened up, shooting directly at the students. A police colonel later told foreign reporters: 'We fired into them. It's no use firing over their heads.'

Enraged by the use of deadly force in an essentially peaceful situation, the students chanted freedom slogans, hoisting their banners higher as they surged towards the police: 'We Are Not Boers!', 'Down With Afrikaans', 'Bantu Education – To Hell With It!' Some students carrying dead and wounded colleagues were scared and crying for help, but others were clearly ready for battle.

Bricks, stones and bottles began to fly through the air. More shots rang out and more students fell. Despite the bullets, the angry crowd kept advancing. There were more shots. Wounded students collapsed among their classmates, hysterical screams piercing the roar of indignation and stampeding feet, dust rising everywhere. But the students would not give up, and continued to hurl abuse and missiles at the police. A watching journalist wrote: 'What frightened me more than anything was the attitude of the children. Many seemed oblivious to the danger. They continued running towards the police, dodging and ducking.' The police, numbering around fifty, realised they were about to be overrun and hurriedly retreated across the Klipspruit River. There they blocked the road with their vehicles, calling for urgent reinforcements. Extra men arrived; helicopters dropped rifles and ammunition. By midday, several hundred heavily armed officers were assembled at Orlando police station, watching the sky over Soweto fill with dark clouds of smoke from numerous fires burning all over the township.

Determined to avenge their dead colleagues and strike a blow in the face of white domination, the students were busy setting buildings and cars on fire. A reporter surveying the scene from a helicopter said he felt like a 'war correspondent flying over a city after a bomb attack'. Vehicles belonging to the West Rand Administration Board (WRAB), the official body charged with managing Soweto, were overturned and set alight. WRAB offices throughout the township were burnt to the ground. All government property, the symbols of apartheid, became targets, including post offices, schools, magistrates' courts, and houses inhabited by black policemen.

Convoys of police vehicles roamed the streets around the students' main stronghold in Orlando West, firing periodically into alleys and doorways from which bricks and bottles flew. A white sociologist named Edelstein was dragged from his car and killed by an incensed mob of students; the black municipal policeman accompanying him was beaten unconscious and left to die in the blazing vehicle. At 1.30 in the afternoon two army helicopters flew overhead, dropping teargas into the crowds. Two police riot squads arrived in camouflage uniform, armed with automatic rifles and machine guns. A large force moved through the township to recover the bodies of the sociologist and the black official. Another convoy of police vehicles slowly made its way on to the hills overlooking the Orlando area.

As the afternoon wore on and the smoke grew thicker, police swept the township. Burnt-out cars, trucks and buses began blocking the roads, hindering their patrols. According to eyewitnesses, it was then that they started to fire indiscriminately.

'I tried to help a girl who was nearly shot,' one sixteen-year-old youth told the authors of a book about the uprising, *Whirlwind Before the Storm*. 'A white cop was pointing a pistol at her and I ran to push him down, but two shots hit me in the leg. It happened at about 4.30pm. I arrived at the hospital about 5.45pm. There were a lot of people shot. The injured were being guarded by police guns pointed at us in the passage. The serious cases had to be treated first. I got painkillers.'

As evening fell, workers arrived home from factories and offices in Johannesburg, many of them joining the students. Arson attacks escalated, and fires illuminated the evening sky over Soweto. Rioters ran through the streets, leaving paraffin-splashed buildings and vehicles blazing behind them. Army helicopters, guiding police operations during daylight, were grounded as night enveloped the township. Convoys of police prowled through unlit streets, firing blindly at sounds in the dark.

At 9.30pm fourteen personnel carriers, known as 'hippos', drove into the township. The army was placed on alert and a military detachment arrived to guard the Orlando power station. Heavily armed police stood watch over the railway system.

A photograph of Hector Petersen's limp, bloodied body in the arms of distraught students took the news of the uprising into millions of homes around the world. Winnie Mandela added to numerous accusations being hurled at white South Africa. 'The language issue is merely a spark that lit the resentment that is building up among black people,' she warned.

By dawn the following day 1 500 police armed with sten guns and automatic rifles stood ready to move into Soweto. First reports indicated the disturbances had abated, but by 8.15am it became clear that nothing had changed. Fighting raged; administration buildings blazed throughout the township.

Many of the students' displayed extraordinary courage and bravado. 'We tried to fight the hippos,' said one, 'but we had to retreat.' Police reinforcements rumbling in throughout the day had sealed exits from Soweto by evening. Asked by a newsman if the situation was deteriorating, the commander of the forces in the township replied: 'Can it get worse?'

By the third day Soweto's streets swarmed with police. The large crowds present on 16 and 17 June had disappeared, leaving small groups persisting in arson and attempts to damage police vehicles. Helicopters carried prosecutors and magistrates into heavily guarded courtrooms to hear evidence against arrested students.

However, township life was a long way from returning to normal. Students in Alexandra, meeting during the previous two days to plan a campaign of solidarity with the Soweto uprising, began to mount pickets at hostels and bus terminals for a mass stay-at-home on 18 June. Crowds marched through the streets carrying placards: 'Why kill kids for Afrikaans?' they demanded.

The police responded swiftly. After ordering the crowds to disperse, officers leading a contingent of 200 men began to shoot. Four people were killed and six wounded. Reacting exactly as their colleagues had done two days earlier in Soweto, the students charged forward, pelting the police with bottles and stones and forcing them to withdraw. Then they set Alexandra alight. By nine o'clock that morning 'everything was going', according to a student's description of the fire and mayhem.

Within days, the disturbances were widespread. 'Townships blaze all over the Reef' announced one newspaper headline. Reports of violence and arson came from every corner of the country: the eastern Transvaal, the Orange Free State, the northern Cape and Cape Town itself. During July, they spread through the Vaal Triangle and the eastern Cape. By August, two months after the uprising began in Soweto, eighty black townships had joined the furious revolt. By October, the number had doubled.

At least 150 lives were lost during the first week of the Soweto uprising, most of them black schoolchildren and most of them shot by police. By October the following year a total of 700 had died in disturbances arising out of the language issue and other apartheid grievances. Over ninety per cent of the dead were less than twenty-three years old.

However, South Africa's black youth had scored significant political victories in return for the blood of their fallen colleagues. Following repeated boycotts of classes throughout the country, 500 secondary school teachers in Soweto resigned their posts, signalling not only the collapse of high school education in the township but the unprecedented power of the students. A campaign organised by the students against proposed rent increases in Soweto was so successful that it led to the collapse of the government-appointed civic administration and the establishment in its place of the most democratic local authority ever seen in the township, a body known as the Committee of Ten.

Another result of the rebellion was the achievement of political solidarity across the generation gap previously dividing conservative older blacks and their militant children. Part of the impetus for the revolt had come from the students' rejection of their parents' authority. Many held their parents responsible for the continuing iniquities of apartheid, declaring that virtually no protests had arisen from the older generation since the Nationalists had introduced a state of emergency in 1960. 'It is our parents who have let things go on far too long without doing anything. They have failed,' a Soweto youth told a newspaper reporter in the early months of 1976.

Claiming that their parents had been seduced into political passivity in the numerous beerhalls provided by township municipalities, students had singled out the drinking establishments as arson targets: sixty-seven of them had been burnt down by the end of June alone. Explaining his hatred of beerhalls to a sociologist, one student said: 'Every evening all beerhalls are packed to capacity – not to make mention of the multitudes who spend most of Saturday and Sunday at the beerhalls ... Some intoxicated people get themselves hurt or make a disgrace of themselves, lying hopeless on the ground, sometimes badly hurt, talking endless jargon, and perhaps retching or even vomiting. Indeed this makes every decent African feel ashamed and gives the African's enemies grounds for maintaining that the African is a very wild and uncultured people.'

On 4 August 1976 around 10 000 adults, eager to atone for fifteen years of submissiveness, supported 12 000 students in the country's first political strike since Nelson Mandela's work stayaway in 1961. Marching from various points in Soweto towards the centre of Johannesburg, they planned to converge on John Vorster Square police station and demand the release of students detained without trial. But they were blocked by a police cordon near New Canada station. Teargas canisters flew into their midst and a policeman suddenly opened fire. Screaming demonstrators began to stampede, some running away, others chasing the police. Three people were killed and thirteen injured.

Dozens were arrested, joining the detained students whose releases they had been trying to secure. They were held under the Terrorism Act or, in some cases, under a new law replacing the Suppression of Communism Act (ironically gazetted in its final form on 16 June, the day the uprising began). The police were empowered to keep them in detention until satisfied they had answered all questions put to them. Prohibiting detainees access to persons other than officers of the state, the laws forbade the release of any information about the people detained under them: 2 430 students by September 1977. Black teenagers simply disappeared. Conducting agonising searches of hospitals and mortuaries, parents would discover weeks or often months later that their children were being held in police cells.

The shootings of 4 August provoked further riots in Soweto. A student meeting at Morris Isaacson School, which attracted a crowd of 3 000, decided to march to John Vorster Square. Numbering 5 000 by the time they were stopped by police, the marchers were again attacked. After failing to disperse them with teargas and batons, the police opened fire. Student leaders immediately called for reprisals: 'Don't mourn – mobilise' they told parents of the dead children.

By mid-August it became obvious that students were leading not only the ongoing revolt but the black community as a whole. 'Young blacks clearly are not as afraid of the police as their parents are,' wrote one journalist. 'This is a significant factor in the new situation. They have taken the leadership of the township almost entirely into their own hands, sometimes against opposition from older Africans, but on other occasions apparently with their support.' A member of the ANC's underground movement, which was slowly regrouping after the long political silence of the 1960s, explained: 'What really got the parents into action was the brutal police killings. Though the police had always been ruthless with peaceful demonstrators, nobody expected they would immediately and cold-bloodedly murder young children.'

The man whose influence dominated events leading up to 16 June 1976 was Stephen Bantu Biko. A dynamic young medical student of outstanding political acumen, he was elected the first president of the South African Students' Organisation (SASO), an exclusively black group formed in 1968 when black students rejected the predominantly white leadership of the National Union of South African Students (NUSAS).

Born a few months before the Nationalist government came to power in 1948, Biko had lived all his life 'in the framework of institutionalised separate development. My friendships, my love, my education, my thinking and every other facet of my life have been carved and shaped within the context of separate development.' So conscious was Biko of the pervasive influence apartheid had exerted on the spirit of his own generation, that he gave up his hopes of a medical career in order to devote himself to SASO's belief 'that the emancipation of the black people in this country depends entirely on the role black people themselves are prepared to play'. Echoing the self-reliance sentiments expressed by Anton Lembede nearly thirty years earlier, he declared: 'Blacks are tired of standing at the touchlines to witness a game that they should be playing ... They want to do things for themselves and all by themselves.'

With SASO colleagues like Barney Pityana, Harry Nengwekhulu, Petrus Machaka, Aubrey Mokoape and Strini Moodley, Biko fashioned a philosophy, later known as black consciousness, from the premise that oppression was essentially a psychological problem. In his opinion, blacks had to shake off the inferiority complex bequeathed to them by generations of white masters demanding subservience. Though an essentially African movement, much of black consciousness's impetus hailed from an international backdrop of emergent youth power: the anti-Vietnam war campaign was raging in the United States, where civil rights campaigns had created black power groups, and students in France had nearly toppled de Gaulle's government a few years earlier.

Achieving a new mood of militant pride in South Africa required that blacks be disabused of their historical dependence on white liberals, Biko believed. Writing in SASO's *Newsletter* of August 1970, he explained his attitude towards 'that curious bunch of nonconformists ... that bunch of do-gooders that goes under all sorts of names – liberals, leftists, etc.

'These are the people who argue that they are not responsible for white racism ... These are the people who claim that they too feel the oppression just as acutely as the blacks and therefore should be jointly involved in the black man's struggle ... In short, these are the people who say that they have black souls wrapped up in white skins.

'... the integration they talk about is ... artificial ... [because] the people forming the integrated complex have been extracted from various segregated societies with their in-built complexes of superiority and inferiority, and these continue to manifest themselves even in the "non-racial" set-up of the integrated complex. As a result, the integration so achieved is a one-way course, with the whites doing all the talking and the blacks the listening.

'... [Blacks] have been made to feel inferior for so long that for them it is comforting to drink tea, wine or beer with whites who seem to treat them as equals. This serves to boost up their own egos to the extent of making them feel slightly superior to those blacks who do not get similar treatment from whites. These are the sort of blacks who are a danger to the community. Instead of directing themselves at their black brothers and looking at their common problems from a common platform, they choose to sing out their lamentations to an apparently sympathetic audience that has become proficient in saying the chorus of "shame!" '

In a later article, Biko urged blacks to find their own response to white racism, instead of a response calculated to appease liberal whites. 'Not only have the whites been guilty of being on the offensive,' he wrote, 'but, by some skilful manoeuvres, they have managed to control the responses of the blacks to the provocation. Not only have they kicked the black but they have also told him how to react to the kick. For a long time, the black has been listening with patience to the advice he has been receiving ... With painful slowness he is now beginning to show signs that it is his right and duty to respond to the kick in the way he sees fit ... The liberals must understand that the days of the noble savage are gone; that the blacks do not need a go-between in this struggle for their own emancipation.'

SASO's hostility towards white liberals was greeted with dismay by the South African media. It was, said the East London *Daily Dispatch*, 'one of the sad manifestations of racist policy at government level ... The result is the emergence of a "blacks only" mentality among blacks ... The promoters of SASO are wrong in what they are doing. They are promoting apartheid. They are entrenching the idea of racial exclusivity and therefore doing the government's work ... Fortunately they represent only a small minority of black students.'

Far from appealing to 'a small minority', black consciousness was sweeping campuses throughout the country. Achieving an unprecedented level of political education, it had by 1972 spread beyond the universities into thousands of schools. Few whites were aware of it: WRAB's chairman, Manie Mulder, speaking shortly before 16 June, assured newsmen that 'the broad masses of Soweto are perfectly content, perfectly happy'.

Indeed, the extent of the uprising stunned SASO almost as much as it shocked WRAB's officials. Particularly surprising to Biko and his colleagues was the willingness of grown men and women to obey the instructions of youths leading the revolt. The generation gap between the young and their elders had always been pronounced in African society; tribal custom venerated age and expected youth to defer to it. The prospect of student leaders attracting mass support had seemed so unlikely to SASO in 1972 that it decided to help form an adult wing of the black consciousness movement, the Black People's Convention, in July that year.

No group was more surprised by the fury of the student rebellion than the ANC, though it had been monitoring the mood of young township dwellers and had by 1975 begun to move from its distant administrative headquarters in London to bases in Zambia, Tanzania, Mozambique and Angola. As the militant youth began organising themselves in a conspiratorial cellular fashion, they were sometimes prompted to do so by ANC 'elders' – former activists from the 1950s as well as ex-Robben Islanders. By the time the student uprising broke out in June 1976, the ANC – though well aware that the philosophy of black exclusivity propounded by Biko conflicted with its own non-racial policy – had realised it was in danger of losing control of the struggle and was seizing every opportunity to enlist the unexpected power of the student force.

Other factors added to the galvanising effect black consciousness had on student confidence and black solidarity, helping to shift discontent into action during the months leading up to the youth rebellion.

Early in 1976 defence minister P W Botha ordered the largest military mobilisation since the Second World War deep into Angola to intervene in a civil war there. Under pressure from America, the mission proved a humiliating defeat for the Nationalists, with captured white South African soldiers paraded before television cameras in a number of black African countries. News of the army's defeat in combat with black soldiers was received gleefully by Africans in South Africa. Coupled with the victory secured by the Front for the Liberation of Mozambique (Frelimo) against Portuguese colonial rule in 1975, it began to seem possible for blacks to challenge white domination militarily – and win.

Another factor spurring the students on was a severe recession in the South

African economy. With unemployment expected to top two million by the end of 1976, black workers began to resist trade union protests, a development which helped fuel student rage against their elders as well as against a state that was clearly unable to offer them adequate job opportunities when they left their schools and universities. Resentment swelled as they contemplated the injustice of an education leading nowhere: not only was the economy closing against them, but they were handicapped by an education system deliberately designed to preclude them from competing with whites for available jobs.

The amount of money invested by the government in the education of every white child was over six times higher than that spent on a black student. Despite the truth of assertions by state officials claiming South Africa offered its black people more in the way of education than did most neighbouring African countries, the continent as a whole was not the standard by which black South Africans measured their own conditions: they compared themselves with the whites in their environment.

Since 1955 blacks had been required to pay taxes towards education but these did not entitle black children to the free books received by white children. Two years before the uprising, the government finally promised to provide free textbooks to black children, but by February 1976 none had been issued. Many students realised the promise of textbooks had been a ploy to help the Bantu education minister implement the dual-language system first announced years earlier, whereby blacks were to be taught in their mother tongue until they reached Standard Four and thereafter in English and Afrikaans on a fifty/fifty basis.

The impending introduction of compulsory tuition in Afrikaans had brought sustained protest from black educators and students. Ignoring their reaction, the government began to deliver Afrikaans textbooks in 1974. The books arrived in large crates at Morris Isaacson School in Soweto, where they were hidden away after students warned the headmaster they would boycott any lessons delivered in Afrikaans.

'At first when we saw the books arriving, we were excited because we thought the government was at last supplying the free ones it had promised us,' recalled Sikosi Mji, a prefect at the school. 'But then we saw they were all written in Afrikaans, a language we hated because it is the language of our oppressors. After hearing that the government had sent out a circular telling all principals to enforce Afrikaans by 1975, we decided we had to act. We had already been trying to introduce some democratic structures in the school, with some success. For example, we'd succeeded in having half the prefects popularly elected and only half appointed by the authorities. I was appointed, part of the system, but I worked against it because I couldn't support it. None of us could. We got to work, lobbying among the parents and the teachers until eventually so much pressure had built up that the principal assured us he wouldn't introduce Afrikaans in 1975.

'The language problem was a very unfair one in black schools. Where else in the world would a child have to be educated in three different languages? In the primary school, we were supposed to be taught in our African language, Xhosa, Zulu, Sotho or whichever. In the secondary school, we had to switch to English and Afrikaans. It was another way for the whites to keep us backward and uneducated. We decided not to let them do this to us.'

The increasingly explosive situation was compounded after South Africa's ambassador to the United Nations, Pik Botha, made a speech to the world body in 1974, announcing that his country would in future be moving away from discrimination based on colour to a new policy of developing the barren tribal reserves occupied by rural blacks. These areas were henceforth to be known as bantustans, he said. As the *Financial Mail* saw it: 'Government's ultimate aim is to force each and every African in the Republic ostensibly to become a citizen of one or other bantustan, so that it can legitimate its refusal to grant them political rights in "white" South Africa. They will then be "foreigners" present temporarily in the "white" areas as guest workers. The Transkei is the first step in this direction. Discrimination will no longer be based on race or colour, so the government will claim, but on nationality.'

Although the shift to the bantustan policy created more school places overall and also had the effect of strengthening political communication between black town and country dwellers, it was bitterly resented, especially by students. The introduction of a 'pink card' system in 1974, designed to ensure that only children living legally in urban areas could find places in city schools, was chaotic: 60 000 out of a group of 111 000 children reporting for enrolment in Soweto were declared illegal residents. Such a large number of pupils could not be accommodated in bantustan schools and the programme was hastily rescheduled, but not before earning the contempt of the entire black student population.

Accumulating assaults on an already inferior education system left thousands of black students with a driving desire for retaliation. Sikosi Mji was typical, in her attitudes if not in her family background, of the young leaders who began to seek ways of mobilising the student masses against Bantu education in particular and apartheid in general. Her father, Diliza, a founder member of the ANC's Youth League, had taken over from Walter Sisulu as secretary-general of the ANC when Sisulu was banned. Her brother, a medical student, became president of SASO. Both Sikosi's parents were medical practitioners.

'I talked to a close school friend of mine, a boy called Naledi Tsiki. He and I went to meet with some people in the location who were spreading the word that the ANC still existed even though it had been quiet underground for a long time. They gave us a copy of the Freedom Charter and asked us to study it and then report back to them. We found it was a general blueprint of what we would like to see in our country. When we told them this, they asked us to work for the ANC in an underground cell and we agreed.'

The two friends then helped organise protests and boycotts at Morris Isaacson in the months leading up to the showdown on 16 June. Appointed head girl of the school in 1975, Mji was particularly effective as an underground leader until the police uncovered her mission and she went into hiding. Naledi Tsiki left the country in December 1975, an embittered, angry twenty-year-old determined to undergo guerrilla training and return to South Africa with weapons of war.

Numerous other students disappeared into police cells or across the country's borders. Walter and Albertina Sisulu's daughter Lindiwe was arrested on 13 June, a few days before the uprising began, and held for eleven months.

Having first been arrested before her tenth birthday and often left at home in later years to look after her young siblings during long periods when her father, her mother and her two brothers were in detention, she expected to cope calmly in prison. But nothing could have prepared her for carefully applied mental torture. 'They would say they had arrested my mother and two brothers and that there was nobody at home except the small children. [Albertina was guardian to her dead sister-in-law's offspring.] I believed them and it upset me. They also said my mother was critically ill and wanted to see me, but they would not let me go to her unless I talked. Later, they told me she had passed away ... I wrote to the minister of justice complaining that I had not been allowed to attend my mother's funeral. After that my treatment changed. I was allowed clothes and books sent in from outside and I immediately realised the police had been lying because, from the way my things were packed, I knew that nobody could have packed them except my mother.'

While Lindiwe Sisulu and hundreds of other students were still in detention, the exodus of disillusioned teenagers grew from a trickle in 1975 to a flood by the end of the following year. Though there were serious ideological differences between the philosophies of black consciousness and the ANC's policy of non-racialism, students fleeing the country ahead of police reprisals found they had no practical alternative but to seek refuge and further the struggle from the only available exile sanctuary: that provided by the ANC. The PAC, though ideologically more compatible with black consciousness, was in complete disarray and unable to offer many of them refuge outside South Africa.

Solomon Mahlangu decided to join the students in exile a few days after his twentieth birthday in October 1976. Crossing the Swaziland border, often trudging for miles on foot, he journeyed to Tanzania, and was later to become the most celebrated guerrilla in the history of Umkhonto we Sizwe.

Many of the fleeing students were much younger than Mahlangu, including one ten-year-old whose courage in combat with police had become a legend at ANC headquarters in Dar es Salaam. Reporting to the ANC, he insisted on immediate military training. Told to resume his education instead, he demanded the right to return to South Africa as a trained soldier. After successive attempts to reason with the child had failed, word of his tenacity reached Oliver Tambo, who invited the boy to supper at his home. The fatherly ANC supremo sat with the invincible ten-year-old for hours until the child was finally convinced he could best serve the revolution by growing a little older and wiser before being infiltrated back to South Africa as an armed fighter.

By the time Lindiwe Sisulu was released from detention, she had also decided to leave the country to join the ANC in exile. Her only remaining mission in South Africa was a final visit to Robben Island to say goodbye to her father. Walter, whom she described at the time as her 'continual inspiration', had difficulty fighting back his tears when he realised he might never see his daughter again, but he managed a smile and a thumbs up sign when she left him.

Sikosi Mji also decided to become a guerrilla fighter. Crossing the Swaziland border on a borrowed passport, she received her travel instructions from an ANC contact on the other side and made her way to Mozambique. Checking into a cheap hotel in Maputo, she was delighted to spot her old friend Naledi Tsiki in the dining room. Although instructed by the ANC not to talk to anyone she might recognise during her journey, she could not resist greeting Naledi. Equally pleased to see her, Tsiki described his military training, telling her he was on his way back to South Africa. She wished him luck, saying she would soon be a guerrilla herself.

However, on reaching Tanzania, she was told she was too immature and hot-headed for immediate military training. Instead, being an articulate and personable girl, she was chosen to accompany Oliver Tambo and other ANC leaders on a lengthy lecture tour of the United States and Europe. 'South Africa can never be the same again after the events of 16 June 1976,' Congress secretary-general Alfred Nzo told the United Nations general assembly. Sikosi Mji added: 'Even though we face heavy odds, we are resolved to pay the highest sacrifice. Help us hasten the triumph of justice by enabling us to meet the enemy on at least relatively equal terms.'

While she and her ANC leaders were telling the world about the injustices of apartheid, Steve Biko died in detention in Pretoria after being tortured and beaten by police. A massive security crackdown resulted in the imprisonment of dozens of government opponents, the banning of numerous organisations and people associated with the students' uprising, and the banishment of Winnie Mandela to Brandfort, a small town in the Orange Free State.

By the time Mji returned to Africa, her friend Naledi Tsiki was a prisoner standing trial as a member of a guerrilla group known as the 'Pretoria Twelve', accused of assisting the underground activities of the ANC and conspiring to overthrow the government of South Africa by violence. Six in the group, which included elderly nationalists like sixty-seven-year-old Martin Ramokgadi as well as young men who had left the country during the student rebellion, were acquitted, but Tsiki was found guilty. 'The African National Congress for years fought for freedom for the black people, without the use of any type of violence,' he told the court. 'Deputations, delegations and peaceful demonstrations were the order of the day ... Most unfortunately, my lord, this meekness was met in most cases with overwhelming shows of strength and violence ... [but] ... our people led by the ANC kept on waging a non-violent struggle ... until it was forcibly sent underground.'

When the sentences were handed down, Tsiki stood in the dock in chains, hearing that he was to spend the next fourteen years on Robben Island. Raising his clenched fist, he shouted '*Amandla!*', to which blacks packed into the public gallery replied: '*Ngawethu!*'

The following June, exactly two years after the Soweto students' uprising, Solomon Mahlangu became the first ANC guerrilla to be sentenced to death. Arrested after a shoot-out in Johannesburg's Gogh Street, he spent a year on death row at the centre of an international campaign to save him from the gallows. For months capturing headlines abroad and in South Africa, his name represented the most hated of all forms of life to whites: a gun-wielding terrorist – but the most revered of all symbols of resistance to blacks: a freedom fighter.

By the time he was executed on 6 April 1979, Mahlangu had become so beloved a black hero that the police decided to bury him in secret lest his funeral provoke what Pik Botha called 'the tensions that lie below the surface in the townships'. While thousands of mourners waited for his body at Mamelodi cemetery, his coffin was carried to Atteridgeville and dumped in an unmarked grave.

Amid the ensuing uproar, a prison psychiatrist announced that Mahlangu had been 'scared' of dying. The unseemly revelation enraged blacks. 'I see the [psychiatrist's] report as mere propaganda designed to instil fear into those youths who may follow in his footsteps,' declared Mahlangu's mother. The issue was threatening to erupt into violence when the Reverend Nyathi, who had administered the last rites, came forward to reveal that Mahlangu had given the ANC salute, stood upright and smiling, and finally walked tall to the gallows.

13

BLOODSHED AND BACKLASH: THE 1980s

The idea of forming a new popular front rather than a political organisation to unite protest inside South Africa was first discussed by the ANC in 1981. Two years later, when the government published its proposals for a constitution giving coloureds and Indians a limited role in the legislature but excluding blacks, a prominent coloured priest, Dr Allan Boesak, head of the Geneva-based World Alliance of Reformed Churches, called a meeting at Mitchells Plain, a township near Cape Town. It drew an enthusiastic crowd of 12 000, many clutching copies of the Freedom Charter and displaying ANC colours. Delegates representing some 300 civic associations, churches, trade unions, student organisations and sports bodies launched the United Democratic Front (UDF), the widest alliance of anti-apartheid opposition ever seen in the country.

The UDF's aims, indistinguishable from those of the ANC except in their repudiation of violence, were supported by underground ANC members as well as by many among the black consciousness generation of the 1970s. Sixty-nine-year-old Archibald Gumede, an ANC veteran whose father Josiah had been a founder member of the ANC in 1912, was elected president of the new umbrella organisation. Boesak was elected a patron, as were Nelson Mandela, Govan Mbeki, Walter and Albertina Sisulu and Helen Joseph.

General secretary was thirty-one-year-old Popo Molefe, the son of parents too poor to send him to school until he was ten. During a childhood of perpetual hunger, hawking peanuts on railway platforms, caddying at golf clubs and packing parcels for supermarket shoppers to make ends meet, Molefe once walked to school barefoot through a freak snowstorm on the Reef in 1964. As head prefect at Soweto's Naledi High School during 1976, he was at the forefront of the student rebellion, which resulted in his detention for seven months.

Other UDF members, representing a cross-section of people involved in the liberation struggle since the early 1940s, were Zollie Malindi (fifty-nine years old), who had fled from police at the Congress of the People in Kliptown with the sole Xhosa translation of the Freedom Charter; Edgar Ngoyi (fifty-seven), one of Umkhonto we Sizwe's chief contacts in the eastern Cape in the days before the Rivonia arrests of 1963; Murphy Morobe (twenty-seven) and Stone Sizane (twenty-nine), typical of the student leaders who had once subscribed to the racial exclusivity of black consciousness but had joined the ANC on being persuaded to accept its non-racial policies by other political prisoners on Robben Island or, in Sizane's case, after listening regularly to ANC broadcasts from Lusaka on Radio Freedom.

Calling on whites and blacks to unite against apartheid, the UDF launched a number of campaigns to persuade voters to reject the proposed three racially separate chambers of parliament and an executive state president with far wider powers than P W Botha already held as prime minister. In the event, voters endorsed the changes by a 2-to-1 majority, bringing a note of triumph to Botha's voice as he declared: 'We have a vote in favour of evolutionary reform.' Leader of the largest right-wing group of white opponents, Dr Andries Treurnicht of the Conservative Party, angrily condemned the result, saying it would 'end the whites' reign' as a sovereign nation in South Africa.

Early the following year Botha dealt the liberation movement another blow, announcing that the government had held secret talks with Mozambique's Marxist leader, Samora Machel, which had led to a joint security pact, the Nkomati Accord. Machel undertook to prevent the ANC using Mozambique as a base from which to launch guerrilla attacks against South Africa in exchange for Botha's agreement to withhold support from the 10 000-member Mozambique National Resistance (MNR) movement which had been creating havoc in Machel's country for five years.

Turning its attention to more immediate matters, the UDF began organising opposition to a new system of local government for townships, whereby the government delegated black municipal councillors to collect taxes and rents, and run beerhalls and other local amenities. Told by Pretoria that they must be self-financing, the municipalities soon ran into trouble, increasing rents and service charges to cover their losses and alienating township residents in the process. Hit by the worst economic recession in fifty years, which was accompanied by high inflation and severe drought in the rural areas, blacks grew increasingly angry. 'People are at the end of their tether,' warned Black Sash, a civil rights movement. 'They just can't make ends meet any more.' Combined with continuing discontent over inferior education, the situation eventually became explosive.

Outbreaks of violence, beginning in the latter part of 1984, spread through townships nationwide. Initially ignited by local grievances, they were intensified by thousands of black youths known as 'comrades', who saw themselves as the vanguard of the revolution and defied the police and the army with stones and home-made petrol bombs.

The first of many major confrontations occurred in the Vaal Triangle on 3 September 1984, the day Botha was sworn into office as the country's first state president. Roving comrades, protesting against increased rates, attacked property in Sharpeville, hacking to death the deputy mayor and killing three other councillors. Numerous buildings were set alight and five people were killed by rampaging mobs of demonstrators. In nearby Evaton township, Indian shops were singled out for destruction. By the end of the week, thirty-one people had died and at least 300 had been injured. Funerals for the victims became occasions for further protest and rioting. Attacks on the homes of black councillors continued.

A massive offensive was launched in October, when a combined force of

7 000 police and soldiers moved into Sebokeng township near Sharpeville, raiding nearly 20 000 homes in a search for 'criminal and revolutionary elements'. They arrested 350 people. The deployment of the army served only to heighten tension, giving the comrades a platform for further protest.

The UDF and a number of trade unions met to organise a massive labour stayaway in the Transvaal on 5 November. Timed to coincide with a boycott of schools, and accompanied by demands for the withdrawal of armed forces from the townships, the resignations of councillors, a freeze on rents and bus fares, and the release of political prisoners and detainees, the strike proved the most successful in over thirty years. Causing severe losses to industries and commerce, it brought unprecedented criticism of the government from the white business sector. 'Not in modern times in this country have businessmen been so united in their condemnation of government and its social and economic policies,' wrote the influential *Financial Mail*. But 6 000 of the 800 000 who had failed to report for work were subsequently sacked by their employers, providing yet another cause for protest.

It wasn't until the year's end that an uneasy calm descended over the townships. By then, 160 people had been killed and hundreds more injured, most of them victims of the security forces. More than a thousand people were detained, compared with 453 arrests without trial the previous year. 'I see an ongoing situation of unrest that will have flashpoints,' predicted Helen Suzman, a veteran liberal politician.

The violence had for months secured front-page attention internationally. As pressure began to mount on Botha to quell discontent by making meaningful concessions to blacks, he offered to free Nelson Mandela from his prison cell provided the ANC leader agreed not to 'plan, instigate or commit acts of violence for the furtherance of his political objectives'.

Mandela's reply was read by his daughter Zinzi to a crowd of 9 000 at Soweto's Jabulani Stadium. 'I cannot and will not give any undertaking at a time when I and you, the people, are not free,' Mandela said. '... what freedom am I being offered when I must ask permission to live in an urban area? What freedom am I being offered when I need a stamp in my pass to seek work? ... Only free men can negotiate; prisoners cannot enter into contracts. Your freedom and mine cannot be separated.'

Botha later told parliament: 'It is ... not the South African government which now stands in the way of Mr Mandela's freedom. It is himself.'

A week later, violence erupted again, this time in Crossroads, a sprawling squatter camp outside Cape Town where homeless blacks and coloureds had over ten years built patchwork shelters from scraps of wood, flattened petrol drums, cardboard boxes and plastic bags. Frequently raided by police in attempts to force its residents back into homelands devoid of employment opportunities, Crossroads was suddenly ignited into an inferno by a rumour that the government was about to shift its 60 000 residents by force. Erecting barricades of broken furniture, old motor car tyres and heaps of rubbish, the squatters blocked the entrances to their settlement. They set the barricades alight, then waited for the government's removal squads to arrive.

Met by around 3 000 demonstrators, many chanting the ANC's slogan, 'Amandla' and throwing stones, the police fired rubber bullets into the crowd and chased fleeing demonstrators. Numerous street battles followed until the authorities finally withdrew; twenty-six policemen were injured, eighteen of the squatters were killed and around 250 were wounded.

Shortly afterwards the authorities mounted a countrywide crackdown against their opponents, particularly those in the UDF. Swooping into seventy homes and offices, they arrested and detained hundreds of activists, charging some of them with treason.

The twenty-fifth anniversary of the police massacre at Sharpeville, 21 March 1985, was a day the authorities knew they could expect demonstrations, despite their attempts to counter what they termed 'unrest' by issuing bans on public meetings. In Langa, a black township near Port Elizabeth, a crowd began to gather with the intention of staging a funeral procession to honour five blacks killed the previous weekend in clashes with police during a boycott of shops, buses and factories. The procession swelled until it numbered about 4 000 and became a protest march commemorating Sharpeville as well as a funeral train.

Striding along a highway leading from Langa to the white town of Uitenhage, the demonstrators were blocked by police vehicles. The officer in charge, speaking into a loudhailer, told the marchers to go home. When they continued to move forward, a warning shot was fired, hitting the ground in front of the procession's leaders. Ignoring it, they surged onward. The young lieutenant in charge of the police contingent panicked, ordering his men to fire. In the ensuing hail of bullets nineteen blacks died.

The killings at Uitenhage brought a wave of counter-violence, establishing a pattern which was to last for over a year longer: repression provoked violence and violence provoked more repression. Added to the bloody cycle was another cause for killing: the decision by some comrades to curtail police informers' activities by murdering known collaborators. In the aftermath of the Uitenhage shootings, enraged mobs in townships near Langa killed seven blacks suspected of helping the police. In one particularly brutal incident, a crowd hacked to death a black town councillor, his son and two of his employees; then set fire to his house. Later they dragged the burnt bodies out of the house and danced around them. 'This country is tearing itself apart,' protested the *Rand Daily Mail*. 'We are writing our history in blood.' By the end of March, just over a year since the township turmoil began, 240 people had lost their lives.

In June 1985 the ANC called a meeting to review its policies. Held in Kabwe, Zambia, and known as the second consultative conference, it noted that the ANC had achieved considerable success in the decade since the Soweto schoolchildren's revolt. The movement had established a formidable presence within the country; Umkhonto's sabotage attacks on government buildings and installations had won the support of disaffected township youth; and popular, legal protest in South Africa had become centred around ANC slogans and symbols. What the ANC lacked, delegates agreed, was internal organisation sufficient to exploit its popularity fully.

Umkhonto's 'armed propaganda' campaign had been borne by a few hundred guerrillas, mainly trained abroad. The Nkomati Accord had demonstrated the vulnerability of such a campaign, which relied on getting activists over the country's borders. Deciding on a new course in the future, the conference resolved to intensify the 'people's war', a programme aimed towards arming the masses. The ANC particularly wanted to organise and direct militant youths, in order to harness the energies of the autonomous insurrectionary movement which had grown out of street fights between township residents and police in the months following the Vaal uprising the previous year.

Discussing at length the question of targets for Umkhonto's violence, the conference – chaired by Oliver Tambo, who once said he personally abhorred violence to such an extent that 'I even take insects out of the bath' – agreed not to take such pains as in the past to avoid civilian casualties. This was not least because of the difficulty of upholding the former embargo on 'soft' targets once the armed conflict spread beyond disciplined MK guerrillas to ill-trained township street-fighters.

The situation inside South Africa remained explosive but racist whites did not hesitate to fuel it further. Appalled at Botha's apartheid reform in April, scrapping the Mixed Marriages Act and the Immorality Act (which had together outlawed marriage and sexual intercourse across apartheid's colour barrier), Eugene Terre'Blanche, head of the growing Afrikaanse Weerstandsbeweging (AWB) which promised to keep South Africa white, declared: 'I think apartheid is the most fair and just principle on earth. It is the only way in which two clashing cultures can exist without friction and conflict … government and government alone will be responsible for the bloodiest revolution Africa has ever seen because the government forces people together who do not belong together. The Afrikaner is not going to accept it. He will assert himself in a counter-offensive with all the power he can muster.'

Tempers in the townships rose when medical evidence presented to the commission of inquiry into the Uitenhage police killings showed, as the Sharpeville inquiry had done twenty-five years earlier, that most of the dead demonstrators had been shot in the back.

Temperatures in South Africa's ruling party also soared after the United

States Congress passed a bill to impose economic sanctions against the country unless explicit measures were taken to reform the apartheid system. Ignoring President Ronald Reagan's calls for restraint in preceding months, the House returned a vote of 295 to 127, which the US Senate was expected to endorse when it voted later in the year.

Botha's mood swung from cautious conciliation to outright defiance of the growing international hostility towards his policies. In mid-June, South African soldiers mounted a dawn raid on nine homes and an office in the capital city of a neighbouring black state, Botswana. Targets of the commando strike were members of the ANC, which had claimed responsibility for a number of sabotage incidents within South Africa during preceding months. The Botswana attack followed the ambush by Angolan troops of a nine-man South African commando unit acting in contravention of a US-mediated ceasefire. Washington's outraged response was to call its Pretoria-based ambassador home for consultations. Botha commented: 'If there are elements in Washington who think that South Africa is going to be run by the United States, then it must be made quite clear that those elements are heading for a confrontation with the South African government and people.'

Township clashes continued throughout the first half of 1985, by which time the government had decided on harsh action. In a bizarre public relations stunt on state-owned national television, the six o'clock evening news on 20 July exposed the full horror of 'necklacing', a barbaric act of vengeance whereby a burning car-tyre was thrown around a victim's neck by militants punishing collaborators. A black crowd was shown stoning, beating, stripping and burning to death a young black woman after the mob had turned on her in response to a lone shout of 'Informer!' The incident occurred at a black funeral in Duduza, near Johannesburg, where South Africa's best-known churchman, Bishop Desmond Tutu, had a few days earlier shielded a terrified suspected informer from a crowd which set the man's car alight and then tried to throw him into the flames. Two hours after the broadcast, Botha appeared on television saying, 'This state of affairs can no longer be tolerated.' He then announced emergency laws to govern thirty-six of the most strife-torn magisterial districts in the country.

Armed with the new laws, police launched a countrywide purge at the month's end. Swooping into homes unannounced, they seized property and detained men, women and children without charge. In some cases they ordered activists to leave the townships in which they had become leaders and move to distant parts of the country. Those arrested included many church leaders, trade unionists and some whites, most affiliated to the UDF. But though the number of arrests grew daily, the violence continued, with the ANC's Radio Freedom exhorting activists to 'make the townships ungovernable'. Second-tier leaders came up through the UDF's ranks to take over the roles of the imprisoned men and women.

Within a week of the emergency declaration – the first time such a measure had been used since the Sharpeville massacre triggered civil unrest in 1960 – sixteen blacks had been killed in clashes with police. Observers at home and abroad lashed Botha with criticism. The Afrikaner leader of the Progressive Federal Party, Dr Frederik van Zyl Slabbert, demanded an explanation in parliament: 'I ask this government, what in heaven's name are you doing?' Dr Allan Boesak urged Botha to negotiate political reform with blacks, warning that the emergency would lead only to more deaths. 'The days when force could be used to suppress opponents of apartheid have gone,' he said.

However, the government was intent on heeding the lessons of its own history: in 1960 and again in 1977, following the Sharpeville and Soweto riots, mass revolt had been controlled by the arrest of township leaders and the banning of activist organisations. Botha planned to deal with the current uprising by once again marshalling all the repressive forces at his disposal.

Within weeks of the clampdown, rioting broke out in the black township with over a million residents and a turbulent record of violent upheaval: Soweto. Students stormed municipal buses, demanding to be transported to the court where over a hundred of their colleagues were being charged with holding an illegal demonstration. Police arrived on horseback, chasing demonstrators with teargas and rubber bullets and arresting 500. Released soon afterwards, they joined massive crowds setting fire to buildings and stoning vehicles in a splurge of mayhem reminiscent of the darkest days of 1976.

The third week of the state of emergency began with the number of blacks in detention exceeding 1 300 and the government announcing another ban. This time its goal was to end the frequent mass funerals which, as the sole legal rallying point for black protest, had remained occasions for displays of resistance. Often numbering up to 50 000, demonstrators at political funerals sang freedom songs and waved ANC flags. On one occasion mourners were filmed beneath the Marxist emblem of Russia, much to the consternation of white television viewers.

A new decree stated that black funerals could only be held indoors for one victim at a time and that they must be conducted by an ordained minister who refrained from political or security references. Those attending funerals must travel to and from them by vehicle only; arriving on foot became an offence. No flags or banners could be displayed; no public address system used. Bishop Tutu, winner of the Nobel Peace Prize in 1984, warned: 'I think that the authorities are really playing with fire, in the sense that they are seeking new points of confrontation and friction with a people who are already embattled by vicious and draconian laws. I'm fearful for what may actually develop. I'm fearful for an explosion one day which we will not be able to control. The consequence of putting the lid on is to allow the steam to build up.'

Early in August, Bishop Tutu defied the ban, leading a procession in Daveyton to the burial site of two young women shot during township violence. When police tried to stop the marchers, Tutu changed his tactics and resorted to a Portia-like plea for pity instead of the outright challenges the authorities had come to expect from him. 'Please allow us to bury our dead with dignity,' he begged the armed officers. 'Please do not rub our noses in the dust. We are already hurt; we are already down. Don't trample on us. We are human beings; we are not animals. And when we have a death we cry like you cry.' The police responded by providing buses to transport the mourners. Afterwards, Tutu approached the colonel in charge, telling him: 'In trying to maintain unreasonable laws, you were reasonable and well behaved today. I want to thank you for that.' Relating the encounter to journalists later, Tutu commented wryly: 'He saluted me. Twice.'

Diplomatic pressure escalated. Twelve European countries, following America's expression of disapproval, withdrew their ambassadors from Pretoria in protest against the emergency regulations and cross-border raids. Pope John Paul II declared that apartheid was weighing on 'the conscience of mankind'. The United States House of Representatives voted 380 to 48 in favour of economic sanctions.

Botha seemed to be verging on concessions to undermine apartheid when he suddenly changed tack, telling his party's Natal provincial congress: 'Reform does not come overnight. We shall not be stampeded into a situation of panic by irresponsible elements. We shall not be forced to sell out our proud heritage.' A White House spokesman, echoing the feelings of millions of disappointed South Africans, observed that 'a crisis of confidence' had overtaken events in the country.

His words were borne out by the value of the South African rand dropping sharply against the US dollar from $1,29 in 1980 to a low of 35 cents in the wake of Botha's Natal speech. The economy began to lose an estimated US$1 billion a month in short-term credit as foreign banks opted out, one New York banker telling *Time* magazine: 'Not since the demise of [the Shah's] Iran has a country fallen out of favour with the international banking community so quickly.'

While gloom and frustration spread through black townships, converted into yet more violence after police arrested over 700 schoolchildren for boycotting their classes, Nelson Mandela's voice was suddenly heard from Pollsmoor, the top-security prison near Cape Town where he had been held since being moved in 1981 from Robben Island. In a rare interview with a journalist from the *Washington Times*, Mandela said he saw 'no room for peaceful struggle' and 'no alternative' to violence. In an earlier interview, again granted by the authorities to an American, who wrote about it in the *New York Times*, Mandela had listed three prerequisites for the peaceful resolution of South Africa's problems. The first was a unified South Africa, 'no artificial homelands'; the second was black representation in the central parliament, 'not membership in the kind of apartheid assemblies that have been newly established for the coloureds and the Asians'; the third was 'one man, one vote'. Dismissing the repeal of laws such as the Immorality Act as 'pinpricks', Mandela said: 'Frankly, it is not my ambition to marry a white woman or to swim in a white pool. The central issue is political equality.'

The interviewer, Samuel Dash, described Mandela as 'a tall, slim, handsome man who looks far younger than his 66 years. Dressed in his own well-fitted khaki shirt and trousers, rather than a regulation blue denim prison uniform, he appeared vigorous and healthy, with a calm, confident manner and dignified bearing that seemed incongruous in our prison surroundings ... I felt that I was in the presence not of a guerrilla fighter or radical ideologue, but of a head of state.'

Dash was particularly impressed with Mandela's sensitivity towards white fears of black majority rule. 'Unlike white people anywhere else in Africa, whites in South Africa belong here – this is their home,' Mandela told him. 'We want them to live here with us and to share power with us.'

At ANC headquarters in Lusaka, lawyers and economists were busy drafting constitutional proposals that translated the broad principles of the Freedom Charter into an explicit blueprint for the future. They advocated a bill of rights, constitutionally entrenched workers' trade union rights and equality for women, and proposed 'corrective action' to redistribute wealth. However, they stopped well short of the socialist reconstruction white businessmen in South Africa had long feared as an inevitability under black rule. Unlike the Freedom Charter, the proposals did not include a specific commitment to nationalise mines, banks and monopoly industries. Prescribing a mixed economy, they envisaged that 'the state shall have the right to determine the general context in which economic life takes place' and the private sector 'shall be obliged to co-operate with the state in realising the objectives of the Freedom Charter'. The economy would be broadened to include co-operative and small-scale family enterprises and the state would direct a programme of land reform.

Its political provisions ruled out federalism in favour of a centralised unitary state and local authorities with delegated rather than autonomous powers. Emphasising popular participation throughout government, the guidelines proposed a majoritarian 'first past the post' electoral system and a judiciary accountable to the people.

In September 1985 one of the most able in the UDF's new generation of leaders was captured by security police after working underground since the start of the townships' rebellion. He was Steve Tshwete, physically a giant of a man who had spent fifteen years on Robben Island. Temperamentally given to wild, often courageous impulses, he had become immensely popular among the comrades. Banished by police orders from his home in King William's Town, near East London, to the impoverished Ciskei homeland nearby, he was not supposed to cross into South Africa without a visa. But he had ignored the ban for months, donning a variety of disguises in order to organise campaigns and boycotts throughout the eastern Cape.

After becoming the most hunted man in the country he was eventually advised by colleagues to escape to exile in Zambia. 'I foolishly decided to go to my home and say goodbye to my father in King William's Town,' recalls Tshwete. 'That evening, I walked into the house and found four members of the security police sitting there waiting for me: it seemed that they had at last caught me red-handed. They told me to collect a change of clothes from the bedroom and, as I was doing this, a friend of mine arrived in a car at the house. He was very drunk.

'I could see policemen ripping UDF posters from the wall in the adjoining room, laughing and joking in Afrikaans, very happy that they'd caught me. Then my friend stumbled in and started shouting and swearing at them, telling them to leave me alone. One of the policemen hit him and I came out of the bedroom to say, "No, leave that man, he's drunk, he's apolitical." But my friend carried on abusing them and tried to hit one of them. A brawl started and I suddenly realised I could make a break for it. I ran out of the door and kept running towards the Ciskei border, which was only about 100 metres away. I got to a store owned by a friend of mine and he immediately drove me to a hideout.'

Daringly addressing a mass political funeral before finally preparing to leave the country, Tshwete shaved his head and beard, dressed in tight jeans and a baseball cap, obtained a passport, and borrowed a friend's sports car. Sitting beside him as he drew up at the Maseru border post in Lesotho was a heavily made-up girl whose outlandish dress was designed to distract police attention from Tshwete. The ploy worked, though not before a nerve-jangling, hour-long delay while South African police scrutinised his forged documents.

As the state of emergency entered its twelfth week, Botha addressed the issue of reform once more, calling for 'co-operative co-existence' through a confederation of ethnic units, each with responsibility for its 'own affairs'. However, he insisted that universal suffrage in a unitary state would cause 'dictatorship of the strongest black group ... greater struggle and more bloodshed'. The ANC in Lusaka condemned the proposals as 'meaningless amendments of the apartheid system', and the mass-circulation *Sowetan* newspaper warned: '[Apartheid] cannot be dressed up in false colours. We are not that stupid.'

Expressing his own disappointment, Botha complained that his reform initiatives had met with nothing but demands for further concessions. 'More than any other national leader, I went out of my way to create an attitude of justice towards other groups,' he said. 'There is no sign of any appreciation for this spirit of justice.'

The following month violence flared up after the hanging of a young black upholsterer and poet, Benjamin Moloise, at Pretoria Central Prison. Convicted of murdering a black policeman in 1982, though the ANC claimed that other unnamed guerrillas had done the killing, Moloise had been passionately dedicated to the struggle, writing in one of his poems: 'A storm of oppression will be followed by the rain of my blood/I am proud to give my life, my solitary life.' News of his death was greeted with fury in Soweto and sent hundreds of Africans on a four-hour rampage through the streets of Johannesburg. Two policemen were stabbed. A number of pedestrians were robbed or beaten, and whites fled in terror. The outrage subsided and then surged again in various parts of the country after Moloise's mother revealed that she had waited outside the prison gates for hours with Winnie Mandela, denied permission to see Benjamin for the last time on the day of his death.

Rioting was particularly severe in the Cape Town area, where a cruel incident occurred on 15 October in Thornton Road, Athlone. Armed police hiding inside packing crates on the back of a railway truck were driven through a suburb where black youths had been stoning vehicles. Unknown to the hidden policemen, an international television crew filmed the truck as it drove along without incident and then as it returned on the same route in order to tempt the stone-throwers again. This time, when the truck was stoned, policemen leapt out of the crates and opened fire. Four people were killed, including a twelve-year-old activist and the entirely innocent occupant of a nearby house. Dubbed the Trojan Horse affair by journalists, it was replayed in living rooms all over the world within hours of the shootings and for months afterwards.

International pressure continued to mount. President Kenneth Kaunda of Zambia warned world leaders attending the fortieth anniversary celebrations of the United Nations: 'If you don't apply sanctions, hundreds of thousands of people will die and [your] investments will go up in flames.' Forty-six member states of the British Commonwealth applauded the Canadian prime minister when he threatened to sever diplomatic and economic ties with South Africa if apartheid persisted.

In Pretoria the government seized the passports of eight Afrikaner university students planning to go to Lusaka for discussions with the ANC. Their proposed trip followed an earlier visit by top South African businessmen to the Zambian capital for talks with an ANC delegation led by Oliver Tambo. Both visits would have been unthinkable, even to the businessmen and students concerned, only a year or two earlier. But a new realisation had dawned on some whites watching the turmoil and the collapse of government-appointed black councils in the townships. Having seen white authorities in the Cape forced to negotiate with UDF affiliates in order to end crippling consumer boycotts, and a threatened school boycott averted after government education officials were left with no alternative but to negotiate with the UDF's boycott committees, they realised that the ANC had succeeded in rendering the townships ungovernable.

What the government saw in white overtures towards the ANC was a new and dangerous respectability for the ANC men and women it preferred to brand as murderers and communists. But the ANC welcomed the development. 'We think it is important for [whites] to come and find out what the ANC is all about,' said Umkhonto we Sizwe's commander, Joe Modise, in a rare interview in Lusaka. 'I think some of them, when they came here, thought they were going to see communists with horns. But they left here knowing they had met South Africans who are no different from themselves.'

While the debate over visits to Lusaka raged, hardliners in the white electorate used the ballot box to tell Botha what they thought of his reforms. Results of five by-elections in various parts of the country showed a marked white backlash as voters swung to right-wing candidates who promised total white supremacy, the repeal of reforms, and harsher police and military action against black rioters and neighbouring states giving support to the ANC.

December 1985 saw the launch of the Congress of South African Trade Unions (COSATU), with a paid-up membership of 500 000 representing thirty-four participating unions. Among those at the forefront of the unity talks creating COSATU were the new organisation's general secretary, thirty-one-year-old Jay Naidoo, a clear-headed former black consciousness leader; Chris Dlamini, a trade unionist since the 1970s; the general secretary of the 150 000-member National Union of Mineworkers, Cyril Ramaphosa, who was a charismatic lawyer detained during the 1976 Soweto riots; and Sydney Mufamadi, whose role as UDF Transvaal publicity secretary had made him so obvious a police target that he helped organise the launch of COSATU from an underground hideout.

Uniting the country's six million black workers had been an ANC goal for many years. Although it shared the ANC's vision of the future in most respects, COSATU opted to retain its autonomy, emerging virtually as a political party seeking political as well as labour reforms. In the months ahead it was to wield its mass labour clout with crushing effect on the economy, despite suffering the state's blows against political opposition, particularly in the form of detentions of its leaders.

Two days before Christmas 1985, holiday shoppers were wandering outside an ice cream parlour in a crowded arcade in the Natal seaside resort of Amanzimtoti when a bomb hidden in a dustbin exploded, killing five whites, among them a two-year-old, and injuring sixty-one people of all races. Referring to his earlier warning that unarmed civilians would not necessarily remain off limits to Umkhonto guerrillas, Oliver Tambo told journalists: 'If I had been approached by an ANC unit and asked whether they should go and plant a bomb at a supermarket, I would have said, "Of course not." But when our units are faced with what is happening all around them, it is understandable that some of them should say, "Well, I may have to face being disciplined, but I am going to do this".'

Christmas Day brought a bloody clash of spears, clubs and shotguns between supporters of the two largest black groups vying for domination in black politics: 2 000 Zulu followers of Chief Gatsha Buthelezi and 3 000 members of the Pondo tribe, close kinsfolk of the Xhosas, who are largely loyal to the ANC. Based on historical rivalries as well as divisions over the extent to which violence should be used to further the struggle and whether blacks should compromise on demands for universal suffrage, the Christmas Day conflict cost fifty-eight people their lives – a death toll which was to multiply manyfold before the fighting ended.

In a speech early in the New Year, Tambo promised to 'continue to make South Africa ungovernable'. The ANC's goal was 'the destruction of the apartheid regime and the transfer of power to the people', he said. Less than a month later the government demonstrated its own power by engineering a military coup in Lesotho, toppling the administration of Chief Leabua Jonathan and installing Major General Justin Lekhanya, who immediately began expelling ANC militants from the country.

While the coup was under way in the neighbouring state, two white policemen were hacked to death by a crowd of 500 unionists resisting a police attempt to ban a meeting near Johannesburg. Armoured vehicles sealed off the nearby black township as police arrested eighty-six people, detaining 250 others for interrogation.

Then violence erupted in Alexandra, a township situated unusually close to white suburbs. Thousands of mourners returning from the funerals of two black victims of clashes with authorities began hurling stones at police. Sealing off the township, troops took up positions on access roads while helicopters hovered overhead and truckloads of soldiers protected roads leading into surrounding white areas. Twenty-three Africans died in four days of street fighting.

An uneasy calm fell over the townships. In March, nine months after first introducing the partial state of emergency, Botha declared that levels of violence had improved enough to rescind the crisis restrictions. But the violence persisted. Three weeks later, thirty Africans were killed in confrontations with police.

The hated pass laws were repealed in April, involving the immediate release from prison of all those held for pass offences. Over 100 000 blacks had been arrested during the previous year for pass violations. In future, said Botha, they would be obliged to carry the same identity documents as were issued to whites. Hailed in Washington as a 'major milestone on the road away from apartheid' and by the respected South African Institute of Race Relations as 'the most important reform in South Africa since World War II', it left black militants unimpressed. 'Apartheid cannot be reformed,' said a UDF spokesman. 'It must be eradicated.' However, the *Sowetan* newspaper conceded that the end of the pass laws would 'affect the person who matters most – the man in the street'.

During 1986 a new form of government-sponsored violence began to escalate: black vigilante activity directed at the destruction of anti-apartheid institutions and activities. Groups of self-seeking, reactionary blacks, willing to serve white masters at the expense of the struggle, began attacking and in some instances killing militant black supporters of the ANC, the UDF, COSATU and other organisations. 'There are right-wing elements of our community ready to be used by the authorities to blunt the edge of liberation forces,' said Murphy Morobe, chief spokesman for the UDF. Brutal fighting between vigilantes and activists broke out at Crossroads, resulting in at least thirty-two deaths and the burning of thousands of shacks.

The toll at Crossroads brought total deaths since violence began in September 1984 to nearly 1 500. In all, 3 477 private black homes, over 7 000 buses and 10 000 other vehicles had been damaged or destroyed. Repairing public losses had cost the South African taxpayer well over 200 million rand. Almost half of the country's black schoolchildren had participated in classroom boycotts. Umkhonto we Sizwe's attacks had escalated from eighty-eight between June and December the previous year to 118 in the first half of 1986.

The violence continued. Four days before the tenth anniversary of the Soweto uprising, one of the most hallowed days on the black opposition's calendar, the government cracked down with a vengeance. Declaring a national state of emergency, Botha aimed to crush the country's 24 million blacks and muzzle the media. Journalists were prevented from reporting anything about the security situation except material released by the government, and they could not name any of the estimated 3 000 mainly black activists arrested and detained immediately after the emergency declaration. Thus 16 June appeared to pass quietly, as far as anyone outside the townships could tell.

However, there was uproar overseas in response to the emergency, which placed the country under virtual martial law. In Paris 1 000 demonstrators marched on the South African embassy; 5 000 staged a protest in The Hague. The House of Representatives in the United States approved a total trade embargo against South Africa except for materials deemed strategically important to the US. As fury raged abroad, tempers grew shorter in the corridors of power at home. Foreign minister Pik Botha, seen as a moderate among Nationalists, railed about 'a Western world that is sick. They could not care less about us ... [They] can hurt us, threaten us, damage our economy, but they cannot kick us out of our own land.'

The liberal newspaper, *Business Day*, commented: 'Few South Africans and fewer foreigners ... have grasped the extent of the gravity of the change that has occurred in the country's affairs in recent weeks ... the hawks in the cabinet ... have finally defeated the doves.'

Stalemate settled in. The preceding years had seen Botha making superficial changes to apartheid, but his position remained light years away from the demands of the ANC and its allies. They insisted that Nelson Mandela and all other political prisoners be released unconditionally; that the ANC and all other banned political groups be legalised; and that the tricameral constitution be replaced with one giving blacks the vote.

During two years of bloody battle, anti-government forces had gone from strength to strength. The ANC's underground organisation, still based on Mandela's M-Plan, had become a national network of secret cells linking one street to another, one township to another, one province to the next. The formation of the UDF had made cohesive nationwide protest campaigns possible by uniting community organisations but leaving responsibility for actual resistance at local level.

However, a strategic turnaround was under way in the ANC, with some favouring a general insurrection. As the constraints on expanding military activities became apparent, though, the ideas of those in the organisation who favoured a negotiated settlement – like Thabo Mbeki – came to the fore.

The UDF and COSATU, having the same political objectives, continued to plan together, enabling strikes in the workplace and boycotts in the townships to be summoned simultaneously for maximum impact. The result was unprecedented grassroots support and a countrywide infrastructure of resistance which, though lying apparently dormant while activists adapted to the state's oppressive laws, would surely rise again.

14

FREEDOM BECKONS

'Those who wish to create the future must not lose sight of the past,' said Boer War leader Paul Kruger on his deathbed in 1904. His final vision was of a past and a future in which Afrikaners stuck together and fought for the right to rule South Africa. Under Kruger's leadership, the Boers had taken up arms rather than surrender to the British. Though divided earlier by a civil war, Afrikaners clung to their 'unity of purpose' under Kruger and, as he predicted, they proceeded after his death to re-establish 'that which now lies in ashes'. But Kruger's guiding philosophy for the future was to be cast aside some eighty years after his death. 'Never forget the serious warning which lies in the saying "divide and rule"', he had said in his final message. 'May these words never be applied to the Afrikaner people.'

By 1987 Kruger's dream of eternal unity among his people had been shattered. Election results that year proved that Afrikaners had divided into two factions: those who had come to realise they were unable to govern South Africa alone, and those who continued to resist change. The split, while heralding dark days of turmoil in the short term, also marked the beginning of the end of the third empire's rule in South African history. In earlier decades the Zulus had relinquished their power to the British Empire; the colonists were succeeded by Afrikaner supremacy. Once Afrikaners began to grope for ways to share power with the disenfranchised majority, they were in effect trying to create political structures to replace those of their own forty-year-old empire.

However, the insurrection that swept through black townships during 1984-86 never threatened the basic power of the South African state. It was smothered by armed repression, ushering in a painful age that spurned liberty and tolerance. Severe press censorship, judicial infringements, bans on opposition organisations, and prolonged detention of thousands of activists cast the country's frail white democratic traditions into mortal danger. United Democratic Front (UDF) official Murphy Morobe, who spoke to a journalist shortly before his arrest in 1987, saw no hope of decisive change for at least a decade. 'Looking at the present scenario here, one could easily come to the belief that there is no prospect that the democratic forces will come to power. The struggle could take another ten to fifteen years – for the pessimistic, twenty. But the events of the past five years show a clear development in a positive direction.'

The gains made by the ANC in the 1980s were indeed substantial when measured in terms of a liberation movement – the oldest in the world – that had struggled for over three-quarters of a century with scant impact on the balance of power in South Africa. The organisation's diplomacy had flourished abroad as never before, shifting world approval firmly away from exclusive white rule to the belief that the ANC alone could negotiate with whites in order to end the conflict in South Africa. This harmony with international opinion, combined with the world's abhorrence of apartheid, enabled the ANC to help orchestrate economic sanctions and disinvestment on a scale that had by 1990 left the average South African, white as well as black, one-third poorer than they would have been without sanctions.

Umkhonto we Sizwe's guerrilla attacks had increased to a point which unnerved the white population. MK's improved skill as an underground movement and the exiled ANC's success in marshalling widespread militancy in tandem with organisations like the UDF and COSATU, gave the ANC the lead among contending black power groups. A marked degree of internal unity flowed from Nelson Mandela's worldwide status as the courageous symbol of the struggle.

These gains were nowhere near sufficient to topple a state which had not even begun to flex its formidable military muscle, though. There was no prospect of a black counter-force capable of challenging the South African army in its own territory. All that remained to secure the revolutionary victory that militant blacks sought, or the more likely negotiated compromise which the ANC might someday accept, was the whites' will to resist change. Power would clearly remain with the whites until the ruling group believed it to be in its own interests to relinquish control. 'There will be a situation of increased conflict for some time to come,' said the ANC's chief spokesman, Thabo Mbeki, 'but in the end the many sensible whites in South Africa will tire of false hopes and promises. They will see that things are going in the opposite direction to the words of their leaders and they will at last realise that it is only a democratic South Africa that will secure the future for Afrikaners.'

Along the way to those negotiations, South Africa's white rulers would continue to offer selected black leaders a role in national affairs. Some accepted personal power and became Pretoria's black limousine bureaucrats. Like Nelson Mandela's cousin and boyhood friend KD Matanzima who, with his brother, George, embezzled some R45-million during his years at the helm of the Transkei's bantustan administration, they would be judged as traitors in the history of the struggle. The ANC's possible alliance with Chief Buthelezi, who controlled nearly a third of the total black population, in order to thwart any viable black/white power axis, would remain vulnerable to the state's strategy of ethnic divide-and-rule, leaving the black population in conflict with itself.

Hopes among whites that the increased black prosperity of the bantustan project would militate against hunger for political power could not be realised in a country throttled by trade bans and deprived of external investment. 'South Africa will never be able to muster the resources needed to provide decent living standards and opportunities for its growing population unless it can attract foreign investment,' said Gavin Relly, chairman of the mighty Anglo American Corporation. International sanctions had left South Africa with the sombre reality of recurring increases of 200 000 jobless people every year. Mass unemployment could only leave the tens of thousands of black youths who called one another 'comrade' without an optimistic vision of the future and with nothing to lose by reckless revolt.

Blacks were psychologically ready for confrontation. Many, many youths were prepared to die in pursuit of freedom. Their frustration with the lack of organised protest action available to them during the repressive calm of the late 1980s was growing. And their observation of hardening attitudes among the scores of whites who had abandoned the marginal reform strategies of the ruling National Party in favour of the reinforced apartheid promised by the Conservative Party was threatening to rise up and challenge the ANC's unwavering non-racial commitment. 'We have to step up the armed struggle,' said Umkhonto we Siswe's chief-of-staff Chris Hani, whose popularity among the ANC's rank and file made him a likely candidate for future leader of the ANC. 'If we don't increase our level of violence, we'll risk losing the support of young blacks in the townships.'

Their volatile support was the wild card in the game. It could have provoked a revival of anti-white sentiment on the lines of the long-eclipsed Pan-Africanist Congress's (PAC) policies. The Africanists' insistence on uncompromising socialism, as opposed to the ANC's preference for a mixed economy, as well as their hostility to the concept of any negotiated settlement, could have impeded progress towards talks between significant white and black leaders. Grim echoes of the PAC army's chant of 'one settler, one bullet' and the Conservative Party leader's declaration that 'the time has come to stop using rubber bullets and birdshot and use real bullets' haunted prospects for peace in South Africa.

Africanists were not a serious threat to the ANC, as it turned out, although the organisation had a powerful anti-negotiation lobby within its own ranks. But the government would not talk to the ANC as long as its right-wing white opponents were a more immediate threat to its survival than the black challenge combined with the world's determination to raise the cost of apartheid through sanctions and disinvestment.

A measure of the hurdles confronting the whites who would decide eventually to negotiate with the ANC was the question of the civil service: what would happen to the whites employed in the state sector, numbering nearly half of the economically active Afrikaner population, when a black government inevitably replaced white bureaucrats with black ones? Another major problem would be convincing whites, who had for so many years trusted their government's anti-ANC propaganda, that the ANC was not, after all, a communist Soviet surrogate hell-bent on red revolution.

Said Thabo Mbeki, son of one of the ANC's most revered leaders, Govan Mbeki, and the man widely favoured alongside Chris Hani as the future leader of the ANC: 'It is not only white South Africans who have to realise that the ANC is not a communist organisation but a national liberation movement. We've struggled in the past with the Americans over this one, and a big battle has raged about it among our own people for decades.

'We have had one goal for seventy-seven years: to get rid of apartheid. Anyone who has accepted that goal has been welcomed into the ANC to join us and help us. The Soviet Union offered us military support, which we accepted because we needed it to achieve our objectives. The South African Communist Party joined us and helped us to confront our common enemy. That does not mean that Christians among us adopted communist ideology, any more than it means we adopted Indian beliefs by working with Indians and accepting their support. It does not mean that communists will prevail in the ANC government. It simply means that we needed to get together and stay together in order to confront this common enemy, apartheid.'

Nevertheless, countless young Africans would continue to study the alternative to a 'mixed economy' that communism offered. The greatest threat to future economic prosperity under majority rule was that blacks might have become so bitterly disillusioned by the capitalist system, identifying it with repression, that they would demand sweeping nationalisation of industry. White businessmen were beginning to realise the urgent need to distance themselves from the apartheid policies which discredited capitalism. But their half-hearted efforts lacked the conviction required to protect the most industrialised economy in Africa from possible nationalisation under ANC rule.

With the richest whites in South Africa – some five per cent of the population – owning eighty-eight per cent of private wealth in the country, and the entire black population owning only two per cent, it was very obvious that any black constituency would demand redistribution of wealth. When racial conciliation was finally negotiated, the ANC would try hard to convince moderately wealthy, skilled whites that the money needed to redress black material grievances would not come from their pockets but from the coffers of the rich. 'We need those whites,' said Umkhonto we Sizwe's commander, Joe Modise. 'We need those skills. We can't run that country alone. We need them to run it. I don't know whether they know how much we need them. But we need them just as much as they need us. They can't run that country alone without us.'

However much whites were eventually reassured that they would not be regarded as aliens in the new country but would proceed with blacks into a mutually prosperous future, Afrikaners would continue to consult the recent history of Africa and despair. Over the previous thirty years, more than seventy leaders in twenty African nations had been deposed in coups and assassinations. Of the forty-one leading black African states at the time, only seven permitted opposition political parties: seventeen were ruled by military juntas and the remainder were one-party states.

The economic picture was equally bleak. With a steady decline in per capita food production in virtually every African country – in a continent with the world's fastest population growth rate – unusual optimism was needed to believe that the future under majority rule would be materially better than the past for most South Africans.

Generally dismal African leadership's inclusion of tyrants like Idi Amin terrified white South Africans. The ANC's own Winnie Mandela, perhaps driven half-mad by security police harassment in response to her often brave resistance during her husband's long years of imprisonment, had become increasingly militant. By the end of 1988, she was criminally involved in child assault and kidnapping. In an infamous case that challenged the judicial system as well as sorely tormenting Nelson Mandela, Winnie had taken a fourteen-year-old called Stompie Seipei Moeketsi to her home and had him beaten to a pulp by her notorious Mandela United Football Club. The boy, suspected of disloyalty to the ANC, was assaulted on Mrs Mandela's orders, as well as by her personally. When he died from his injuries, the Soweto doctor who had unsuccessfully urged her to get Stompie into hospital without delay was shot dead in mysterious circumstances.

Nelson Mandela and his fellow ANC leaders had by this time been moved from Robben Island to a mainland prison, Pollsmoor, where he was kept in isolation and where, in 1985, he began to plan a negotiated settlement with the South African government – but without the knowledge of his colleagues for fear that the initiative would be defeated if leaked to the ANC's rank and file. 'It was clear to me that a military victory was a distant if not impossible dream,' he recalled in his memoirs. 'It simply did not make sense for both sides to lose thousands if not millions of lives in a conflict that was unnecessary. It was time to talk.'

The process had begun somewhat implausibly in 1985 when justice minister Kobie Coetsee visited Mandela at the Cape Town clinic where he was having prostate surgery. 'He dropped by the hospital unannounced, as though he was visiting an old friend who was laid up for a few days,' Mandela recorded in his autobiography. Substantive negotiations began nine months later.

Top South African intelligence officials had been advocating talks with Nelson Mandela since 1984 in the belief that the country would go up in smoke if he died in prison. By Christmas Eve 1986 Coetsee began to prepare the world's most famous prisoner for freedom. Without warning, the deputy commissioner of Pollsmoor told Prisoner 466/64 that the two of them were going for a drive around Cape Town. It was Mandela's first outing in twenty-two years. But when he suddenly found himself alone in the car, he remembers feeling uncomfortably free, his jailer having parked and disappeared into a shop to buy a soft drink.

'As the seconds ticked away, I became more and more agitated ... I had a vision of opening the door, jumping out, and then running and running until

I was out of sight ... I was extremely tense and began to perspire. Where was the colonel? But then I took control of myself; such an action would be unwise and irresponsible, not to mention dangerous ...'

When the official emerged carrying two cans of Coke, Mandela was delighted. Like a tourist, he was driven week after week around the Cape Peninsula, marvelling at its beautiful beaches and stunning mountain views, stopping at cafés for tea, and meeting the family of one of his prison warders. No one recognised him because, though his name was well known throughout the world, no picture of him had been published for a quarter of a century.

Outside the prison's walls, the media saw a state dedicated to ever more brutal repression. People were also dying by Winnie Mandela's vaunted method, the necklace killing. South Africa was in bloody turmoil. Only the country's president, P W Botha, and the ANC's imprisoned leader knew how good the prospects were for peace.

Talking initially to Botha's spymaster Niels Barnard, alongside the genial Coetsee (although some of the ANC's exiled politicians had already made their own contacts with the Nationalists), Mandela asked constantly for a meeting with their leader. He wrote to Botha in 1989, outlining his terms for an honourable peace. The ANC would suspend violence if the government would remove obstacles to negotiation, such as legalising the ANC, releasing prisoners, ending the state of emergency, and withdrawing troops from the townships. First, the two sides would talk about how to create the conditions for talks; then they would enter into full negotiations.

Botha had no intention of accepting such terms – though they were to form the basis of the eventual deal struck with his successor, F W de Klerk – but he decided to meet Mandela. The VIP prisoner's minders were so keen for him to make a good impression on their leader that Pollsmoor's commander insisted on retying Mandela's tie. The tall, intimidating Barnard, whose prominence in the early negotiations had initially disturbed Mandela, stooped to tie the laces of Mandela's shoes, which the stiff, elderly gentleman was no longer able to do on his own.

South Africa's two leaders met on 5 July 1989 in a Cape Town mansion,

Tuynhuys, the official residence of the country's state president – with the old Afrikaner pouring the tea. Mandela was touched by the gesture. 'I came out feeling that I had met a creative, warm head of state who treated me with all the respect and dignity I could expect,' he said later. Botha was 'unfailingly courteous, deferential and friendly ... He completely disarmed me.'

Forty-seven secret meetings were held between a few tight-lipped government officials and 'the Old Man', as they referred to Mandela, over the two years leading to his release on 11 February 1990. Freedom – eventually in the bag after the Convention for a Democratic South Africa (CODESA) ended successfully in 1993 – was mainly the result of Mandela's ability to convince such Afrikaners as Coetsee and Barnard that he had the best interests of their mutual nation, South Africa, at heart. Remarkably, they came to trust him with their own fate.

15

THE ANC IN POWER

South Africa's first democratic election was held in April 1994. Archbishop Desmond Tutu, voting for the first time in his life, declared: 'It is an incredible feeling, like falling in love ... It's like a new birth. We are going to be the rainbow people of the world.'

After an eighty-two-year struggle for a non-racial society, the ANC swept to victory with 252 of the 400 seats in the new parliament. When the new legislators gathered in Cape Town for the first time, they chose Nelson Mandela as their State President. In a stirring climax to a legendary struggle, he was inaugurated the next day in the amphitheatre of Pretoria's Union Buildings before 150 monarchs and heads of government.

The nation's rebirth had come perilously close to collapse over the preceding months, hovering on the brink of civil war as the Zulu Inkatha movement, die-hard white conservatives and 'independent' bantustan governments threatened to use force to thwart inevitable ANC rule. When Chris Hani was found dead in a pool of blood by his young daughter in the driveway of their home on Easter Saturday 1993 the abyss had beckoned particularly alarmingly. But freedom broke through the chaos, and what a joy the post-election celebrations were for struggle weary South Africans.

Everything positive and progressive seemed possible when the triumphant liberation movement took over in 1994. Having won admiration internationally for its peaceful transition to democracy after centuries of conflict, hopes were high that the most admired man on the planet, Nelson Mandela, would conquer the nation's bitter divisions.

During the ANC's early years in power, South Africa was run collaboratively by Nelson Mandela and his deputy, Thabo Mbeki. Madiba, as the elder statesman was affectionately known, concentrated on the reconciliation work that so urgently needed to be done in the racially tormented country, and for which he had unusual talent and enthusiasm. Mbeki took care of the dauntingly diverse administrative reforms involved in dismantling apartheid.

Although the ANC had inherited an economy that was virtually bankrupt after years of sanctions and mismanagement, with the country's assets almost exclusively in white hands, the new government had an array of promising solutions to the world's worst inequality. To spread wealth a little more evenly, it introduced black economic empowerment (BEE), the idea being to create a black middle class. Companies with more than fifty employees and revenues of at least R5 million a year were to be given a rating based on how much of their equity was owned by blacks, how many of the top posts were held by the formerly disadvantaged, what training opportunities were open to them, and so forth. The higher a company's rating, the better its chances of being awarded lucrative public contracts.

Another black empowerment project involved the country's land, which blacks had not even been allowed to rent under the Land Act of 1913. By 1994, eighty-seven per cent of South Africa's agricultural tracts belonged to whites. As the ANC had long intended, the new government quickly announced that it would redistribute thirty per cent of white-owned farms to poor blacks within five years on a 'willing buyer, willing seller' basis. Alongside this reform, it announced an end to the feudal work relationship that had afflicted farm workers for generations.

Clearing out most of the country's white civil servants (including talented teachers and some of South Africa's best-qualified police officers and town planners) by offering generous severance packages, the ANC was soon boasting about the proportion of whites in the public sector having fallen from forty-four per cent to eighteen per cent. That they were usually replaced by inexperienced and often poorly qualified ANC loyalists was not considered a problem compared with the obviously pressing need for the ANC to provide jobs for its supporters.

But although wholesale employment of blacks instead of whites and all manner of affirmative action was understandable and just in the circumstances, the former oppressor had unfortunately set the ANC up to fail in government by withholding quality education from blacks under apartheid and by failing to provide anything more than menial employment opportunities for Africans during half a century of National Party rule.

Perhaps inevitably, given Africa's post-colonial track record of bad governance, things began to go wrong. Not only did inefficiencies and mismanagement escalate in daily life in the form of rampant crime due to poor policing, electricity blackouts, declining education and health facilities and standards, as well as innumerable potholes on roads nationwide, but the ANC's system of 'cadre deployment' – the appointment of loyal party members to well-paid public posts for which they were not necessarily suitably qualified – made matters steadily worse.

Thabo Mbeki, having succeeded Mandela as president in 1999, brought a brief Africanist twist to the ANC's increasingly erratic decisions. An intense, thin-skinned politician who had played an important role in the psychological conquest of Afrikanerdom, Mbeki smoked thoughtfully on a pipe, a habit that came across as urbane and created the sense of a black Englishman whose sophistication was far removed from white stereotypes of Africans. Having been one of the few visible ANC leaders while he was in exile, however, Mbeki's fault lines were apparent early on – control freakery, a soft spot for pompous presentations as well as a tendency to make decisions that were clouded by race.

Bringing his underground paranoia with him from Lusaka, Mbeki's instability at the helm became apparent in 2001 when he accused three of his rivals – Cyril Ramaphosa, Mathews Phosa and Tokyo Sexwale – of plotting to oust him. In exile, the mere mention of internal ANC sabotage or spying would have been enough to destroy an opponent. Furthermore, Mbeki's eccentric ideas on Zimbabwe's rocky road to democracy alienated many of his former admirers. He then made a fool of himself as the entire world condemned his inexplicable and heartless Aids denialism. These were serious blunders which became his legacy, despite a lifetime's dedication to the struggle.

As his popularity waned at home and respect for him died abroad, President Mbeki expressed his acute wariness of whites a few months before being deposed by his beloved ANC. He spoke bitterly and embarrassingly during a public lecture in 2007 of the 'challenge to defeat the centuries-old attempt to dwarf the significance of our manhood, to treat us as children, to define us as subhumans whom nature has condemned to be inferior to white people, an animal-like species characterised by limited intellectual capacity, bestiality, lasciviousness and moral depravity, obliged in our own interest to accept that the white segment of humanity should, in perpetuity, serve as our lord and master.'

Thinking Africans expressed disapproval at the way some of their prominent peers played the race card when things displeased them. But relations between the racial groups were remarkably cordial, on the surface at least and considering the history, though there were still enormous reservations on both sides, to which sparse social mixing testified. Like Mbeki, most South Africans tried to be even-handed but remained racially and ethnically prejudiced. A few months after he was turfed out of office, a series of horrific xenophobia attacks across South Africa left 62 dead and 670 injured.

Mbeki was a talented mediator who brought a long war in the Congo to a close. Since 2003, fighting in that country has been intermittent and localised, and there can be no doubt that Mbeki's 2002 Sun City Agreement saved hundreds of thousands of lives.

He was also an able administrator, introducing masses of vital legislation and human rights reforms. But he drove the country towards centralised control, seriously damaging the efficacy of parliament in the process. His Africanism meant that whites became less evident in the state's top, highly skilled positions even though blacks lacked the skills and experience to fill the gaps. Some whites had emigrated, but a 2007 study found only 1 400 civil engineers left in local government (three for every 100 000 citizens, compared with twenty-one two decades earlier). One-third of local authorities had no engineers of any sort. Only seven per cent of sewage treatment plants met international standards. 'The terrible shortage of human capital is now the single most important reason for questioning South Africa's ability to move forward,' according to Azar Jammine, head of the consultancy Econometrix.

BEE did not spread equality as intended. Creating some extremely wealthy black individuals and a small African middle class very rapidly during Mbeki's presidency, it failed to benefit the masses. Redistribution of land on a consensual basis was so poorly administered that it resulted in only six per cent of farms having changed hands by 2010. The government's attempts to liberate farm labourers by trying to force employers to take material responsibility for resident workers and their families resulted instead in large numbers of unskilled rural black people being evicted by white farmers. The subsequent boiling over of deep resentments − coupled with increased expectations of imminent change from farm dwellers as well as their employers' fears of the new dispensation − so hardened attitudes on both sides that over 3 000 white farmers and members of their families have been murdered in isolated homesteads since 1994 by mainly disaffected, dispossessed former farm workers.

There have been many achievements in South Africa since 1994, the ANC's successes in office outweighing the failures in the eyes of the majority of its citizens − most of whom still vote for the party in regular, well-organised elections. Apart from the ascendancy of black rule having purged South Africans of the pain and indignity of apartheid, the country has provided welfare benefits for 15 million people; been welcomed back into the international community; cut its murder rate by fifty per cent over recent years; almost eradicated severe malnutrition among the under-fives; increased school enrolment to nearly one hundred per cent; and established the world's biggest antiretroviral treatment programme for HIV/AIDS.

The worst problem confronting the ANC in office is corruption, both moral and material. 'I didn't join the struggle to be poor,' said Smuts Ngonyama defensively when accused of unfair business practices in 2007. His remark epitomised a prevailing culture of entitlement in the ruling party. Paul Hoffman of the South African Institute for Accountability estimates that corruption is endemic throughout the public sector, partly because so few cases are prosecuted. 'From top to bottom, the attitude seems to be: if everyone else is able to act with impunity, why shouldn't I?' He estimates that about a third of the ANC's 86-member national executive committee have been investigated for fraud or other criminal activity – including the party's fourth post-apartheid leader, Jacob Zuma.

As the president following Kgalema Motlanthe – the caretaker who stepped elegantly into the job for a few months after Mbeki's unseemly removal from power by a populist alliance at Polokwane in the last days of 2007 – Zuma was a professional spy and former head of ANC Intelligence during the liberation years. A proud Zulu, well liked by most of his political colleagues, he lacked Mbeki's sharp, educated approach but his gentle wit and genuine non-racialism made him a favourite among Afrikaner negotiators in the distrustful atmosphere that prevailed at the time of Nelson Mandela's release from prison.

He was the first of the ANC's exiled leaders to be smuggled into South Africa to make arrangements for the return of the organisation's guerrillas and diplomats in 1990. Descending the steps of the plane from Lusaka, he remembers being shoved into the back seat of a government vehicle alongside the general who headed apartheid's brutal police. 'Basie Smit was very keen to sit next to me,' recalled Zuma, with a typical throaty chuckle, in an interview with author Patti Waldmeir. After sharing copious quantities of grilled meat and hard liquor, he was taken under cover of darkness on a tour of the Voortrekker Monument, the sandstone shrine built to celebrate the triumph of a few hundred Afrikaners over thousands of Zulu warriors at the Battle of Blood River in 1838. Recalling with much laughter the announcement on state radio the following day that police had issued a warrant for his arrest, he realised that the situation in the country was so volatile that the police chief dared not tell even his own men that he had been supping with a terrorist.

Polygamous Zuma, adored by his wives, fiancées, and twenty-one children, is a shrewd politician – but no leader. Having aspired to office in deeply compromised circumstances, with fraud charges looming ahead and a rape acquittal behind him, he cultivated a fickle support base that spanned a good deal of the ANC's political spectrum, persuading each faction that he had its interests at heart. As a result, he was hopelessly indebted for his election as president to more than one powerful grouping, most notably to the head of the ANC Youth League (ANCYL), Julius Malema, a boyish-looking thirty-year-old born, like the majority of South Africans, into poverty, who epitomises a new culture of chaos in the ANC.

In addition to the favours Zuma owed, he struggled constantly with the factionalism that had marked the ANC's transition from revolutionary movement. Trying to satisfy everybody from free-marketeers to out-and-out Marxists, the national power vacuum yawned dangerously. By 2011, Zuma was becoming less popular among rank and file members of the ANC for his failure to improve their living conditions. Pressure began to mount on him from all sides as the country waited for him to prove himself worthy of the presidency. Malema's racist outbursts, random insults, loud demands for Zimbabwe-style land invasions and nationalisation of mines had by then alarmed his old sponsors and embarrassed the government to such an extent, leaving much-needed foreign investment and job creation in the doldrums, that the youth leader was eventually charged with bringing the party into disrepute for advocating that the government of Botswana be overthrown.

But the conflicts of interest in Zuma's populist administration continued to pile up. Whether reflected in foreign policy bungles and hypocrisy – such as barring the Dalai Lama from the country lest South Africa's partner in the BRICS trade alliance, China, take offence; or the ANC's inability under successive leaders to broker democracy in neighbouring Zimbabwe; or its failure to take a coherent position on Libya's revolution – or in the continuing service delivery impotence due to 'cadre deployment' that so infuriated ANC voters, Zuma failed to lead on just about every occasion that the country most needed his guidance. In some respects it was not entirely his fault, since the message sent out by the party's shabby treatment of former president Mbeki was that it did not want a leader who led from the front, especially if the market-friendly direction he chose was not popular. However, South Africa's social, political and economic circumstances – in which progress towards a fairer society had by most measures been superficial – created a fertile environment for demagogues like Malema.

Sadly, things had begun to fall apart. The ANC in-fighting that has characterised its governance had become evident in many public institutions, notably the SABC. Walter Sisulu's journalist son Zwelakhe did a good job of trying to transform the state broadcaster during the 1990s, but he left amid acrimony. Not a single CEO of the corporation has since enjoyed a term of office without controversy. For that matter, no fewer than a dozen big state-owned companies have found themselves without a chief executive over recent years after their black bosses were sacked or forced to resign amid allegations of mismanagement, corruption – or both.

Corruption at all levels had begun to seem unstoppable. The infamous arms deal in the late 1990s, especially in respect of who got what share of the loot and how much of it went into ANC leadership campaigns, has haunted the government since the Mandela era. Both Swedish and German arms dealers have admitted paying vast 'consultation fees' for contracts in South Africa, but the truth of who benefited remains a closely guarded secret. Zuma's personal opportunism has led to calls for greater scrutiny of state tenders awarded to his extended family, dubbed Zuma Inc for its questionable business dealings in sectors of the economy where the state plays a key role, like mining and telecommunications. Nothing speaks more damningly of corruption and 'cadre deployment' than Zuma's appointment to the post of police commissioner of a loyal but completely inexperienced man to replace the previously disgraced and imprisoned incumbent, Jackie Selebi.

Another post-apartheid failure with tragic consequences for the poor and for the country's future is education. With forty per cent unemployment and a crippling skills shortage, the ANC might reasonably have been expected to focus more political energy on improving the inferior schools it inherited in formerly blacks-only areas. Instead, despite spending six per cent of its GDP and the biggest chunk of its annual budget on education, school results have actually declined under ANC rule, not least because most teachers in the public sector are not properly trained. Graeme Bloch of the Development Bank of Southern Africa describes South Africa's education system as 'a national disaster'. He estimates that eighty per cent of schools are 'dysfunctional'. Even education minister Angie Motshekga admits that black schools are 'in crisis'. Half of all pupils drop out before taking their final exams, and only eleven per cent get good enough passes to qualify for university. Alarmingly, this implies that an under-educated class will lead the country for some time to come.

Largely to blame for its education debacle were inappropriate ANC policies, such as outcomes-based schooling, which had already been discredited elsewhere by the time it was adopted in South Africa. In addition, a narrow focus on BEE as empowerment, whereas education is the most obviously effective empowerment tool in the country's circumstances, discredits the ANC's policy priorities.

Further mocking the ANC's long struggle for equality is the state's declining health system, South Africa's health record being among the worst in the world. An ambitious national health insurance scheme with upgraded facilities has been proposed, but there are widespread doubts as to its funding and management viability.

With one of the world's most admired constitutions to South Africa's credit, Zuma's manipulation of legal checks and balances and of media freedom are shamelessly self-serving. While threatened repressive measures targeting journalists and whistleblowers will surely breach the constitution and be challenged in its court in due course, there is barely any plausible defence of the ANC's integrity left under Zuma's leadership. Having fared badly as an individual at the hands of both jurists and journalists due to his own criminal activities, Zuma simply decided to reshape South Africa's institutional landscape to suit himself. Because he was preoccupied with ensuring that fraud charges – which he had managed to sweep away unlawfully in order to become president – would not be reinstated, he appointed some blindly loyal and questionably qualified political allies to positions that matter in the judicial cluster, including those of police commissioner, public prosecutor and chief justice. These moves ensured that, as long as Zuma remained in charge, he would not be arrested again.

The Institute for Democracy in South Africa (IDASA) reckons that prolonged dominant-party rule by the ANC is already eroding many of the safeguards enshrined in the constitution, including the separation of powers. Accountability is being weakened, public watchdogs are being undermined and party and state are becoming increasingly conflated. Nevertheless, free and fair elections are held on schedule and the country does not suffer from despotic rule or personality cult, IDASA notes.

A year away from what he hopes will be his re-election for a second term in 2012, Zuma suffered the humiliation of seeing his own image being burnt outside ANC headquarters at Johannesburg's Luthuli House during violent demonstrations against Julius Malema's disciplinary hearing. More significantly, and to the consternation of many ANC stalwarts, the young demonstrators also set fire to the party's famous black, green and gold flag. The following day, a spokesperson for the ANC Veterans' Association, Kebby Maphatsoe, expressed astonishment at such turmoil within the organisation. 'We believe that the movement of Nelson Mandela is under threat by those who are supposed to inherit it,' he said. 'Our hearts are still in pain for the unforgivable act of burning the ANC flag and the raiding of Luthuli House.'

Despite the ANC being at the height of its powers, its future is today less certain than at any time in its long history. In the past, the organisation went through two enormous transformations with remarkable agility; the first at the instigation of the hot-headed young rebel, Nelson Mandela. He brought about changes that drove the organisation from gentlemanly protests to armed resistance.

The second great shake-up in the ANC occurred twenty-two years ago as

Mandela emerged from prison, when the liberation movement transformed itself from deep socialist militancy to centre-left political conformity. It was at the time dominated by realistic and courageous leaders like Mandela, Sisulu and Tambo, who are no longer steering the great juggernaut through the third revolution that is now under way. Whether the ANC, with its current leadership, still has the flexibility to transform itself and survive the anarchistic onslaught of politicians like Julius Malema remains to be seen.

The ANC's struggle for liberty and equality was supposed to have ended with its election to office in 1994, when it defeated apartheid. But rampant unemployment, income distribution as skewed as anywhere on earth, and lingering racial tensions cast shadows that lengthen by the year. Many of the organisation's supporters decry today's ANC because South Africa has not yet been transformed into the proud rainbow nation for which Nelson Mandela fought and suffered nearly three decades of imprisonment. A hundred years of struggle, but for whom? they ask. While the country came together exuberantly to host a successful football World Cup in 2010, it seems that even a hundred years of struggle – and it *has* been a monumental struggle – against inhumanity, greed and abuse of power has not been long enough to secure a 'better life for all', as the ANC promised.

EPILOGUE

Nelson Mandela was a vivid presence for me long before he came out of prison. Although the picture I had of him in my mind, with a slightly off-centre middle parting, was no longer his hairstyle when he walked from jail to freedom in February 1990, he looked as familiar as the world's greatest celebrity – which he had become.

Madiba, as South Africans call him, impacted a lot of lives, including mine. I doubt he will ever fade into the mists of fame as some stars do, certainly not in my heart. His biggest idea was to liberate the oppressor as well as the oppressed, thereby setting us all free. At first, he was a potentially life-changing force beckoning from afar but later, on his release after twenty-seven years behind bars, he became the single most important conqueror of apartheid.

He was the father not only of his own nation but of a universe deprived of true heroes. Actually, he was like nothing on earth when he appeared, smiling, outside those prison gates. As the best man in the world, what a reputation he had to uphold. And how fortunate we were as South Africans, a troubled lot, to have such a wonderful person to guide us.

This is why, when I began to analyse the ANC's record in power and found that its greatest defect was corruption, I had to think hard about the fact that

South Africa's shameful arms deal — the start of its faulty governance — was sealed during Mandela's presidency.

Like other journalists, I had long known of a couple of lapses in Madiba's moral leadership, which had become virtually unmentionable in the legacy of his towering achievements. I debated the worrying matter of referring to them with various people, some of whom thought I should shut up.

It was painful, I must say, to reach the conclusion nevertheless that Madiba had made some bad calls during his otherwise exemplary life and that these should be aired. So rarely are they discussed due to global admiration for him that one shrinks from the burden of including his worst decisions in the crisis of corruption that currently undermines the ANC's long struggle for equality. But the truth ought not to be a variable for some and not others, even though in Madiba's case the wrongs are so overwhelmingly dwarfed by the rights.

If Nelson Mandela has slowly begun to lose his aura of sainthood as a result of the odd whispered revelation — just as corruption and incompetence have emerged to taint the ANC administration he once led — it is largely due to his attempts to protect his wife from the consequences of her recklessness and cruelty. He always insisted he was a mere mortal, saying firmly on one occasion: 'I'm an ordinary person, I have made serious mistakes, I have serious weaknesses.' As to persistent rumours of mismanaged money, one has to bear in mind that the struggle generation, especially those who were imprisoned for long periods, had absolutely no money to use or misuse. As Madiba once told Ghaleb Cachalia in response to a question about spiralling corruption among state officials, those ANC members grabbing whatever they could lay hands on from government coffers were like deprived kids let loose in a sweetshop for the first time. If Mandela was soft on corruption, turning a blind eye to fraudulent activities such as the trend-setting arms deal that occurred on his watch, it may have been because they seemed relatively inconsequential compared to the huge things he had fought for and against all his life.

His former wife Winnie had wantonly squandered the international respect she once enjoyed, though many South Africans remain loyal to her regardless of the criminality for which she became infamous. Dispassionate commentators have speculated that Nelson Mandela was made by nearly three decades of imprisonment, in the sense that his human weaknesses – the alleged womanising some journalists have lately investigated, for example – could not discredit his admirable political resolve; whereas Winnie was destroyed by too much 'freedom' for similar reasons of human frailty.

I remember Ruth Bhengu, a reporter from the *Sowetan*, telling a group of journalists about her first encounter with Madiba. She had been called to Winnie's house in March 1992 after hearing that Mrs Mandela, drunkenly brandishing a firearm, was causing a commotion. On arrival in the early morning gloom, with notebook in hand, Ruth found Winnie forcibly evicting one of her lodgers, Xoliswa Falati, from an outside room after an argument in which Winnie's former friend had threatened to rescind untrue legal evidence she had given in court on Mrs Mandela's behalf. The woman's possessions were flying through the air while Winnie shouted obscenities. One bystander found an uncashed cheque for a large sum of money made out to Mrs Mandela and signed by pop singer Lionel Richie blowing in the wind amid hundreds of scattered documents.

Arriving almost simultaneously at the scene was ANC President Nelson Mandela. Summoned, like Ruth Bhengu, by Winnie's victim, he had not expected to find a journalist there. Madiba had come to save Winnie from herself, bringing a locksmith to enable the tenant to get back into her room. While the man was busy with the door, Mandela strolled up to Bhengu, telling her he would rather she did not write about the affair despite his belief in a strong and free press: this particular story was a domestic issue and would only cause trouble, he said.

Bhengu told her editor, Moegsien Williams, about Madiba's warning but she went ahead and wrote the story. Before it had gone to press, however, Williams received a call from 'the Old Man' to ascertain that it would not appear. Mandela told the editor that exposure of Winnie's behaviour could jeopardise her chances of being acquitted on an upcoming appeal against the kidnapping and assault of a little boy from Tumahole called Stompie Seipei Moeketsi. Williams knew from a conversation he had had earlier in the day with Winnie's evicted tenant that some sort of cover-up had occurred, and he realised that the internationally respected Nelson Mandela was endorsing the deception, but he courageously went ahead and published the report.

Not long afterwards, Ruth Bhengu met Madiba at a social event. He remembered her and said so, putting his arm around her rather pointedly as if commending her integrity, or so she felt.

By that time Mandela had separated from the mesmerisingly beautiful Winnie, which must have been incredibly hard for him to do when he had loved and admired her so much during his lonely years in prison. That he felt a profound sense of guilt for the hardships she had endured in his absence was reflected in the lengths to which he went in trying to spare her the punishment she was due in the ghastly Stompie case. Included was the strange disappearance on the eve of Winnie's trial of key prosecution witness Katiza Cebekhulu, who was later found on the verge of death in a Zambian prison. A British MP who questioned Kenneth Kaunda, Zambia's president at the time of Cebekhulu's incarceration, was told that he had been jailed without charge because Nelson Mandela 'wanted Katiza Cebekhulu here and out of South Africa ... He didn't give me any reason at all. What I did was to work on trust.'

Mandela met Cebekhulu during a visit to Zambia in September 1992, listened attentively to his story, and promised to get him out of jail without delay. But nothing happened until the prisoner went on a hunger strike a year later and the United Nations High Commission for Refugees eventually secured his release in December 1993.

Madiba's status as a moral giant will doubtless survive such lapses of judgement and pity, to which all human beings occasionally succumb while negotiating the many contradictions of life. That he was known, furthermore, as a bit of an autocrat is not surprising given his age and royal Xhosa ancestry. It explains, for instance, why he began negotiations with the apartheid government despite not having a mandate from his colleagues in the ANC: such secret decisions might be undemocratic but they are occasionally necessary for brave leaders to take.

There were times in Mandela's presence far from the limelight when you could see how honourable he was by nature. An incident following the death of his struggle colleague Maulvi Cachalia during his presidency is a good example. I had gone straight to a community hall in Mayfair on hearing that people were gathering there to salute the human rights activist.

Madiba was flying to an official function when he was informed that his old friend and ally had passed away, but he immediately changed course. We all stood up as soon as Nelson Mandela walked into the crowded room. Someone started singing *Nkosi Sikilel' iAfrika*. Most of the hastily assembled group were South Africans of Indian descent; every one a staunch ANC supporter. As had been customary throughout the liberation years, they sang the African part of the moving hymn-cum-anthem that day, although the ANC had negotiated a new national anthem incorporating it as well as the Afrikaans equivalent and a bit of English. Then we sat down to hear our president speak.

Madiba tended to treat the deaths of his old comrades as a natural part of life, perhaps even in those days preparing us for the time when we would have to bid him farewell. He had been smiling at Amina Cachalia when he walked in. But when the singing stopped, he was suddenly looking furious. He sprang to his feet, saying we had gathered to honour a great democrat, and describing how disappointed he believed Maulvi would have been to hear us singing a 'truncated' version of the country's anthem. 'You negate our achievement,' he scolded us, referring to the civil war he and the other ANC negotiators had averted when they'd made a deal with the former oppressor which included a cumbersome new anthem. I always felt Madiba was my own father, not just the father of the nation, but never more so than when he ticked us off so bluntly that day. It was not a public speech and, in its obvious spontaneity, showed how principled Madiba was generally and how honourable he expected us to be if we'd given our word.

What struck me about the man was how formal yet warm he was. Although interested in all of us when we'd gather around the lunch or dinner table, and especially in his close friends like Amina and Yusuf, of course, he was simultaneously remote. Spending twenty-seven years of his life in a cell not much bigger than a dog kennel and returning to the world as its most revered citizen meant he seldom relaxed, I guess. Once, at Yusuf's eightieth birthday party, when Mandela was still the president of South Africa, he walked onto the veranda and looked around at the Cachalias' guests, who were all hanging back in silence, completely awestruck in his presence. Standing still for a moment, he asked jocularly, 'Doesn't anybody want to clasp me?' I stepped forward, saying, 'I do, Madiba,' and put my arms around him briefly, though he was as stiff as a tree. His use of the odd, old-fashioned word 'clasp' might have been meant as a handshake but I took it as a hug.

When Madiba left the presidency, my friend Amina knew he had not done enough towards HIV/Aids awareness while in office. She and I sometimes talked about this missed opportunity, the result no doubt of South Africa being the only country in the world to face the pandemic while grappling with major political upheaval. It was a blot on Madiba's legacy, we agreed, and I knew Amina had talked to him about it. So when Adam Roberts, the Johannesburg-based correspondent of *The Economist*, asked me at the height of Thabo Mbeki's denialism how best he might approach Mandela to see if he wanted to avail himself of three pages in order to discuss the subject of Aids in one of the world's top newspapers, I took his proposal straight to Amina – who thought it a good idea. She set up a lunch for Roberts to discuss the matter with Madiba a couple of months hence. In the meantime, however, Mbeki made statements suggesting he might finally be remedying his disastrous position on the disease and its causes. So it no longer seemed appropriate for Madiba, always a staunch party man, to challenge Mbeki as we had intended.

Amina went ahead with the lunch that was booked in Madiba's busy diary and to which Roberts and I had already been invited. Changing its purpose from Aids activism to a celebration of Bram Fischer's birthday, she invited a number of other guests, including Arthur Chaskalson, the head of the Constitutional Court. Madiba brought his third wife Graça, who dominated the conversation at her end of the table. Adam Roberts and I were delighted to be next to Madiba, who was wonderfully relaxed that day.

I watched him closely, enjoying his impish jokes and feeling lucky to have such rare access to the world's most admired man. While several women guests were putting the food on the dining room table, he playfully told a mining magnate among us: 'It's not a politically correct thing to say, but I've always thought women's place was in the kitchen.' After insisting on having Perrier water rather than the brand available, he guffawed when Amina asked him loudly, 'Did you have Perrier on Robben Island, Nelson?' He stayed for several hours and kept glancing at Chaskalson, a shy legal boffin who was a nightmare to sit beside socially because he struggled to make small talk and was therefore silent much of the time. Having been a member of the legal team, led by Bram Fischer, that had defended Mandela on treason charges during the Rivonia trial in 1964, he and Mandela knew each other well so when Madiba began to stare at Chaskalson, he looked up and smiled. Mandela then put his hands together and, without looking away from the jurist, joked: 'For those of you who do not know Arthur, he is the man who got me life imprisonment.' To which Chaskalson replied in an instant: 'If I hadn't, you would have been assassinated.'

Once, I showed a charming painting of Madiba with dreadlocks, which my son had given me as a present, to Madiba's legal adviser, Professor 'Fink' Haysom – who used to stay at my Johannesburg guest house during Mandela's presidency. He commented that, despite being told continually that people who used his image commercially ought to pay to do so, Madiba always responded dismissively, saying simply, 'They do it with love'.

I can't tell you how often I have looked at his benign expression in the painting and consciously swept trivia or petty grievances from my mind. It never ceases to amaze me that a man who saw too much of the dark side of humanity could forgive those who had wronged him so grotesquely. Having been driven almost beyond endurance at times in prison, I'm sure, it's hardly surprising that he lost his way now and then. When I see the picture of his kind face amid the unruly dreads, I often think the ultimate meaning of Nelson Mandela for me is that he made the hapless villains among us – who had been raised to be racists – believe that even they were lovable.

AUTHOR'S NOTES

Research for this book began in August 1986 and was conducted in the
Transkei, Lesotho, Zambia, Zimbabwe, London and South Africa. My sources
of information included interviews, books, magazines and newspapers, as
well as documents and commissions of inquiry. The principal published
reference works for each chapter are listed below, together with the interviews
I conducted myself. Further sources, such as numerous copies of the African
National Congress's *Sechaba* magazine, publications from the South African
Institute of Race Relations and other periodicals and documents, have not been
noted individually. Although some of the books listed contributed to more than
one chapter, I have noted each title only once, whereas some of the interviews
provided information for two or more chapters and have been noted in each
instance.

CHAPTER ONE

Research material was gathered in 1986 in and around a village called Qunu, near Umtata, Transkei, where Nelson Mandela grew up. With the help of a translator, I talked to No Ta Tsumbana, a seventy-eight-year-old cousin of Nelson's who spent her early childhood with him, and to Stumo Mandela, aged seventy-seven, another of his cousins who still lived in Qunu. Nelson's older sister Mabel, who lived in her husband's family village in the mountains beyond Qunu, provided most of the material. I also interviewed Kaiser 'KD' Matanzima in Umtata in 1986.

CHAPTER TWO

Research material came from Albertina Sisulu, interviewed in Soweto in 1987; Harry Brigish, in a brief telephone interview in 1987; Jaydev Nasib 'JN' Singh, who spoke with me in Johannesburg in 1988.

Books contributing to this chapter include Burger, J (pseudonym of Leo Marquard), *The Black Man's Burden* (Victor Gollancz, London, 1943); Huddleston, Trevor, *Naught For Your Comfort* (Collins, London, 1956); Desmond, Cosmas, *The Discarded People: An Account of African Resettlement in South Africa* (Penguin, London, 1971); de Ridder, J C, *The Personality of the Urban African in South Africa* (Routledge and Kegan Paul, London, 1961).

CHAPTER THREE

Chief book sources include: Jabavu, D D T, *The Black Problem: Papers and Addresses on Various Native Problems* (Lovedale Press, Alice, 1921); Jabavu, D D T, *Native Disabilities in South Africa* (Lovedale Press, Alice, 1932); Plaatje, Solomon T, *Native Life in South Africa: Before and Since the European War and the Boer Rebellion* (P S King, London, 1916); Davenport, T R H, *The Beginnings of Urban Segregation in South Africa: The Natives (Urban Areas) Act of 1923 and Its Background* (Institute of Social and Economic Research, Rhodes University, Grahamstown, 1971).

CHAPTER FOUR

A comprehensive account of this period came from an interview with Peter 'AP' Mda, who lived in Mafeteng, a small town in the mountains south of Maseru, Lesotho. Ellen Kuzwayo, a South African author who was the Congress Youth League's first secretary, gave me an interview in Soweto in 1987, as did Godfrey Pitje, an early ANCYL member, who talked with me in his Johannesburg law office in 1987.

Principal book sources include: Lodge, Tom, *Black Politics in South Africa since 1945* (Ravan Press, Johannesburg, 1983); Karis, Thomas G and Carter, Gwendolen M, *From Protest To Challenge: A Documentary History of African Politics in South Africa 1882-1964* (4 volumes) (Hoover Institution Press, Stanford, 1972-1977); Walshe, Peter, *The Rise of African Nationalism in South Africa: The African National Congress 1912-1952* (University of California Press, Berkeley and Los Angeles, 1971); Gerhart, Gail M, *Black Power in South Africa: The Evolution of an Ideology* (University of California Press, Berkeley and Los Angeles, 1978); Callinicos, Luli, *Oliver Tambo: His Life and Legacy* (STE Publishers, 2006); Sisulu, Elinor, *Walter and Albertina Sisulu: In Our Lifetime* (David Philip Publishers, 2002).

CHAPTER FIVE

Yusuf Cachalia was an eloquent source of information in an interview I conducted with him in Johannesburg in 1987. David Bopape and Amin Kajee, both leading activists in the 1950s, gave me interviews in Johannesburg in 1987 and 1988 respectively. Betty Shein, a housewife, recalled the days when she worked with Oliver Tambo during an interview in Johannesburg in 1987. Robert Matje, a prominent eastern Cape organiser of numerous ANC campaigns, discussed them with me in a long interview in 1987.

Book references include Kuper, Leo, *Passive Resistance in South Africa* (Yale University Press, New Haven, 1957); Roux, Edward, *Time Longer Than Rope: A History of the Black Man's Struggle for Freedom in South Africa* (University of Wisconsin Press, Madison, 1966); Lodge, Tom, *Mandela, A Critical Life* (Oxford University Press, 2006).

CHAPTER SIX

Helen Joseph and Amina Cachalia supplied information and anecdotal material in a number of interviews in Johannesburg during 1987 and 1988. Indres Naidoo talked to me about the Congress of the People in one of several interviews conducted in Lusaka, Zambia in 1988.

Books on the period which proved enlightening include: Joseph, Helen, *Side By Side: The Autobiography of Helen Joseph* (Zed Books, London, 1986); Matthews, Z K, *Freedom For My People* (David Philip, Cape Town and Johannesburg, 1983); Suttner, Raymond and Cronin, Jeremy, *Thirty Years of the Freedom Charter* (Ravan Press, Johannesburg, 1986); Legum, Colin and Legum, Margaret, *The Bitter Choice: Eight South Africans' Resistance to Tyranny* (Word Publishing, Cleveland, 1968); Lerumo, A (pseudonym of Michael Harmel), *Fifty Fighting Years: The Communist Party of South Africa 1921-1971* (Inkululeko Publications, London, 1971).

CHAPTER SEVEN

Several of the interviewees listed above contributed to my research for this section, including Helen Joseph and Amina Cachalia. I also talked to Suliman Esakjee, a treason trialist, in Johannesburg in 1988.

Books include: Sampson, Anthony, *The Treason Cage: The Opposition on Trial in South Africa* (Heinemann, London, 1958); Hutchinson, Alfred, *The Road to Ghana* (Victor Gollancz, London, 1960); Joseph, Helen, *If This Be Treason* (André Deutsch, London, 1963).

CHAPTER EIGHT

An interview in Lesotho in 1987 with journalist Joe Molefi, a Pan-Africanist Congress activist during the 1960s, and a telephone conversation with Colonel Ignatius Terblanche in 1987 provided material for this chapter.

Book references include: Luthuli, Albert, *Let My People Go: An Autobiography* (Collins, London, 1962); Reeves, Ambrose, *Shooting at Sharpeville: The Agony of South Africa* (Victor Gollancz, London, 1960); Segal, Ronald, *Into Exile* (Jonathan

Cape, London, 1963); Sowden, Lewis, *The Land of Afternoon* (Elek, London, 1968); First, Ruth, *117 Days: An Account of Confinement and Interrogation Under the South African Ninety-Day Detention Law* (Penguin, London, 1965); Joseph, Helen, *Tomorrow's Sun: A Smuggled Journal from South Africa* (Hutchinson, London, 1966); Paton, Alan, *South African Tragedy* (Charles Scribner's Sons, New York, 1965); Lodge, Tom, *Sharpeville: A Massacre and its Consequences* (Oxford University Press, 2011).

CHAPTER NINE

A four-hour discussion in Lusaka in 1987 with Joe Modise, who seldom granted interviews, contributed to this section, as did an interview with Indres Naidoo in Lusaka in 1988. The bulk of the material came from a special edition of a magazine called *Dawn*, published by the ANC in 1986 on the occasion of the twenty-fifty anniversary of the formation of Umkhonto we Sizwe.

Book references include: Feit, Edward, *Urban Revolt in South Africa 1960-1964: A Case Study* (Northwestern University Press, Evanston, 1971); Mtolo, Bruno, *Umkhonto we Sizwe: The Road to the Left* (Drakensberg Press, Durban, 1966).

CHAPTER TEN

An interview with Ruth Rice, daughter of Bram Fischer, in Johannesburg in 1988 provided useful background material.

Books include: de Villiers, H H W, *Rivonia: Operation Mayibuye* (Afrikaanse Pers-Boekhandel, Johannesburg, 1964); Mandela, Nelson, *No Easy Walk to Freedom: Articles, Speeches and Trial Addresses of Nelson Mandela* (Heinemann, London, 1965); *The Anatomist: The Autobiography of Anthony Sampson* (Jonathan Ball Publishers, Cape Town 2008).

CHAPTER ELEVEN

Indres Naidoo, interviewed in Lusaka in 1988, was a rich source of information about Robben Island. Steve Tshwete contributed to this section during an interview in Lusaka in 1988. Caroline Motsoaledi and June Mlangeni gave me interviews in Johannesburg in 1988. The interview with Albertina Sisulu in 1987 also contributed to this chapter.

Book references include: Naidoo, Indres (as told to Albie Sachs), *Island in Chains* (Penguin, London, 1982); Breytenbach, Breyten, *The True Confessions of an Albino Terrorist* (Faber, London, 1985); Mitcheson, Naomi, *A Life for Africa: The Story of Bram Fischer* (Merlin Press, London, 1973); Buntsman, Fran, *Robben Island and Prisoner Resistance* (Cambridge University Press, 2003).

CHAPTER TWELVE

Sikosi Mji was interviewed in Lusaka in 1987. A prominent ANC organiser, a white woman who did not wish to be named, gave me useful background information. I spoke to a former Baragwanath Hospital doctor, who also requested anonymity. The quotation from Lindiwe Sisulu (page 162) came from an article she wrote in *Sechaba*.

Books include: Biko, Steve, *I Write What I Like* (Heinemann, London, 1979); Brooks, Alan and Brickhill, Jeremy, *Whirlwind Before the Storm* (International Defence and Aid Fund for Southern Africa, London, 1980); Kane-Berman, John, *Soweto: Black Revolt, White Reaction* (Ravan Press, Johannesburg, 1978); Hirson, Baruch, *Year of Fire, Year of Ash: The Soweto Revolt, Roots of a Revolution* (Zed Books, London, 1979); Lodge, Tom, *Resistance and Reform 1973-1994* (Cambridge University Press, Volume Two, 2011).

CHAPTER THIRTEEN

I interviewed Steve Tshwete in Lusaka in 1988. Albertina Sisulu, interviewed in 1987, provided material for this chapter, as did Thabo Mbeki, interviewed in Lusaka in 1988.

Books include: Davis, Stephen, *Apartheid's Rebels: Inside South Africa's Hidden War* (Yale University Press, New Haven, 1987); Gastrow, Sheila, *Who's Who in South African Politics* (Ravan Press, Johannesburg, 1987); Leach, Graham, *South Africa* (Century Hutchinson, London, 1986); Meredith, Martin, *In the Name of Apartheid: South Africa in the Post-War Period* (Hamish Hamilton, London, 1988).

CHAPTER FOURTEEN

Thabo Mbeki was interviewed in Lusaka in 1988. Joe Modise talked to me in Lusaka in 1987, and I spoke briefly with Chris Hani during the ANC's seventy-fifth anniversary celebrations in Lusaka in 1987. My last interview for the first edition of this book, arranged over many months, was to be with the president of the African National Congress in exile, Oliver Tambo. Due to take place on 28 April 1989, it was wiped out at the eleventh hour by an explosion in Lusaka and the simultaneous expiry of my final copy deadline in London. I was waiting at my hotel in the Zambian capital for an ANC car to collect me for the meeting when I was informed that a grenade had blown up an ANC house not far from where I was due to see Tambo. On such occasions a tight security cordon closed around the organisation and its president in particular, so my interview had to be cancelled.

Interviews with Walter Sisulu and Andrew Mlangeni shortly after their release from prison in 1989 produced material for this chapter.

Books used for my research on this chapter include: Mandela, Nelson, *Long Walk to Freedom* (Macdonald Purnell, 1994); Bridgland, Fred, *Katiza's Journey: Beneath the Surface of South Africa's Shame* (Sidgwick & Jackson, 1997); Waldmeir, Patti, *Anatomy of a Miracle: The End of Apartheid and the Birth of the New South Africa* (Viking, 1997).

CHAPTER FIFTEEN

Numerous publications and other research – conducted by the author as a journalist in the years since the ANC became the country's first democratic government in 1994 – contributed to this chapter. In particular, a special report on South Africa called *The Price of Freedom* and published by *The Economist* on 5 June 2010 yielded a lot of information.

SELECTED INDEX